Optimizing AdWords

Optimizing AdWords provides the information marketers and future marketers need to harness the power of Google's AdWords search engine marketing applications. It provides a big picture overview of the AdWords system, helping businesses and individuals decide how to advertise their products or their clients' products. *Optimizing AdWords* was written for those at every rung of the ladder, from marketing directors to small business owners to students just starting out in marketing.

This volume is organized around accessibility and ease of use. Author Paige Miller, co-founder of MultiPlanet Marketing Inc., has written this how-to guide to be super easy and fast to read and absorb. It moves you straight to the salient points of the text, allowing readers to take on AdWords in overview before coming back and collecting the finer details. Chapters 1 through 4 cover the basics, while the rest acts as a reference that readers can come back to in building and growing campaigns.

Using this book, professional marketers and other business professionals can utilize Google AdWords and optimize it for existing marketing strategies, or create whole new campaigns based around the system. Today, given the level of competition for ad positions on Google search pages, success hinges on understanding Google AdWords well enough to outperform competition. This book will provide readers with the knowledge necessary to master Google AdWords.

Paige Miller is a former software developer, marketing director of a successful dot.com and co-founder of MultiPlanet Marketing Inc., a company that uses the latest Internet marketing techniques in client marketing strategies.

Optimizing AdWords

A Guide to Using, Mastering, and Maximizing Google AdWords

WITHDRAWN

Paige Miller

Routledge
Taylor & Francis Group

NEW YORK AND LONDON

First published 2016
by Routledge
711 Third Avenue, New York, NY 10017

and by Routledge
2 Park Square, Milton Park, Abingdon, Oxon, OX14 4RN

Routledge is an imprint of the Taylor & Francis Group, an informa business

Library of Congress Cataloging in Publication Data
Miller, Page W., author.
Optimizing AdWords : a guide to using, mastering, and maximizing Google
AdWords / Paige Miller.
pages cm
Includes bibliographical references and index.
ISBN 978-1-138-94857-0 (hardback) — ISBN 978-1-138-94858-7 (pbk.)
— ISBN 978-1-315-66955-7 (ebook)
1. Google AdWords. 2. Internet advertising. 3. Internet marketing. I. Title.
HF6146.I58M55 2015
658.8'72—dc23
2015027895

ISBN: 978-1-138-94857-0 (hbk)
ISBN: 978-1-138-94858-7 (pbk)
ISBN: 978-1-315-66955-7 (ebk)

Typeset in Perpetua and Bell Gothic
by Florence Production Ltd, Stoodleigh, Devon, UK

Dedicated to my daughter Lauren,
who got me started on this project,
and to my husband Steve,
who helped me survive it.

Contents

Figures

Introduction

When it began, AdWords was a simple application. However, over the years, it has become a sophisticated and robust application. Today, given the level of competition for ad positions on Google search pages, success hinges on understanding the application well enough to outperform your competitors—and increasingly your competitors are national brands.

This document is for:

1. **Chief marketing officers, marketing directors and marketers.** People who need to understand Google AdWords in order to incorporate its capabilities into their marketing strategy, oversee or manage a staff that will execute the strategy or execute ads themselves.

2. **Marketing students.** Future marketers who already know the basic principles of marketing and want to apply that knowledge to AdWords and future marketing employees who want to understand one of the most powerful marketing tools in the industry.

3. **Small business owners.** People who know their customers and what they want to sell but need to know how to use AdWords.

The information in this document:

- **Gives you a "big picture overview" of AdWords.** You need the big picture if you are to make decisions about what you want to do to advertise your product(s) or your clients' products.
  - **Google does not provide an overview of AdWords capabilities.** That means you do not get the opportunity to devise a growth path—building on increasingly sophisticated AdWords features. More people stumble upon different types of ad and haphazardly try them out, never knowing about the obscure features that could make a real difference in their success.

— **Google uses a learn-as-you-go approach to teach AdWords.** This means they start you off with the easy stuff. That's fine, but most people never go beyond the easy stuff to learn—and use—the full power of AdWords.

- **Tells you where to find more information in AdWords Help.**
  — **Google information is vast and diverse.** Google provides write-ups about AdWords' capabilities, along with blog posts about features and applications. Thus, the information about a topic may be spread over dozens of articles. Knowing the exact name of the article addressing your issue can save you hours of reading time and frustration.
  — **Google personalizes AdWords Help.** It may not show you articles about certain features if your Account does not use those features.
- **Moves you straight to the salient points, so you don't waste time reading lots of words.**
  — Time is money. The less time it takes you to absorb an idea the better.

The conventions used in this document include:

- **Boldface**—to indicate major concepts. In this document, you can read only the boldface sentences and have an overview of the whole AdWords system.
- *Italics*—to designate an AdWords function, capability or menu choice. AdWords has a vocabulary all of its own, and you need to become familiar with these terms. Without italics, the terms make for confusing, even mind-boggling, sentences. The italics let you know when "AdWord-ese" is in use.
- **Indentation and bullets**—to highlight important details related to a concept, practices, etc., which can impact your success.

This book is guaranteed to have out-of-date material, and gaps.

- **AdWords changes every day**. AdWords changes, renames, moves and deprecates features often. Sometimes, it provides in-depth explanations and sometimes it offers little or no notice.
- **AdWords is a huge application to master.** Few, if any, people use all its features. Few people know all the capabilities available. It's not possible to describe every possible combination of features. Nevertheless, once you know the basics you can shuffle the pieces around and still predict the outcome.

All that being said, I love AdWords. It has changed the game of advertising.

- **Learning AdWords takes time and patience.** (Most marketers have neither.) It can feel like an abyss, because of it capabilities, and it can feel like a maze, because of its always-one-more-link Help articles. If you have unfortunate timing and tackle it when big changes are being released, it can feel like changing a tire on a moving car.

I wrote this to be a super-easy, super-fast book to read that works as a learning tool and as a reference.

- Chapter 1: What AdWords Offers. Tells you what AdWords can do so you can plan the types of ads that will help your business most.

- Chapter 2: How AdWords Works. Explains the basic concepts that govern the way AdWords works. Knowing how AdWords makes decisions helps you control your own success.

- Chapter 3: Key Concepts of Ads. Shows you the path for setting up a campaign (without losing a lot of money!), gives you the important details about developing campaigns and shows you how to measure results.

- Chapter 4: Getting Started. Gives you the insights, secrets and rules for starting, growing and monitoring successful campaigns.

Save yourself some time:

1. **Blast through the document reading only the boldface sentences for a quick overview of the whole AdWords system.** Then go back to a section when you need the details.

2. **Read Chapters 1 to 4, then use the rest of the book as a reference as you grow your campaign(s).**

For those of you who blast ahead to develop ads after reading only a few sections, use the Index to find answers to the problems you encounter.

WELCOME TO MASTERING ADWORDS

AdWords is a Search Engine Marketing (SEM) tool for advertising on the Internet.

- AdWords lets you use Google's search engine to show paid advertisements on the Internet to people either conducting searches or reading websites.

- When people see your ad, they can click it and visit your webpage where they can buy your products, sign-up for your newsletter, download an app or take whatever action you requested.

AdWords is a sophisticated marketing tool capable of bringing significant traffic and revenue to a business owner.

- Jumping into AdWords without a basic understanding of its operation and capabilities can be frustrating, confusing and expensive.

- Few companies want a total novice responsible for their AdWords budget, so it pays to learn the AdWords system.

AdWords is somewhat of a mystery. Google provides Help pages, with snippets of information about each AdWords function and individual prompts, and a blog that discusses various topics. Neither AdWords Help nor the blog gives you a full overview, and you may remain apprehensive about the way you are spending your money on AdWords.

AdWords is complex, like working a big jigsaw puzzle with no picture. AdWords has a lot of features that you must fit together in many different combinations. Once you understand the pieces more capabilities become obvious.

With AdWords, a lack of vigilance and knowledge can be expensive. AdWords is highly profitable for many businesses but, left unattended, AdWords can be a steady, unproductive drain of money out of your advertising budget with few or no results.

Unless you understand AdWords, you can spend a great deal of time and money trying to solve the most common problems, such as:

1. Why ads are not appearing or are not receiving clicks.

2. How to target websites that reach the prospects for your product.

3. How to control the cost of your clicks.

AdWords is multi-layered. Executing an AdWords campaign requires many more steps than most people realize. Just look at them:

1. Understand how AdWords works.

2. Determine your business goals and AdWords strategy.

3. Determine your ad types.

4. Review the AdWords landscape.

5. Identify lucrative keywords.

6. Create a compelling landing page.

7. Write a compelling ad.

8. Select the best campaign options.

9. Select the best ad group options.

10. Run a preliminary campaign.

11. Measure your results and profit.

12. Optimize good ads.

13. Improve poor ads.

14. Grow your campaigns.

15. Introduce advanced AdWords features.

16. Track your billings.

The more steps you skip the more money it costs you!

Chapter 1

What AdWords Offers

This chapter describes the advertising channels available (the advertising "networks," as Google calls them) and the benefits and major features of the 22 different ad types that Google offers. Such an overview enables you to align your campaign ads with your marketing objectives from the beginning, rather than running simple ads until you stumble upon better ad types as you learn the AdWords application.

More specifically, the chapter covers the Search Network and the Display Network, along with the Google Shopping, Ad/Mod and YouTube "networks" that Google considers part of the Display Network. It covers the most common uses and major capabilities for the AdWords ad types, and notes special technical, marketing or timing characteristics that require upfront consideration before use.

AdWords currently offers four major networks (a network being a set of designated Internet sites) and many different types of ads within each network. The networks have different technical requirements for ads, through some networks overlap.

The four networks are shown on p. 2.

When you create an ad, you must specify which network you want to use.

Note that Local and Mobile Ads run on all networks. Google does not consider these ad types but, rather, options that work with the various ad types.

However, because Local and Mobile Ads are so important to marketers, we discuss them separately for each network, so you have the setup information you need to accomplish your specific goals.

The following pages describe the major benefits and features of the many ad types that show on each network.

1

The *Google Search Network* – which shows ads on the Google.com results pages after you enter a search query. The network also includes *Google's Search Partner sites*, a group of web sites specially designated by Google to show search ads.	 *Search Network Ad*
The *Google Display Network* - which includes millions of websites whose owners have agreed to show ads on their pages, along pages on YouTube, Gmail, Google Financial pages and various other Google-owned sites.	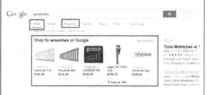 *Display Ad (beside arrow)*
The *Google Shopping Network* – which shows thumbnail-size ads on the Google.com search results page when you enter a search term for a product. Ads also show when you enter a search term and click the *Shopping* menu option.	 *Google Shopping Ads*
The *Google/AdMob Network* – technically part of the Display Network, this network shows ads as overlays on mobile apps, as well as ads for downloading mobile apps.	*An AdMob ad on a news app and another on a gaming app*

FIGURE 1.0 Google networks overview

SELECTING THE RIGHT NETWORK FOR YOUR CAMPAIGN

Selecting the right network for your ads is one of the most important decisions you make. Use these best practices guidelines to help you make your choice:

1. **Use only Search Network Ads until your ads are bringing buyers (buyers, not visitors) to your site.**

   • Search Ads bring more traffic, faster, since the searcher is actively looking for your product, service, etc. Thus, you have a more focused opportunity to test and refine your ads. Once your ads are making money for you, you can expand your campaign and budget.

2. **The Search Network is your first choice if you want to sell a product.**

   • The Search Network puts your ad before people who are actively searching for your product, service, organization, etc.

   • The Display Network is a less attractive channel for *selling* a product than the Search Network because it targets people not actively looking to buy.

3. **The Shopping Network is your best choice if you sell scores of different products.** The Shopping Network lets you connect an e-commerce site with AdWords, making it practical to run ads for hundreds of products.

   • The Shopping Network requires creation of a file (a feed) of product information that you must upload and maintain. This may be a daunting task for someone with limited technical skills or support. The number of products you want to advertise must be large enough to merit the labor required to support Shopping Network Ads.

4. **The Display Network is your best choice if you want to:**

   a. **Generate leads, reach new groups of prospects or spread the word about special events and sales promotions.** The Display Network is also useful for services, expensive or complex products that people research, evaluate and contemplate before buying.

      — Display Network ads are attractive for lead generation because people reading about a topic related to your product often respond to an ad offering more information about that topic. Further, the ads are inexpensive in comparison to other lead generation channels, such as trade shows and telemarketing.

3

— To use Display Network ads effectively, you must know your audience and keywords reasonably well. Otherwise, you pay for many clicks that do not bring buyers. Use Search Ads to learn about your prospects for a period of time before you move to Display Network ads.

b. **Sell a product or service that has a long sales cycle.** Display Network ads keep your name in front of your prospects, so they remember you when it is time to research or purchase your product.

c. **Research your market and find your prospects.** The Display Network lets you reach prospects outside the sites you already know. By using *automatic placements, a choice within* targeting method for Display Network ads, AdWords finds sites your prospects frequent and gives you the list of those sites. This enables you to learn of sites where you can advertise directly or, possibly, contribute content likely to be read by your prospects.

d. **Test different value propositions, messages and ad copy to determine which resonate best with your market**. Display Network ads are an inexpensive alternative to surveys or focus groups for researching your best, most lucrative positioning, value proposition and messaging. By experimenting with different ad copy, you gain valuable insights into the messaging that resonates with prospects, though you may or may not gain sales.

e. **Target websites where your prospects gather.** Display Network ads provide five targeting methods: keywords, audience (gender, age), topic, interests, managed placement (i.e., website or webpage you specify) and congressional district. By experimenting with different demographics, psychographic and geographic targets, you can gain valuable insights into prospects, enthusiasts, followers, constituents, etc.

f. **Target viewers by age, gender and interest.** You can select interest categories from AdWords' predefined category and sub-category lists to reflect the interests of your existing customers if you know them.

Note that "in market" is an interest category. Thus, you can target people who are in the market for your product. AdWords determines a searcher is in the market for your product from his or her search history.

g. **Personalize your landing page for your visitor based on the website or webpage sending the visitor to you.** For managed placements, you can set a different destination URL than the one associated with the ad copy. This lets you customize your landing page based on the website sending you the visitor.

h. **Sell a new, revolutionary product (as the iPad tablet was in 2010), since no one searches for items that never existed before!**

5. **Mobile Ads on the Display Network is the choice for reaching people on the go, snaring nearby customers and building brand awareness.** Targeting cell phone users with ads that include a clickable phone number and driving directions can bring people to your store.

6 **The Google AdMob Network with its Mobile Apps partners is your choice for advertising your company's mobile application, whether your app is a game, a productivity tool, a news service or a self-help program.**

THE SEARCH NETWORK

The Search Network is the one most familiar to Internet users.

- Search Network Ads show on Google.com results pages after someone enters a search query.
- Search Network Ads appear at the top, right-hand side and bottom of search engine report pages (SERPS).
- Search Network Ads are text-only ads.

Search Network ad types share the same basic attributes. Obviously, each variation has a few differences, but knowing the Basic Search Ad capabilities provides a solid foundation for branching out into other Search Network ad types.

Basic Search Ads

Basic Search Ads **are the ads most familiar to everyone, and they are the ads most businesses use when starting to use AdWords.**

- *Basic Search Ads* **are most valuable for selling products (as opposed to selling services).** Concrete tangible items sell well on Search Ads, while services require more explanation and thus have a somewhat lower conversion rate (sales rate).

5

> ### Women's Shoes
> www.------.com/ ▾
> Up to 70% Off Trendy Shoes
> for Women. Shop Now!

FIGURE 1.1 Basic Search Ad placements
Only the small yellow Ads icon indicates the information is a paid ad.

- **By default, *Basic Search Ads* show on all devices.** That includes desktops, laptops, tablets, music devices (iPods, etc.), smart phones (Android, iPhones, etc.), feature phones (flip phones) and phablets (large smartphone).

- **When you set up a *Basic Search Ad*, you create a list of words and phrases, called *keywords*, that describe your product.** When someone uses one of your keywords in a search, your ad is eligible to appear.

- **AdWords charges you only if the searcher clicks on your ad.** You pay for each click (thus, the phrases "pay-per-click" and "PPC").

- **You set the maximum amount you are willing to pay for a click, which is called the *max cost-per-click (max CPC).*** You set this amount for your campaign and it applies to all your ads and keywords, but you can override it in various places.

- **The amount you *actually pay* for an ad is called the *average cost-per-click.*** This number is an *average* for the period of time you specify. Google does not tell you the *actual cost* of a single, individual click.

- **When you set up a *Basic Search Ad*, you specify conditions for showing your ads,** including: (1) the geographic area where a searcher must be, (2) the device a searcher must be using (desktop/laptop/tablet or mobile phone) and (3) the language a searcher must speak.

- **Clicking a *Basic Search Ad* takes the searcher to the landing page you specified.** Your homepage can be your landing page; however, it is better to develop a special page just for your product.

- **You can (and should) add *ad extensions* to Search Ads, to show your address, phone number, promotional offers, sitelinks or Google +1 page.**

(See Basic Search Ads, p. 180, for instructions on creating Search Ads.)

Leather Jacket
www. _____ .com/Leather-Jackets ▾
★★★★★ 26,104 seller reviews
Huge Selection of **Leather Jackets**
Free Overnight Shipping on **Jackets**

FIGURE 1.2 Google Search Ads

Dynamic Search Ads (DSA)

For *Dynamic Search Ads (DSA)*, **AdWords auto-fills the headline of the ad with the search term being queried.** Otherwise, *DSAs* look like a Basic Search Ad.

Dynamic Search Ads **are great for major retailers who have hundreds of products and hundreds of webpages.** *DSAs* save retailers many hours of tedious copy-writing and keyword research, setup and monitoring. They are also powerful tools for artists and craftsmen who sell one-of-a-kind items.

Plastic Kid Pool
www_____com/
Find **Plastic Kid Pool** Today.
Shop **Plastic Kid Pool** at
1200 _____, Springfield, PA
(_____)   - Directions

FIGURE 1.3 Dynamic Search Ad
AdWords inserts the search term into the ad where you specify.
Note the boldface keywords in description lines one and two in the image above.

DSAs **serve as a reminder to searchers that your store has the product they seek.** Thus, *DSAs* build brand awareness, as well as bring traffic to your website.

- *Dynamic Search Ads* **use** *keyword insertions,* **a way of automatically embedding the searcher's keyword phrase where you want it within your ad description.** Note the boldface keywords in description lines one and two in Figure 1.3.

  Thus, you can setup *DSAs* for each type of product you sell and provide a two line description relevant to that product. (You define the type of product using a category, URL, page title or page-content-tag.)

For example, when someone searches for "brown strappy sandals," your ad reads:

Brown Sandals
www._____.com
Big Savings on Brown Sandals.
Free Shipping Over $99.

When someone searches for black pumps, your ad reads:

Black Pumps
www._____.com
Big Savings on Black Pumps.
Free Shipping Over $99.

- **For *Dynamic Search Ads*, AdWords generates a headline using the searcher's query words and searches your website for a URL containing the query word(s).** It combines the headline and URL with the description you provided and any other *ad extension* information (such as an address, phone number or coupon offer) you provided.

- *Dynamic Search Ads* **do not compete with other AdWords ads you run.** Thus, if you create an ad for lawn toys, AdWords will not create a DSA for lawn toys but, rather, will use your existing ad.

- *Dynamic Search Ads* **work with the *Remarketing* features.** This produces ads that appear only to previous visitors, automatically presenting them with images of items they considered previously or similar/better items they might consider.

- *Dynamic Search Ads* **also work with *Google Shopping*.** Retailers upload an inventory file into AdWords, and AdWords creates ads that use the searcher's query term in the product description.

(See Dynamic Search Ads, p. 198, for details about creating Dynamic Search Ads.)

Local Ads—Google My Business

One of the most effective ads for a local business is not an AdWords ad at all, but rather an information listing created through *Google My*

FIGURE 1.4 Google My Business

Because Multiplanet Marketing holds the top organic search result, Google shows the Google My Business information and location on the map at the top of the left column.

Business. Formerly, Google called this feature Google Places for Business and Google Places.

- A *Google My Business* **account requires you to have a Google Account and a Gmail address.**

- A *Google My Business* **account is required if you want to use** *location extensions* **in your AdWords ads.** *Location extensions* **add your address and phone number to AdWords ads.**
  Further, having a *Google My Business* panel increases your AdWords *quality score* and, thus, helps your AdWords ads achieve higher ad positions on a search results page. For those reasons, *Google My Business* is presented here.

(See Ad Rank and Quality Score, p. 97, for more about quality scores.)

A *Google My Business* **ad:**

- **Is free and does not require the use of AdWords.** It appears when your company is the top organic entry on the search results page.

- **Provides a top-right column of information about the first business on the SERP.**

- **Appears on all devices—smartphones, tablets and desktops.**

- **Includes a map, which is particularly helpful for people looking for your business as they shop.**

9

In addition, a *Google My Business* account lets you:

- **Post updates that show on your Google+ page.** This lets you:
  — Post greetings.
  — Announce sales.
  — Show pictures.
  — Link to content.
  — Upload videos.
  — Create events.

  You can show your posts to your circle of followers, people who have mentioned your business on Google+, people who have added you to their circle of friends, or all of these groups.

- **Review data about searchers and followers.** You can see how many online searchers and Google+ users viewed your listing, viewed your listing on a mobile device, clicked on your directions, went to your webpage, shared your post, commented on your post, etc.

  You can also see where people were when they clicked your listing for directions.

  You can track your followers by age, gender and country.

  Different *Insight Cards,* as Google calls its data pages, give you different sorts of your data for the last 7, 30 or 90 days.

Local Ads—Google AdWords Express

For small business owners with no marketing expertise or time to learn AdWords, Google has a special, no-expertise-needed, simplified version of AdWords called *AdWords Express.*

AdWords Express lets you advertise in your city, state or zip code area. Thus, it is great for small businesses selling in their local area.

- **Google provides phone support for people setting up** *AdWords Express* **accounts.**

- **With** *AdWords Express* **you write three lines about your business and set a budget.**

- **You can use your own website, a Google+ site or a free website from Google as your landing page.** Google's free websites use templates, with pre-set formats and stock photography, so technical knowledge is not required.

- **For a small, very reasonable fee, Google registers your domain name and provides hosting.**

- *AdWords Express* determines your keywords (based on your website, Google+ business category and/or Google My Business information) and runs your ads.

- *AdWords Express* shows your ad to people who are in your area (based on IP address, the searcher's Google Profile, mobile device location service, etc.) or who specify your area in their search terms.

- As with AdWords search ads, *AdWords Express* ads appear in search results and on Google maps. They also appear on all devices—desktops, mobile phones, tablets, laptops, etc.

For more information, enter *AdWords Express* into Google.com.

Local Ads—AdWords Search Network

Local Ads let you compete aggressively with national companies when a person in your area searches for your product or when a searcher specifies your geographic area in his or her search query.

Essentially, *Local Ads* are Search Network Ads targeted to people in your business' geographic area. They show on Google.com results pages after someone enters a search query for your product, provided:

1. That person resides in your area based on information Google has (IP address, Google profile, etc. or his or her Google.com setting). The Google.com location setting appears under the Search Tool menu.)

2. That person is in your local area based on mobile phone location data.

3. The search query includes your city/state or zip code in the search query.

    - You can create highly localized campaigns for each geographic area in your market. For example, a *Local Ad* might read "Go Westtown High School. 10% Off Sports Equipment," while a regular search ad might read "10% Off Sports Equipment. Online. This week only."

    - As with all Search Network campaigns, you specify the geographic, language and device requirements the searcher must meet before you allow your ad to show.

    - For each individual *Local Ad* you create, you specify a list of keywords describing your product. A searcher must use one of your keywords for your ad to appear.

    - AdWords charges you only if the searcher clicks on your ad.

    - Clicking the ad takes the searcher to the landing page you specified.

(See Local Ads—AdWords Search Network, p. 204, for instructions on setting up a Local Ad.)

11

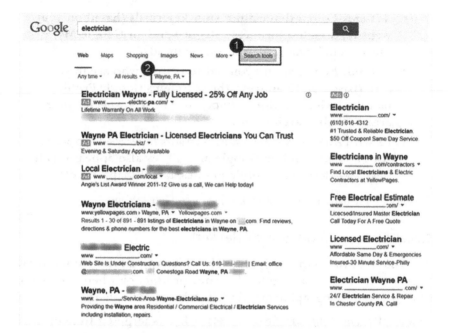

FIGURE 1.5 Local Ads

AdWords show Local Ads to people near your store. Click the *Search Tools* menu choice (#1) to shows your location (#2) that Google uses for your searches. You can change it to search in other areas (#3).

Mobile Ads on the Search Network

Mobile Ads are especially useful for contacting people as they research products or shop near your store.

Ads on mobile devices make it easy for viewers to call you, find your business or take advantage of a special mobile-only coupon.

- According to Google, 77 percent of mobile searches take place at home or at work. Seventeen percent take place on the go. Three out of four searches result in a *secondary action*, either continued research, a visit to a website or a sharing of information.

Mobile devices include smartphones, feature phones (flip phones) and phablets (devices with cell phone technology but between tablets and phones in size).

- Smartphones have full browsers (such as iPhone using the iOS operating system and Android devices using the Android OS system).

- Likewise, tablets have full browsers.
- Feature phones (also called flip phones) use the Wireless Application Protocol (WAP), which supports the small screen of the flip phone.

FIGURE 1.6 Mobile Search Ad with ad extensions

Call Extension, Download Buttons and *Sitelinks* are *ad extensions* that provide value to shopper near your store. AdWords sometimes removes a description line from your ad in favor of more *ad extension* information.

FIGURE 1.7 Feature phone (flip phone)

Ads for WAP-based phones must have WAP-based landing pages. They show on either the Search Network or the Display Network but only on feature phones.

Ads run on the Search, Display and AdMob Networks run on mobile devices.

- **The Search Network supports text-ads on Google.com.**
- **The Display Network supports text, image, animated and rich-media formats across the many Display Network Partner sites.**

- Note: If you are advertising a mobile app, use the *Mobile App Install* and *Mobile App Engagement* ad types available in AdWords. They offer more features and are a better ad type choice for apps. (These ad types are explained later.)

On the Search Network, all ads appear on smartphones, tablets and mobile apps by default; however, you can create Search Network Ads that run only on mobile devices.

Mobile Search Ads let you:

- Link to the mobile version of your website (if you have one—and increasingly you should have a mobile version of your website).

- Set a *bid adjustment* for a Mobile Ads, so you bid higher or lower for an ad on mobile devices than if the ad appeared on a desktop.

- Include *ad extensions* to add your phone number, address, directions sitelinks, and/or a map to your store. With one click, your searcher can call you, go to your website, or jump to your sale or promotional landing page.
  — AdWords sometimes shows your ad extensions instead of the second description line if your ad extensions have garnered clicks in the past. (You can force the second description line to always show.)

- Use *callout extensions* to add information about your business practices (e.g., "24/7 service," "Price matching"). Callouts are not clickable.

- Use the *Conversion Tracking* and *Conversion Optimization* features with *Mobile Ads*. *Conversion Tracking* captures data about ad viewers, visitors and buyers, while *Conversion Optimization* adjusts your bid to help you obtain more visitors, with Mobile Ads.

- Use *Remarketing* with *Mobile Ads*. *Remarketing* lets you show ads only to people who have visited your site before (whether they bought anything or not).

To get the most out of your *Mobile Search Ads,*

- Address your customers' needs in the first line.

- Size your image for the smaller screen.

- Use different, often shorter, keywords, since people often use different keywords on mobile devices.

Remarketing Lists for Search Ads (RLSA)

Remarketing Lists for Search Ads, or just RLSAs as Google calls them, let you target previous visitors to your website as they search on Google.com or *Google Shopping* for other items.

- You must activate the *Remarketing* feature to create *Remarketing Lists for Search Ads*.

- Remarketing Ads combine the keyword search capability of Search Network ad with AdWords' Remarketing capability, which uses cookies to create lists of visitors to your webpages and track visitors as they surf the Internet.

  For example, you could create Remarketing lists for Visitors and Buyers, or fine-tune your lists for Shoe Buyers, Shoe Shoppers, Dress Buyers, Dress Shoppers, etc.

- To protect the privacy of the visitors, AdWords requires that your Remarketing lists have 1,000 cookies before ads are eligible to show.

(See Remarketing Ads, page 282, under the Display Network for a fuller explanation of Remarketing.)

Using *Remarketing Lists for Search Ads*, you can:

- Create a special ad target exclusively for people who previously looked at the product on your website; for example:

> **Those Shoes You Love**
> *www._____.com*
> Are On Sale! Get Yours
> Before Your Size is Gone.

- Create special ads for previous buyers to encourage them to return for different items; for example:

> **If You Like Our Shoes**
> *www._____.com*
> You will Love our Purses!
> Checkout Our Latest Arrivals Now.

- Create an ad with generic keywords but target the ads only to previous visitors; generic keywords are usually expensive but targeting only previous visitors can keep them affordable.

- Create ads that target previous visitors who viewed a particular page, abandoned a shopping cart or visited multiple webpages.

- Increase your bid for existing ads when the searcher is a previous visitor.

Remarketing Lists for Search Ads are very flexible and support:

- Visitors being on multiple Remarketing lists (especially if they visit multiple pages).

- Using multiple ads for the same list (as when you advertise a product and a site-wide sale).

- Multiple ads qualifying to show to a visitor, but AdWords uses the ad with the highest *ad rank* (a measure AdWords computes). (See Ad Rank and Quality Score, page 97, for more information.)

RLSAs look like any other ad on the Search Network.

RLSAs use the cost-per-click bidding model. You can bid at the Ad Group Level for all underlying ads or at the *Remarketing List* Level for all ads using a particular list.

AdWords provides performance data for each Remarketing Ad and for each *Remarketing List*.

(See Remarketing Lists for Search Ads (RLSA), page 212, for setup instructions.)

Search-Ads-with-Display-Select

Search-Ads-with-Display-Select **appear on the** *Search Network* **as well as** *Display Network* **webpages where relevant keywords appear.**

- Google cites a 35 percent increase in click-throughs and a 35 percent lower cost-per-customer purchase (i.e., more customer visited and they spent more), on average, using this ad type when it was introduced. (Be leery, however, and monitor your results closely. Your ads may not be average.)

- According to Google, *Search-Ads-with-Display-Select* appear on "highly appropriate" websites. Google states that it applies "higher standards" for selecting ad *placements* on Display Network Partner websites for these ads, but Google does not describe its standards.

The *Search-Ads-with-Display-Select* option lets you:

- Show a text ad on the Search Network but show an image, mobile apps, digital content, shopping or dynamic search ad on the Display Network.

- **Use *Target Methods* for the Display Network.** Just as with other Display Network ads, you can specify the exact webpages you want used (which augments the highly appropriate ones AdWords selects for you).

You can switch *Search Network Ads* to the *Search-Ads-with-Display-Select* option where you want to add Display Network websites to your placements. (Google states it has 2 million publisher sites on the Display Network.)

Note: *Search-Ads-with-Display-Select* replaces the *Search Network and Display Network ads* available before 2014. Google expects to convert all legacy *Search Network and Display Network* campaigns to this option.

(See Search-Ads-with-Display-Select, page 215, for setup instructions.)

THE DISPLAY NETWORK

The Google Display Network includes millions of websites whose owners have agreed to show ads on their webpages. It also includes YouTube, Gmail, Groups and Google Financial pages.

- **The website owners are called *Google Display Network Partners*, and they receive a portion of the revenues generated from ads appearing on their webpages.** (*AdSense* is the name of the product Partners use to tell Google which of their web pages have ad space available.)

- Google dictates the placement of ads on YouTube, Gmail and other Google-owned sites, but the Google Display Network Partners say where ads appear on their websites.

- According to independent sources, Display Network ads drive roughly 40 percent of the total conversions for most advertisers, while Search Network Ads drive roughly 60 percent.

If you are building brand awareness, Display Network ads may be a less expensive and more valuable means of capturing more "eyeballs."

Because the viewer is not actively looking for your product, a Display Network ad may be less valuable than a Search Network ad if you are selling a product.

The following discusses each type of Display Ad.

17

Basic Display Ads

Basic Display Ads **differ from Search Ads in several important ways:**

- *Basic Display Ads* **appear on webpages, in Gmail, on YouTube and on apps.** They never appear on the search results pages of Google.com.

- *Basic Display Ads* **come in many forms, sizes and webpage locations.** They are text only, image, animated and interactive ads.

   They show in different sizes and locations on a webpage depending on the publisher's page layout and preference.

   They can appear across the top of a page as a banner, down the right-hand column or within the body of a webpage.

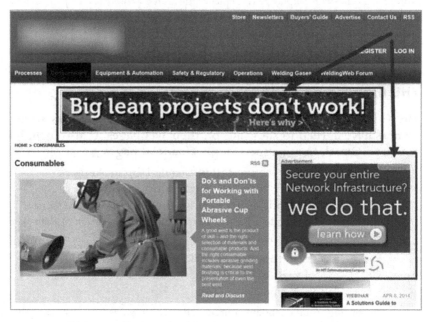

FIGURE 1.8 Webpage display ads placements

Display Ads appear in the right-hand column and across the top of the page, as shown here, and within the webpage.

You can target display ads more precisely than search ads.

- *Basic Display Ad* campaigns let you specify geographic, device and language requirements that the viewer must meet (just as Search Network campaigns do).

- *Basic Display Ads* target websites by keywords, but they also support several *targeting methods* that let you target your prospects more closely, including:
  — *Automatic placements*: AdWords places your ad on websites where one of your keywords appears.
  — *Managed placements*: AdWords lets you specify the websites where you want your ad to appear. The Display Planner tool suggests appropriate websites.
  — *Topics*: where you specify, from AdWords' pre-defined list of topics and sub-topics, the topics that a webpage must show to be appropriate for your ad.
  — *Demographics*: where you select the age groups, genders and parental status of the desired viewers for your ad. (Not all websites can accommodate this criterion.)
  — *Interests*: where you select interests from AdWords' predefined list of interests and sub-interests that you want searchers to have.
  — *Remarketing Lists*: where you select the *Remarketing Lists* you want AdWords to use. (*Remarketing Lists* are part of the advanced AdWords feature, Remarketing, page 182.)

  Targeting methods are cumulative. If you use two *targeting methods*, a website must meet criterion for both methods.
- Further, you can exclude your ad from certain categories of sites (e.g., parked sites, error message pages, video game sites or sites involving sensitive topics such as deaths and disasters).

For Display Ads, you have a choice of the *cost-per-click* (CPC) or the *cost-per-thousand-impressions* (CPM) pricing options.

- **With *cost-per-click* (CPC) impressions, AdWords charges you only if a viewer clicks on your ad.** Clicking the ad takes the searcher to the landing page you specified.
- **With *cost-per-thousand* (CPM), AdWords charges you each time at least 50 percent of your ad appears to the viewer.** (Note: the M in CPM stands for the Roman numeral M, which means 1,000.)
  — **Impression Ads are useful for getting the word out about your brand, your upcoming events or your promotional offer.** You are not required to have a landing page if it has a complete message, so they are quick and easy to set up.
  — Because CPM ads use the same flat-rate bidding model that most magazines and newspapers use, they make it easy to compare costs between AdWords ads and print ads.

FIGURE 1.9 Impression-based display ad

Like the Search Network, the Display Network supports options to:

- Deliver ads as fast as possible.
- Add location and phone information.
- Schedule ads to start and stop at specified times.
- Run only on certain days or hours.
- Link viewers to your Google+ site.
- Show the number of Google+ followers you have.

(See Display Network Ads, page 241, or watching for instructions for creating Display Ads.)

Ads on Mobile Apps

Ads on Mobile Apps **reach people using apps on their smartphones.** The owners of the apps where your ad appears have opted into Google's AdMob Network, which is part of the Display Network.

- App viewers could be playing a game, reading news, or watching a movie or YouTube video when your ad appears.

You determine the apps where your ad appears. You can specify categories of apps or individual apps where you want your ad to show.

Your ad can be a text, image or app/ digital (animated or video template) ad.

FIGURE 1.10 Ad on mobile app

You can use *Ads on Mobile Apps to:*

- *Remarket* to people who have visited your website previously.
- Advertise to people based on their *interests.*
- Show your ad on *YouTube's mobile app* (m.youtube.com).
- Advertise *your own* mobile app—an excellent way to reach people who own your app and to advertise your new app.

(See Ads on Mobile Apps, page 304, for instructions.)

Engagement Ads

Engagement Ads engage viewers and build brand awareness. For the most part, large advertisers and advertising agencies use them for their clients.

- **Engagement Ads use a *Cost-per-Engagement* (CPE) bidding model**. AdWords charges you only when a viewer clicks your ad. This makes the ads very cost effective.
- **You can use all the Display Network targeting methods with Engagement Ads.** However, not all Display Network Partner websites can accommodate Engagement Ads.
- **The AdWords auction algorithm attempts to show your ad to viewers most likely to click it.**

Engagement Ads come in these major types:

1. **Standard expandable**: when the viewer rolls over the ad for two full seconds, it expands to a larger size and shows your message. The two-second delay prevents accidental opens.

2. **Hover-to-play**: when the viewer hovers over the ad for two seconds, a visual appears that can include sound, animation or video. You create Hover-to-Play Ads in AdWords, using Ad Gallery templates.

3. **Lightbox**: when the viewer clicks the ad, the ad expands into a large canvas and your ad or video appears.

Lightbox Ads use rich media capabilities (i.e., special effects) to:

- Show animation.
- Show a video (see Figure 1.11).
- Show a video in a masthead ad space.
- Flip open to double its size and show an ad or video.
- Show a catalog of products with pages that flip (see Figure 1.12).

FIGURE 1.11 Rich media display ad

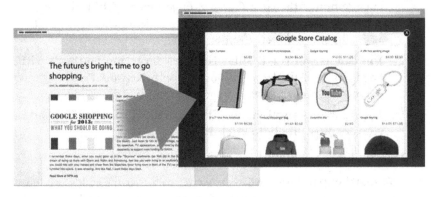

FIGURE 1.12 Engagement Ad—catalog lightbox
When clicked the catalog ad enlarges to a multi-panel ad.

- Swipe like a touch screen to a different image or swipe across a single, extra-wide image.
- Show a video mosaic (i.e., a grid with a different video in each cell).
- Dissolve (i.e., a fade out/fade in transition) through a series of pictures.
- Show a landing page (as shown on Gmail in the Figures 1.13–1.15).
- Move the webpage to the side to make room for a large ad.
- Include buttons to show multiple images.
- Include a sliding bar or rotating carousel to show items.
- Include sound, scrolling, hot spots, tap-to-call, countdown clock and many more effects.

(See Engagement Ads, page 250, for setup instructions.)

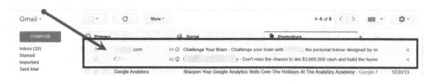

FIGURE 1.13 Engagement Ad

When clicked, a one-line Gmail ad unfolds as a larger ad and, finally, as a full-page landing page (see Figures 1.11 and 1.12).

FIGURE 1.14 Gmail ad unfolded one level

For live examples of rich media ads, go to DoubleClick's Rich Media Gallery (www.richmediagallery.com/resources/engagement_ads).

- **You create lightbox ads using templates that are part of DoubleClick Studio, an online software application developed and operated by Google's DoubleClick division.** DoubleClick also hosts lightbox ads (i.e., stores the ads and serves them to the Internet upon request from a site).

- **Rich media ads are technically sophisticated with many requirements.** Depending on the Engagement Ad type, you may need a DoubleClick Studio programmer, an HTML programmer, a graphic designer or a videographer to help you create your Engagement Ad.

- Technical requirements depend on such things as whether your ad uses video, Flash, borders or frames, whether it runs on desktops, tablets or smartphones, whether it requires user prompts such as "mouseover here," etc. Search in AdWords Help for "AdWords policies—Engagement Ads" for a full list of requirements.

For more about DoubleClick rich media ads, see "Engagement Ads" in *Google's Think Insights and Trends* blog.

23

FIGURE 1.15 Gmail ad fully unfolded

This ad unfolded into a full landing page

Local Ads—AdWords Display Network

Local Ads on the Display Network let you show your ad on websites frequented by your prospects and customers.

This is especially useful for reaching people in your neighborhood who are reading local magazines or viewing local event sites. However, you can also reach people who live in your neighborhood as they visit websites across the Internet.

FIGURE 1.16 Local Ad on Display Network

A Local Ad on a local news site can reach many potential customers.

You can run a Local Ad simply by defining your geographic area within your campaign. You can use city, state, metropolitan area, congressional district, a radius around an area and points of interest to define your market.

For Display Network ads, AdWords shows your ad on websites visited by people in your geographic area, based on such information as IP address, location designation on their smartphone, Google map location, etc.

Be aware that Local Ads on the Display Network run on all devices, but some Display Network ads can be difficult to read on a smartphone. Know that text ads work well.

- You can restrict your campaign to mobile devices and show your Local Ad only to people using smartphones, phablets or tablets.

Mobile Ads on the Display Network

As you know, all Display Network ads run on mobile devices with full browsers—smartphones, phablets and tablets. Display Network ads, whether designated mobile or not, show on desktop-sized websites and on mobile-optimized websites, whichever is appropriate for the device the viewer is using, without your doing anything different to your ad.

You may, however, want to setup separate Mobile Ads for smartphones and phablets to accommodate their smaller screens.

- *Mobile Ads on the Display Network* **show best if they are text ads or image ads.** (See Display Ads, page 241, for examples of the different ad types.)
- **Image-based, animated and rich-media ads are quite small on smartphones.** For them, you need to do one of the following:
  — Design your ad using large type and fewer words, and test it on small screens.
  — Eliminate all but banner sizes for your ad.
  — Eliminate small screen devices from your campaign.
  — Switch to Search Network text-based ads or *Google Shopping.* Listings for smartphones and phablets, since they show better.

For *Mobile Ads* on the Display Network, you can:

- **Specify that your ad runs only on mobile devices.** Further, you can specify exactly which devices, operating systems and carriers you want to target with a Mobile Ad campaign.
- **Specify that your ad runs only on YouTube.**
- **Specify that your ad runs only on YouTube's smartphone app.**
- **Run image ads on mobile apps as banner ads and/or as interstitial ads.** (Interstitial ads appear between screens as a viewer moves from one place to another.) Interstitial ads tend to be more expensive but have higher click-through rates.
- **Add *promotional offers* to your Mobile Ad.** This lets you use promo codes to give viewers special coupons.
- **Use *ad extensions* in your Mobile Ads to help you attract customers.** Ad extensions include business address, phone number, sitelinks, Google+ followers and seller-ratings (collected by Google).
- **Use *display optimizer* features with Mobile Ads.** *Display optimizer* looks for placements outside your target methods to help you obtain more visitors with Mobile Ads.
- **Use Remarketing with Mobile Ads.**

You can see performance data for each device on the statistics table.

Mobile App Install Ads

Mobile App Install Ads **send people from your ad directly to an app store where they can buy or download your app.** The more people download your app the better your store ranking and, in return, the more people are likely to download your app.

Mobile App Install Ads **run on the Search Network and the Display Network.**

- *Mobile App Install Ads* **show only on phones and tablets.** They do not show on desktops.

- *Mobile App Install Ads* **on the Display Network can target people based on age, gender, managed placement (webpages you specify) and these special app-related targets:**
  — *Installed app categories*: people who have downloaded other apps in a category that you're interested in targeting. Further, you can limit it to people who have paid for at least one app from the targeted category.
  — *New mobile devices*: people who have activated phones between 7 and 90 days.
  — *Apps*: specific apps in certain categories, such as "Games" or "Health." Also, you can input a list of apps.

- **For** *Mobile App Install Ads* **running on the Display Network, image ads can show as banners and interstitial ads or just as interstitial ads on apps.** (Interstitial ads appearing between screens of an app as the viewer transitions from one place to another.) Interstitial ads tend to be more expensive but have higher click-through rates.

- **You can exclude your** *Mobile Install Ad* **from running on apps, in which case it runs on the Search pages or Display Network websites on phone and tablets.**

- **You can use** *Remarketing* **with Display Network** *Mobile App Install Ads.* If you use *Remarketing*, you can target people who have visited your website previously and/or people who have search patterns similar to your previous visitors.

- **You can use** *Conversion Tracking* **with Display Network** *Mobile App Install Ads.* If you use Conversion Tracking, you can use the CPA bidding model and set a CPA *Bid Limit* (a ceiling) or a Target CPA (an amount you do not want AdWords to exceed when averaged over all your clicks).

- *Mobile App Install Ads* on the Display Network and can run on YouTube. These ads require a link to your YouTube video, and they use the *cost-per-view* (CPV) bidding model.

- For *Mobile App Install Ads* AdWords tracks downloads of Android-based apps through *Conversion Tracking* and reports downloads as *conversions* on the statistics table. Thus, the *cost per acquisition* (CPA) bidding model applies. If you use Conversion Tracking, you can enter a CPA *Bid Limit*, and AdWords will optimize your bid to improve your results.

- *Mobile App Install Ads* also run on the Search Network, appearing before people searching on Google.com for apps like yours or searching for something that your app does. The ads link to the app store for searchers looking for an app and to your app itself if the search is for something your app does.

FIGURE 1.17 Mobile App Install Ad showing on a mobile app

Note the Mobile App Install Ad at the bottom of the screen on this news app.

- If you are selling mobile apps such as ringtones, wallpapers, quizzes, etc., you must clearly state the price, billing interval and the fact it is a subscription on your webpage.

If you inherit the legacy version of these ads, called *Promote in Mobile App* ads, Google recommends replacing them with *Mobile App Install Ads*, which offer more features.

Mobile App Engagement Ads

Mobile App Engagement Ads help you keep people engaged with your app. Keeping users engaged is important since more than 80 percent of the time people use an app only once.

- When someone who previously downloaded your app clicks your ad, AdWords opens your app to the screen you specify. For example, you can run an ad asking your app users to check out your latest article. When someone clicks the ad, the app opens to your article.

Mobile App Engagement Ads **are being rolled out to AdWords users during late 2014, and it may not be available to you yet. (You can apply to Google to use it.)** *Ads in Mobile Apps* **offer a legacy—and much less robust—version of these ads.**

Mobile App Engagement Ads **run on the Search Network and the Display Network.**

Mobile App Engagement Ads **on the Search Network show in search results on mobile phones and tablets to people who have installed your app.** Your ad should entice the user to return to your app to find what they were searching for on Google.

Best Apple Strudel Ever
www.goglutenfree.com
Gluten free. In our Recipe App.
Click Here To View.

For example, if one of your app users is searching for a recipe for apple strudel and you are running *Mobile App Engagement Ads* for your Gluten-Free Recipes app, your ad could appear in the search results on the user's mobile phone.

- If the user clicks your ad, your app opens to your apple strudel recipe.
- If your app is closed at the time the user clicks your ad, AdWords sends a request to your app to launch. AdWords opens the URL you specified in the ad. Similarly, if the user has deleted your app, AdWords treats the ad click like a Mobile App Install Ad and begins the download process.

This scenario is particularly useful for ecommerce apps.

Mobile App Engagement Ads **on the Search Network also offer these capabilities:**

- **They run for Android apps only, but will include other app platforms soon.**

- **They use the *Maximize clicks* flexible bidding strategy.** This strategy lets AdWords bid on your behalf to get your ad as many clicks as possible within the *target spend amount* (budget) you set. You can set a *CPC bid limit* as the maximum amount you will pay.
- **AdWords provides keyword suggestions and search volumes to help you choose the most productive keywords.**

Mobile App Engagement Ads on the Display Network offer the following capabilities:

- **They have the ability to show ads to:**
  — People who downloaded your app, to advise them of a new version.
  — People who use a certain version of your app, to try certain features or to encourage them to upgrade to a new version.
  — People who have not used your app recently, to encourage them to use the app.
  — People who visited certain screens in your app, to tell them changes to the content.
  — People who took specific actions in an app (such as starting an application, reaching a higher level in a game or abandoning a shopping cart), to remind them to return to the app.
  — People who meet a combination of the above options (e.g., people who use Version 7.0 of your app but have not used it in the last 25 days), to try out a new feature.

To enable these capabilities, you must activate the *Conversion Tracking* and *Remarketing* features. Consequently, you will need to:
  — Determine which pages of your app you want to track for. *Remarketing* purposes before tags are added.
  — Add *tags* (snippets of code) to your application; you may need support from your app programmer.
  — Re-release your app after the Conversion Tracking and *Remarketing* tags are added.

- **You can specify the operating system(s), device(s) and carrier(s) for your campaign.** This is especially important if your app works with only some brands of smartphones, tablets, etc.
- **You can set ads to take users to *deep links,* a specific screen within your app or website.**

In programming parlance, a *deep link* is a uniform resource identifier (URI) for a specific screen in the app. It is composed of a domain, a scheme, a host and a path. You must enter the URI when you setup an ad and it is visible when you edit your ad. Consult your app program about deep links in your app.

30

Remarketing Ads

Remarketing **Ads enable you to reach people who previously visited your site or your YouTube channel or video.** *Remarketing* is especially valuable for e-commerce sites.

Remarketing **Ads are very effective because they can present your message again to people who have already shown an interest.**

- With *Remarketing*, you have opportunities to stay in touch with previous visitors and coax them back for a second look at your product by showing them ads as they surf the web and visit Display Network Partner sites.

- You can develop special *Remarketing* Ads for previous visitors based on the webpage(s) they visited or whether they abandoned a shopping cart on your site. Note: If they visited multiple pages, your *Remarketing* Ads could bid against each other.

- You can fine-tune your targeting of previous visitors using Display Network targeting methods (keywords, topics, managed placements and interest categories). For example, you can direct ads to women aged 25 to 34 who are parents.

- You can construct sophisticated strategies in line with your sales funnel.

  For example, you can use Search Ads with keywords used by people not-ready-to-buy to bring similar prospects to your website. Then, you can follow-up with Display Network-*Remarketing* Ads using keywords for more sales-ready prospects.

- You can learn about your prospects and customers by reviewing the Display Network sites they visit. Subsequently, you could target your *Remarketing* to those sites (i.e., to *managed placement* sites) with specific ads.

- Your *Remarketing* Ad can promise a special offer if the visitor returns to your website, and you can use a different landing page to deliver the offer.

- You can use *Remarketing* Ads in conjunction with the *Conversion Tracking* feature (discussed later) to gain more impressions.

- You can use *Remarketing* with YouTube videos and take advantage of the cost-per-view bidding model under which you pay only if the viewer watches your video.

- *Remarketing* Ads use the cost-per-click (CPC) bidding model for Search Network Ads and Display Network ads (except for YouTube ads, which

31

use cost-per-view (CPV) bidding model). However, if you also use Conversion Tracking, the cost per acquisition (CPA) bidding model applies.

- *Remarketing* Ads do not look different from Search Network or Display Network ads.

Remarketing Ads—Interest-Based Ads

Interest-Based *Remarketing* Ads are a powerful tool for targeting new people who have interests similar to your existing visitors and customers.

- For example, if you sell mountain bikes online, you may find that many of your customers are interested in environmental issues, healthful eating or yoga. You can target your ads to appear on sites related to those interests.

Interest-Based *Remarketing* Ads let you use psychographics (personality attributes) and techno-graphics (technical and online behaviors) to target your prospects. These are much more powerful than basic Display Network ads, which limit you to people that match demographic characteristics and websites that match keywords, topics or managed placements.

Use of Interest-Based *Remarketing* Ads requires a privacy policy on your landing page. Google prescribes the content, which must reveal AdWords usage, the use of cookies and a description of your use of *Remarketing* for similar audiences.

- To review Google's privacy requirements, search on AdWords Help for the topic, "Information to include in your privacy policy."
- People who do not want their browsing activity tracked can opt out using Google's ads preferences manager. Review these options by searching on Google for the topic, "Make the ads you see on the web more interesting."
- For more information about using *Remarketing* lists, search on AdWords Help for the topic, "Interest-Based advertising policy."

Third-party vendors (i.e., vendors other than Google) can interface with Interest-Based *Remarketing* Ads to provide even greater access to new people based on interests.

- Any agreement you make with a third-party ad vendor must meet Google's *third-party ad serving policy.* For example, the vendor must disclose data collection and usage practices and meet Google's privacy and notice requirements. For more information, search in AdWords Help for "Requirements for third-party ad serving."

Video Ads

Video Ads reach people who watch videos online on YouTube or on those Display Network websites where videos are accepted. Video Ads let small businesses look like large businesses, at a much more affordable rate than other visual media, such as TV.

According to Google:

- Nearly one-third of the time people spend online is spent watching videos.
- People remember Video Ads better than static ads.
- A Nielsen study found people remember the brand and the message better and like online ads better than television ads.
- Nielsen also found that Video Ad recall is roughly 40 percent higher online than on TV in the U.S.
- A 2009 Online Video Engagement Consortium study found that people in the U.S. who watch online TV shows pay closer attention to the ads than people who watch live TV shows.

Five Video Ad types are available within AdWords, and more formats are available through DoubleClick, Google's rich-media software and service division. Be aware, however, that you can also:

- **Buy a** *contract-based inventory* **of ads on the Display Network from Google.** Ad agencies have access to additional targeting capabilities. Contact YouTube Ad Sales directly to learn more.

- **Buy a** *reservation-based inventory* **of ads on YouTube that runs outside of AdWords' control.** The inventory available is different from that offered by AdWords. High purchase commitments are expected. YouTube scales the CPC price of reserved ads based on the number of impressions you buy. You must buy these ads directly from YouTube. Go to YouTube.com and click the Advertising link at the bottom of the page or contact YouTube ad sales directly at 866–246–6453 to learn more.

The video formats available in AdWords include:

1. *In-Stream Video Ads*, which are, essentially, 15- or 60-second commercials that show on the Display Network and/or YouTube.

2. *YouTube overlay banners*, which show as static ads across the bottom of video clips, mostly on YouTube. Google now calls these ads *in-video static image ads*.

3. *YouTube promotional ads*, which show as a static image that advertises your video on YouTube.

4. *Hover-to-play Video Ads,* which show only when the viewer clicks the ad. Google previously called these *click-to-play* ads.

5. *Expanding Video Ads*, which show on the Display Network as ads that expand and offer video content when a viewer clicks them. These are also called *Lightbox Ads*.

The following describes each Video Ad type.

In-Stream Video Ads

In-stream Video Ads **are commercials that show before, during or after the featured content.** Many agencies use *in-stream Video Ads* to re-purpose their TV commercial.

In-stream Video Ads **appear on YouTube, YouTube Watch pages and on many Google Display Network Partner websites.** You can omit any of the three placements.

Not all website owners accept *in-stream Video Ads.* Those that do, determine when and where the ad runs on their websites.

In-stream Video Ads **can be short video clips or TV-like commercials.**

- **Short-clip Video Ads:**
  — Are videos of 20 seconds or less that, generally, supplement your online ads by using sound and motion to attract attention.
  — Can use the *cost-per-click* or *cost-per-thousand* bidding options.
  — Are non-skip-able Video Ads.
  — Can target the audience by Display Network targeting methods (keywords, placements, topics, interests, *Remarketing Lists* and site categories).
  — Can be in the same campaign with other Display Network ads—which makes setup faster and tracking of the overall campaign easier.

- **TV-like commercials:**
  — Are videos that often have appeared on TV and the financial investment in the production is large. These Video Ads were called *in-search ads* in previous years.
  — Are called "pre-roll" Video Ads if they run before the featured video or "mid-roll" Video Ads if they run during a featured video (like a commercial break). The website owner decides whether to accept Video Ads of this type and determines where the video runs.
  — Use the cost-per-view (CPV) basis, and you can customize your CPV bid for each video size.

34

FIGURE 1.18 In-stream Video Ad (pre-roll) before a YouTube content video

— Start automatically and can be skipped (i.e., closed) by the viewer after five seconds. AdWords charges you only if the viewer watches the full video or 30 seconds, whichever is shorter.

— Can target the audience by target group (i.e., gender, parental status).

— Can be up to 60 seconds long. Video Ads over 15 seconds run before, during or after video content of 10 minutes or more. Video Ads of 15 seconds or less run before, during or after shorter clips or long content videos.

— Can provide performance data segmented by format, network, device, time, click type and conversion status.

— Cannot be in the same campaign with other Display Network ad types and are not associated with an ad group. (Thus, each video is its own campaign, ad group and ad).

— Can include a call-to-action (static image) image at the end of your Video Ad. This further encourages a viewer to click your ad and go to your website or YouTube channel.

— Can include your own overlay banner on YouTube. You can make your In-Stream Video Ad do double duty. By adding a companion image or a commercial to your In-Stream ad, you now have a YouTube promotion ad.

Because people can copy YouTube videos to their own websites and blogs, your Video Ads might appear outside the Google Display Network.

Overlay Banners (In-Video Static Image Ads)

Overlay banner ads **were the original type of ad shown on YouTube in 2000 when Google bought YouTube.** Note that the ad itself is not a video, but rather a link to your website, YouTube channel or YouTube video.

Google calls these ads *in-video static image overlay.* We call them *overlay banners* in this document, because that says what they look like.

Overlay banners show on top of a video, either your own video or someone else's video, the owner of which has opted-in to Google AdSense to permit ads to show on their videos. The ads occupy the bottom 20 percent of the screen.

- **Overlay banner ads show on YouTube, which lets you take advantage of the huge audience watching videos each day without requiring you to create or submit a video.** Overlay banner ads also show on the Google's Display Partner websites that permit videos.

- **An overlay banner ad for your local business on a popular YouTube video is a great way to remind people of your business or to announce a Grand Opening.**

- **Overlay banner ads appear at any point during the YouTube video.** The YouTube owner (i.e., the publisher) sets the time when the overlay ad appears, and it is not necessarily at the start of a video.

- **Overlay banner ads are text, image or interactive Flash**. Flash is currently limited to certain customers.

FIGURE 1.19 Display Network—overlay banner ad on YouTube watch page

Overlay banners offer three bidding methods: *cost-per-click* (CPC), *cost-per-thousand* (CPM) or *cost-per-view* (CPV) bidding methods.

- With CPC you pay only if the viewer clicks your ad. With CPM, you pay each time your ad appears whether the viewer clicks it or not.
- With *cost-per-click* (CPC) or *cost-per-thousand* (CPM) ads, you can:
  — Mix Video Ads with other types of Display Network ads.
  — Use *targeting methods* (keywords, placements, topics, interests, *Remarketing Lists* and site categories) to define who sees your ad and where your ad appears.
- With *cost-per-view* (CPV) ads, you can:
  — **Customize your bid for each ad size**.
  — View performance data by format, network, device, click-type, time of day and conversion for a deeper understanding of your audience.
  — Add a call-to-action to the end of your video.
  — Target the videos that your ad shows on by target groups defined by:
    (1) Placement (i.e., on YouTube video, videos on a particular. YouTube channel, videos on a particular website, and/or real-time, live-streaming videos on a publisher sites).
    (2) Keywords.
    (3) Age.
    (4) Gender.
  — With CPV, you cannot mix Video Ads with other types of Display ads.

YouTube Promotions

YouTube promotions advertise your YouTube videos on the YouTube search page and, thus, drive people to your YouTube channel or to a Watch Page to see your video.

- **Google calls these ads** *in-display promotion ads.* In the past, Google called these ads *promoted YouTube videos* and *in-search ads*.
- *YouTube promotion* **ads** appear on YouTube Watch pages and on the Google Display Network.
- *YouTube promotions* use a static image. Note that the ad itself is not a video but, rather, a static image that links to your video.
- *YouTube promotions* appear with a small "AD" icon on the YouTube Search page when someone's search query relates to your keywords.

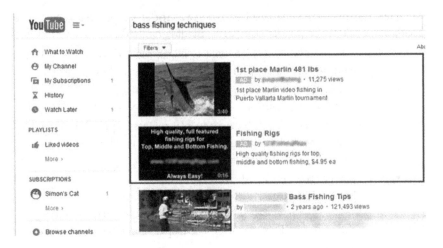

FIGURE 1.20 In-display YouTube promotion ads on search page

Google no longer considers these a separate type of ad, preferring instead to call them simply In-Display Video Ads on the YouTube Search page.

- *YouTube promotions* link to the YouTube video or channel you specify.

- *YouTube promotions* can use the *cost-per-click* (CPC), the *cost-per-thousand* (CPM) or the *cost-per-view* (CPV) bidding options.

    With CPC, AdWords charges you only when a viewer clicks your ad. With CPM, AdWords charges you for each ad impression. With CPV, you pay only if the viewer clicks your ad.

a. With *cost-per-click* (CPC) or *cost-per-thousand* (CPM) ads, you can:
    — Mix Video Ads with other types of Display Network ads.
    — Use *targeting methods* (keywords, placements, topics, interests, *Remarketing Lists* and site categories) to define who sees your ad and where your ad appears.

(These Video Ads use the *all online campaign* screen.)

b. With *cost-per-view* (CPV), you can:
    — **Customize your bid for each ad size**
    — View performance data by *format, network, device, click type, time of day*, and *conversion* for a deeper understanding of your audience
    — Add a call-to-action to the end of your video
    — Target Video Ads by:
        (1) *Target groups* (using age, gender, parental status).
        (2) *Placement* (i.e., on YouTube video, videos on a particular YouTube channel, videos on a particular website, and/or real-time, live-streaming videos on a publisher sites).

FIGURE 1.21 In-display YouTube promotion on side menu

— With CPV, you cannot mix Video Ads with other types of Display ads.

Engagement Video Ads

Engagement Video Ads **expand to twice their width or height when clicked.** This gives the ad more presence on the page.

Because the viewer must take action to see the video, he or she is usually more engaged than a viewer perusing a webpage.

Google must approve *Engagement Video Ads.* Allow two weeks for review, testing and approval.

Engagement Video Ads **let you:**

- Bid on a *cost-per-engagement* basis (i.e., *cost-per-click*). Your ad is considered clicked when someone (1) hovers the mouse over the ad and it expands, (2) clicks to play a video or (3) taps the content.

- Run on the Display Network Partner websites that support engagement formats.

- Define your market using location and language, like Basic Display Network Ads.

- Run on all devices, but you can specify that your ad run only on smartphone or tablets or desktops. This is important since your ad may not show well on some devices. For example, expanding ads do not show well on smartphones.

39

- Target your audience using the Display Network *targeting methods (keywords, audience, topics, interests, site categories and managed placements parameters)*.

Engagement Video Ads **come in three formats:**

1. Hover-to-play.

2. One-video lightbox.

3. Three-video lightboxes.

The following describes each one.

Hover-to-Play Video Ads

Generally, visitors who click *hover-to-play Video Ads* **are more engaged than visitors who see** *in-stream Video Ads,* **which run automatically.** Per Google, click-through rates for *hover-to-play Video Ads* can be higher than usual, sometimes as high as 4 percent.

Hover-to-play Video Ads **include a static cover image and a video.** The viewer must click your ad to see it. After clicking the ad, the viewer cannot skip or close the ad. Previously, Google called these *click-to-play ads*.

For *hover-to-play Video Ads,* **you need:**

- An enticing cover image that piques the viewer's curiosity. This is key to attracting people to your ad. An image that does not look like a commercial often fairs well.

- An interesting, entertaining or informative video is key to keeping people engaged.

- A solid call-to-action on your ending image is key to coaxing people to go to your site, to visit your store or to call you.

FIGURE 1.22 Hover-to-play Engagement Ad

Hover-to-play Video Ads **let you:**

- Show videos of up to four minutes in length. However, 30-second videos receive optimal results.

- Mix *hover-to-play ads* with other ad types in a Basic Display Network campaign.

- Link to your webpage.

- Use the *cost-per-click* bidding method.

One-Video and Three-Video Lightboxes

Lightboxes expand nearly to full screen to show the rich-media contents of your ad, which can be a video of any length.

- After someone hovers over the ad for two seconds or clicks the video your video starts with the sound on.

- Both types of Video Ads run on websites with a 300 x 250 (inline rectangle) space or a 336 × 280 (large rectangle). Not all Display Network Partners can accommodate lightboxes.

THE GOOGLE SHOPPING NETWORK

The *Google Shopping Network* **consists of a panel on Google.com and pages under the Shopping link on the Google.com page.**

- The panel in the upper right-hand corner of the Google.com page shows the top ranked listings for the query entered by the searcher. Clicking on a listing takes you to the advertiser's website. Clicking on the "Shop for <search term> on Google" takes you to the Shopping page.

- The Shopping page shows dozens of small listings.

Only *Google Shopping Ads* appear on the *Google Shopping Network*.

Google Shopping Ads

Google Shopping Ads **appear in a panel of images on Google.com or in a page of image ads on** *Google Shopping,* **an option on the Google.com query entry page.**

Google Shopping Ads are excellent for retailers who sell hundreds of products. They are also valuable for advertisers of custom goods, such as an artist or artisan, who have many one-of-a-kind items.

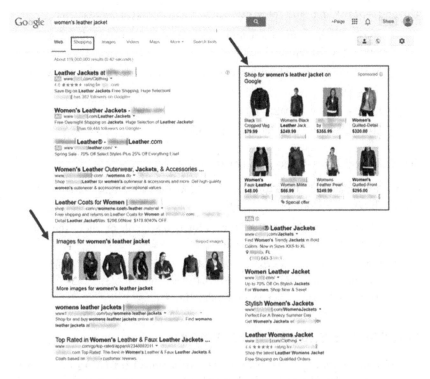

FIGURE 1.23 Google Shopping/product listings

This Google.com page shows the Google Shopping product listings immediately at the top of the page, within the organic results or on the right above the Search Network ads.

Google claims many businesses experience significant increases in click-through rates using *Google Shopping* and some businesses even double or triple their traffic.

- When the searcher clicks on *Shopping* in the top menu of Google.com, the *Google Shopping* page appears. Thus, a search for a product brings up pictures and prices of dozens of the product submitted by advertisers.

- When a shopper clicks on an item, the ad box expands, revealing a larger image of the item along with color, sizes, price and buyer reviews. The shopper can add the item to a *shortlist*, where it is stored along with other items under consideration. The shopper can add or delete items from the shortlist over time.

- When a shopper clicks the *visually similar items* button, numerous items of the same type appear. This dramatically changes the shopper's options and the level of competition. It makes advertising via product listings more necessary but, perhaps, less cost-effective than before.

FIGURE 1.24 Google Shopping page showing Google Shopping/product listings

The Google Shopping page (#1 above) provides a specially formatted page that shows only products—no organic search entries—for the search term entered by the shopper, and it provides the shopper with a couple of tools to track products under consideration, (#3) view items on the shopper's shortlist, (#4) and filters to narrow the choices on the page and (#5) options for sorting the page. Other Search ads (#6) appear at the bottom of the page.

- Google Shopping accommodates multiple pictures of a product (usually taken at different angles). This gives a shopper a simulated 360-degree view of the item. Google restricts this capability to brand owners.

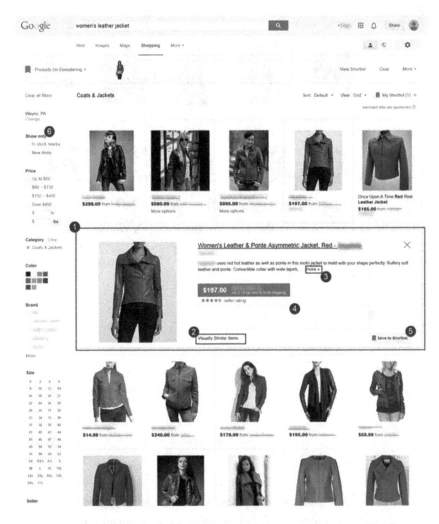

FIGURE 1.25 Google Shopping showing an item clicked by the shopper

Note that the ad box expands (#1) and additional information and options show, such as see *visually similar* items (#2), see *more* (#3), see *Seller Ratings* (#4), *Save to Shortlist* (#5) and narrow choices via *filters* (#6). This dramatically changes the shopper's options. Items saved to the *shortlist* appear at the top. These options make advertising via product listings more of a necessity because of the overt competition.

Listings for *Google Shopping* are setup very differently than other AdWords ads.

- *Google Shopping* supports only *cost-per-click*, manual bidding. AdWords charges you only if a searcher clicks on your ad and goes to the landing page you specified.

- To run *Google Shopping Ads* you create a file (or spreadsheet), called a *feed*, containing a line item for each product you want to sell and then upload it to Google.

- Google places your inventory in an ad group called *all products*. You can sub-divide the *all products* ad group into smaller *product groups* so you can give each its own max CPC bid.

- Your feed must follow Google's exacting standards; you must keep information in your feed in sync with information on your website (especially price and availability), and you must re-load your feed at least once every 30 days.
    - The Google Merchant Center supports an *automatic item update* feature to keep your website and feed in sync. You embed special HTML tags, called *schema.org microdata*, into your webpages to designate product prices and availability information. Google then uses your website data rather than the data in your feed to create listings.
    - The Google Merchant Center also supports an application program interface (API) that lets you update your feed online within the merchant center, which is especially helpful if your prices change intraday.

- When someone searches on Google.com or *Google Shopping* for a specific product, AdWords conducts an auction among the advertisers who have feed information for that specific product and creates a panel on the search page showing the top-ranked items. It also creates a *Google Shopping* page showing all the relevant listings.

- If the searcher clicks your product listing for an enlarged view, you are not charged. However, if the searcher clicks your listing to go to you website, you are charged.

ptGoogle Shopping* makes running sales, special promotions and offers easy, one of its greatest benefits.

- **You can attach a *promotional message* to a *product grouping*.** A promotional message should be an alert, rather than additional ad copy. For example, you can add a promotional message such as "Limited quantities available" to your product listings for dress shirts.

You can create multiple product groupings within an ad group, so each grouping can have its own promotional message.

- **You can submit a *special offer feed* that lets you attach a promo code to your listing so your buyer can receive a cash discount, percentage discount or a free gift at checkout.** You must contact Google to apply and be approved for this feature. Search on Google.com for "Merchant promotions" for more information.

***Google Shopping* gives customers an extra measure of confidence.**

- **Google offers a Trusted Store program for qualifying merchants that offer superior service.** Trusted Store merchants must meet rigid delivery standards, which Google monitors. They display the Trusted Store badge and their customers can purchase order protection from Google. If a dispute occurs, the customer can ask for Google's help in resolving the issue. (Search in Google.com for Trusted Stores Merchant Guidelines for details.)

FIGURE 1.26 Google Trusted Store badge

- **If you show ratings stars or reviews on your website, you can also show them in your listings.** The *schema.org microdata*, the special HTML tags mentioned previously, let you mark reviews and ratings on your website for use within product listings.

  (See Google Shopping Listings, page 291, for instructions on creating *Google Shopping* listings.)

***Google Shopping* offers detailed tracking data.**

- **Performance data for your *Google Shopping* listings appear under the *Products* tab on the main menu.** You can view other facets of the data using the Shopping views in the *dimensions* tab.

- **AdWords also provides *benchmark data* for max CPC, impression share and CTR.** Benchmark data lets you compare your bid, share of available impressions and click-though rate for a product to the overall average of all advertisers for a similar product.

Google's subsidiary DoubleClick offers additional benefits for *Google Shopping* advertisers.

- Through Google's DoubleClick division, you can run *Google Shopping* campaigns with DoubleClick updating it automatically based on changes to your Google Merchant feed. This saves time and ensures accuracy. For example, the DoubleClick system ensures that a product is paused if it is out of stock or if the price on the landing page is not the same as the price in your feed.

  (Search in DoubleClick's Search Blog for "Inventory-aware campaigns: automatically create and optimize search campaigns.")

Dynamic Remarketing for Google Shopping Ads

Dynamic Remarketing **Ads are a powerful add-on to your** *Google Shopping* **campaigns.** They let you automatically target ads to people who previously visited your website, re-showing them your product for the next 30 days as they visit Display Network Partner sites across the Internet.

With *Dynamic Remarketing*, **you do not need to setup ads for each product.** AdWords constructs the ad using information in your *Google Shopping* feed and shows them to your previous visitors.

Dynamic Remarketing **uses tags, cookies and lists in the same way the Remarketing feature does to identify visitors and the products they viewed.** (See Remarketing Ads, page 282, for more information.)

You can use *Dynamic Remarketing* **Ads in conjunction with the** *Conversion Tracking* **feature to gain more impressions and the** *Conversion Optimizer* **to increase your bid (within the limits of your target CPA).**

In a nutshell, this is how *Dynamic Remarketing* **Ads work:**

1. **You create a feed of product information (category, descriptions, prices, etc.) and upload it to the Google Merchant Center website.**

2. **You setup Remarketing, if you do not already use Remarketing.** You insert a *tag*, a snippet of code created by AdWords, into each webpage and plug-in the product category and other information for each specific webpage.

3. **You set up a Remarketing list for** *All Visitors*, **where AdWords stores the visitor's ID and the product category viewed.** AdWords creates the following lists:

   - General visitors: per Google, "people who visited your website but didn't view specific products."

   - Product viewers: per Google, "people who viewed specific product pages on your site but did not add them to their shopping cart."

47

- Shopping cart abandoners: per Google, "people who added products to the shopping cart but didn't complete the purchase."
- Past buyers: Per Google, "people who purchased products from you in the past."

4. **Next, you setup a Display Network campaign.** That is, you (1) select a geographic area and language for your campaign and (2) create an ad group, setting a *max* CPC for each of four types of visitors (general, product viewer, shopping cart abandoners and past buyers) for each product category and (3) customize the ad templates to match your brand identity or simply upload your logo for AdWords to insert in the standard templates.

When someone visits one of your webpages, AdWords adds a cookie (i.e., a short file) with a unique ID number to the visitor's PC. In addition, AdWords also adds the visitor's ID to an *all visitor* lists and one of the four lists (listed previously).

5. **For the next 30 days, as your visitor surfs across Display Network websites, AdWords includes your ad in the auction for ad positions before your visitor.**

- **If you use a flexible bidding strategy, or the Conversion Optimization feature, AdWords automatically optimizes your bid as dictated by those features and with consideration to how close the visitor was to buying (i.e., which of the four lists he or she is on) and how much time has passed since the visitor's last visit.**

- If you use *Conversion Optimization*, your bidding model is set to enhanced *cost-per-click* (eCPC), and AdWords automatically optimizes your bid based on how close the visitor was to buying (i.e., which of the four lists he or she is on) and how much time has passed.

- If you use the *conversion optimizer* feature to achieve a target *cost-per-acquisition* (CPA), AdWords automatically optimizes your bid based on historic performance and how close the visitor was to buying (i.e., which of the four lists he or she is on).

6. **When you win an auction, AdWords constructs an ad based on the visitor's previously-viewed products.**

For more information about *Dynamic Remarketing*, search in AdWords Help for "Using dynamic Remarketing to show ads tailored to your site visitors."

(See Dynamic Remarketing, page 47, for instructions.)

Chapter 2

How AdWords Works

This chapter describes the AdWords auction process—from the outside and the inside. Understanding the decision-making paths and priorities of AdWords, as it selects and prices ads to be shown, helps you construct a more successful campaign. It brings to light many elements to consider across your campaign— from writing your landing page and ad text to defining your market and CPC bid.

More specifically, the chapter reviews the auction process from the perspective of the Google searcher—a scenario familiar to millions of searchers and web viewers—along with the information you provide to create an ad. It goes on to review the inner workings of the AdWords algorithm (as much as publically known), explaining the key elements and options that determine which advertiser's ad is shown, the ad's position on the web page and the cost-per-click (CPC).

ADWORDS FROM THE SEARCHER'S PERSPECTIVE

The following image is a typical Google search engine results page, with ads at the top and down the right side. Virtually all Google.com users are familiar with AdWords from the perspective of a searcher.

Here's what the searcher sees and does online:

1. When you enter a search term into Google.com, Google provides a series of results pages, called search engine results pages (SERPs). Google calls the search engine pages its *Search Network*.

2. Each SERP includes ads, marked with a small yellow icon, above the search results, down the right side and across the bottom of the page. A list of websites related to your search term appears in the body of the page.

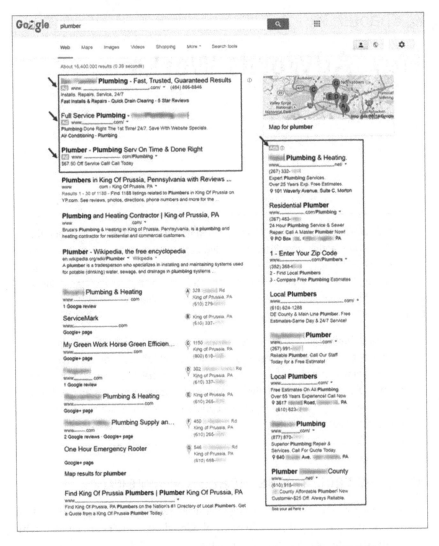

FIGURE 2.1 Search ads on Google search engine results page (SERP)
Each ad or panel of ads is marked with a small yellow icon.

3. The ads relate to either the search term you entered or to interests (products, topics, etc.) you have viewed previously on the Internet.

4. When you click on an ad, Google takes you to the advertiser's *landing page*. There you can take whatever action the advertiser offers, such as:

   • Buy the advertised product.

   • Obtain more information about a topic.

- Sign up for a newsletter, download an application to your smart phone, download a brochure or white paper, etc.

The operation of search ads is straightforward and easy to understand. Less understood by searchers, however, are the ads on the webpages of various news sites, e-magazines, blogs and the Gmail homepage. These, too, are AdWords ads.

FIGURE 2.2 Display ads

5. Google compensates more than a million website owners for showing AdWords ads on their websites. This network of websites composes Google's Display Network.

6. On these sites, Display Network ads relate either to the content on the site or to the interests of the reader. Ads appear only in spaces designated by the site owner.

7. When you click on a Display Network ad, AdWords takes you to the advertiser's landing page.

ADWORDS BEHIND THE SCENES

Google never fully explains how AdWords works. However, a general understanding of the behind-the-scenes functions emerges from AdWords documentation, research conducted by AdWords aficionados and Google's blog.

1. **Before you advertise on AdWords, you must provide AdWords with the specifications for all aspects of your ad, including:**

   a. **The Google Network you want to use (i.e., the Search Network, the Display Network, both the Search and Display Networks, the AdMob Network or the Shopping Network).**

   b. **Your desired market.** You specify the geographic location, language, searcher's location, searcher's device, etc. AdWords assumes you want your ad to show on all devices (PCs, laptops, tablets and mobile devices) unless you specify certain devices.

   c. **The maximum amount of money you agree to spend in one day (the *daily budget*).**

   d. **The headline for your ad, two lines of description, an easy-to-remember *display URL*, and the actual *destination URL* of the landing page where the searcher can purchase your product or learn more about it.**

   e. **The words and phrases you want to trigger your ad (i.e., your *keywords*) and the words and phrases you do not want to trigger your ad (i.e., your *negative keywords*).**

   f. **Additional information appended to your ad, such as your business address, phone number, sitelinks and number of Google+ followers.**

   g. **If you are using Display Network ads, the types of websites appropriate for your ad.** They can be websites AdWords identifies for you (such as websites discussing topics related to your product), or websites you specify (i.e., *managed placements*).

   h. **The types of people you want to see your ad (i.e., age, gender, interests).**

   Once this information is provided and your ad is approved, AdWords makes your ad eligible to compete for an ad space on your selected network.

2. **When a searcher initiates a search or lands on a website that can display ads, AdWords initiates its *auction process*.**

   Google does not reveal the exact process for conducting the auction. However, the following presents a very general overview (many nuances and fine points are omitted). Logically, ads that do not pass a particular criteria drop to the bottom of the list or are dropped completely from the group of ads being considered.

a. **First, AdWords selects the ads with keywords that match, or come closest to matching, the searcher's query term.**

b. **AdWords determines how well the searcher's demographics relate to your desired market.**

   For example, if you want to show ads to females in Philadelphia, the searcher must be female (as far as Google can determine) and either live in Philadelphia or include "Philadelphia" in the search query. If the searcher meets your requirements, your ad continues to compete in the auction.

c. **AdWords computes a *quality score* that represents how well your ad relates to the searcher's query.**

   Google does not reveal the formula for calculating a quality score, saying only that the computation weighs some 200 factors. Three very important factors are:

   — Expected click-through rate: how likely searchers are to click your ad.

   — Ad relevance: how closely the searcher's keyword relates to the keywords for your ad and the keyword(s) in your ad.

   — Landing page experience: how useful your website's landing page is to the searcher (i.e., how long people generally stay on your page).

   At a minimum, we know from Google documentation and experiments conducted by researchers that the following factors are part of the evaluation:

   — Whether your keyword matches the query exactly, partially or broadly. Exact matches add the most value to your quality score. Broad matches add the least to your quality score. (See Level 5: Keywords, Targeting Methods and Targeting Groups, page 81, for more information.)

   — Whether you have more than one ad using the best keyword. Because AdWords permits only one ad per advertiser, AdWords attempts to select your "best" ad. It eliminates all but one of your ads based on the past performance of your ad (i.e., the click-through rate of the ad), your bid, and your *ad rotation* choice. For *Google Shopping* campaigns, where you can prioritize one campaign over another, AdWords uses the ad from the highest prioritized campaign.

— Whether the searcher is looking for a local product, service or business. Ads targeting a narrow geographic area near the searcher's location receive higher quality scores than ads targeted to national markets. For example, in a query for "dry cleaner," an ad targeting the searcher's neighborhood scores higher than an ad targeting the entire United States.

— How high your *click-through rates (CTR)* is. Your click-through rate is the number of visitors to your site divided by the number of ad showings for your products. AdWords considers the CTR is for the keyword, your URL, and the overall click-through rate for this type of ad (search or display) across your account. AdWords researchers indicate *click-through rate* is the major determinant of a quality score. This agrees with Google's stated belief that "success breed's success" and the click-through rate is the most reliable indicator of an advertiser's success.

3. **AdWords determines the *max CPC* you agree to pay if someone clicks your ad.** The maximum amount you agreed to pay includes:

   a. The amount you specified for your keyword (your *maximum cost-per-click*, or max CPC).

   b. Any increase you authorized AdWords to make because you selected one of these bidding options:
      — *Automatic bidding*, which gives AdWords leeway to change your bid to get as many clicks for you as possible each day.
      — *Enhanced CPC* with manual bidding, which gives AdWords leeway to raise your CPC by up to 30 percent to get as many clicks for you as possible each day.
      — *Flexible bid strategy*, which gives AdWords leeway to change your bid to meet a page-location requirement, a targeted spending goal, a return on ad spend goal or an average cost-per-acquisition goal.
      — *Conversion Optimization*, which tries to get as many clicks as possible at the lowest average cost possible during the month.

   c. Any *custom bid* for a particularly attractive keyword or website (e.g., you'll pay 10 percent more if the searcher is near your store, or 10 percent less if the ad is on YouTube).

   d. Any *bid adjustment* you set for a specific device (e.g., a mobile device verses a desktop), location or day/hour.

   AdWords applies the above auxiliary bids (items b., c. and d.) to obtain an adjusted max CPC (my terminology).

Note that bids adjustments are "compounding" in that they are applied on top of each other. For example, the max CPC is increased by the *enhanced CPC* option to set a new max CPC; the new max CPC is increased by the *custom bid* to set a higher max CPC; the higher max CPC is increased further by the *bid adjustment* to set an even higher max CPC, etc.

Google does not reveal the order in which AdWords applies the auxiliary bids. However, it is logical that AdWords applies decreases first and increases last to maximize the CPC and, thus, give your ad its best chance for a high ad position.

4. **Using your quality score and your adjusted max CPC, AdWords next calculates an ad rank for each ad.**

    Again, Google does not reveal the formula for the calculation. However, one AdWords researcher theorizes the formula is simply:

    Quality Score × Adjusted Max CPC

    Such a formula gives equal weight to the bid and the quality score.

Advertiser	Max CPC Bid	Quality Score	Ad rank (Max CPC x Quality Score)
Advertiser A	$0.45	8	$ 3.60
Advertiser C	$0.80	3	$ 2.40
Advertiser D	$0.75	3	$ 2.25
Advertiser B	$0.30	5	$ 1.50
Advertiser E	$0.25	2	$ 0.50

FIGURE 2.3 AdWords calculates an ad rank for each ad
Ad rank is (*quality score* times *bid*).

5. **Next, AdWords sorts the ads in ad rank order, highest to lowest.** (See Figure 2.4) The ad with the highest ranking takes the top ad position, the ad with the next highest-ranking ad takes the next ad position, etc., etc.

    The ad with the highest ad rank takes the top ad position. Note that the highest bidder did not receive the highest ad position.

    AdWords determines the amount each ad pays for a click. The higher your quality score for an ad, the lower the amount you pay when a viewer clicks your ad.

    Again, Google does not reveal the exact algorithm for computing your *actual cost-per-click*, as Google calls it.

Advertiser	Max CPC Bid	Quality Score	Ad rank (Max CPC x Quality Score)	Ad Position
Advertiser A	$0.45	8	$3.60	1
Advertiser C	$0.80	3	$2.40	2
Advertiser D	$0.75	3	$2.25	3
Advertiser B	$0.30	5	$1.50	4
Advertiser E	$0.25	2	$0.50	5

Figure 2.4. AdWords assigns an ad position to each ad

The ad with the highest *ad rank* takes the top ad position. Note that the highest bidder did not receive the highest ad position. The ad with the highest ad rank takes the top ad position.

Advertiser	Max CPC Bid	Quality Score	Ad rank (Max CPC x Quality Score)	Ad Position	Could have bid	Actual CPC charged, if ad is clicked
Advertiser A	$0.45	8	$3.60	1	$ .30	$ .31
Advertiser C	$0.80	3	$2.40	2	$ .75	$ .76
Advertiser D	$0.75	3	$2.25	3	$ .50	$ .51
Advertiser B	$0.30	5	$1.50	4	$ .10	$ .11
Advertiser E	$0.25	2	$0.50	5	*	*

FIGURE 2.5 AdWords assigns a CPC to each ad

A cost-per-click is assigned to each Advertiser before the searcher sees the ads.

However, in theory, AdWords does the following for each advertiser to determine what to charge each advertiser:

a. AdWords determines the amount the top ranked advertiser *could have bid* to achieve the same ad rank as the next highest ad. In our example, if Advertiser A had bid $0.30, his or her *ad rank* would equal that of the next highest Advertiser (Advertiser C) ($2.40 divided by 8 = 30¢).

b. AdWords adds 1¢ to the computed amount the Advertiser *could have bid* to obtain the amount to charge an Advertiser if his or her ad is clicked by the searcher.

Google states in its blog that an advertiser wins an ad position by out-bidding the next best ad by 1¢. The theory discussed previously supports that premise.

Google also does not say how it handles the bid for the lowest ranking ad.

c. For Display Network ads, AdWords may adjust the actual *cost-per-click* downward if AdWords data shows that ads appearing on a particular Partner website are unlikely to result in a conversion.

d. According to one large AdWords agency, AdWords also adjusts the actual *cost-per-click* downward for Advertisers with high quality scores. The algorithm for this type of adjustment is not known.

The agency also claims a quality score of 5 is average, while most first page ads score closer to 7. Further, a higher-than-average score brought the following discounts in 2013:
— Score of 6 = 16.7 percent discount.
— Score of 7 = 28.6 percent discount.
— Score of 8 = 37.5 percent discount.
— Score of 9 = 44.4 percent discount.
— Score of 10 = 50 percent discount.

Based on this data, increasing your *quality score* nets a big cost savings— and potentially an even bigger increase in revenues if you use those savings to buy more ads and to gain more buyers.

6. **AdWords verifies that top ads meet "certain *cost-per-click* thresholds."** Google does not say what the thresholds are (so far as I have found). Consequently, other factors, outside the theoretical mathematical formula described previously, may enter into the final determination of the actual CPC for top ad positions. (One might theorize that a threshold might be the minimum amount Google must pay Google Network Partners for showing ads on their websites, or other legitimate overhead costs.)

7. **AdWords formats your ad for presentation.** If you specify one or more *ad extensions* (address, phone number, sitelinks, offers or Google +1), AdWords adds the appropriate pieces to your ad. AdWords reformats your ad to fit the space available. For example, when the ad position is wide, AdWords runs two lines of the ad's description as one long line of text.

8. **Finally, AdWords displays the ads.** The advertiser with the highest-ranking ad takes the top ad position above the SERPs and the advertiser with the next highest-ranking ad takes the next ad position, usually above the SERPs. The third highest ad takes the top position on the right-hand column, and so on and so, until AdWords fills all the ad slots on the first page. Then AdWords proceeds to fill the following pages.

9. **When the searcher clicks on your ad, AdWords charges the computed actual cost-per-click amount to your account.** AdWords does not charge you if no one clicks your ad unless you are running a cost-per-thousand (CPM) ad.

10. **AdWords stores data about each ad.** It tracks the number of *impressions* (showings) each ad receives, the number of clicks each receives and a running total of the actual CPC paid, among many, many other items.

11. **Periodically, you evaluate your AdWords costs and determine your profits.**

    As you learn which ads and keywords produce results and you become savvier about AdWords features, you can implement advanced features to save time and earn more clicks, as well as conduct experiments to determine more or better ad messages.

As you can see, each step in the AdWords process—from ad creation to the live auction—presents many decision points. Once you have an overall picture of AdWords, you will understand how general the previous overview is.

Chapter 3

Key Concepts of Ads

This chapter discusses the key concepts that drive AdWords' auction logic in greater detail and offers comprehensive explanations of the various data elements and their impact. Understanding these concepts lets you setup ads quickly, correctly and with more confidence, eliminating the many surprises people experience when AdWords does not match their ads, keywords and other parameters as they expect. Some advanced concepts let you tap into AdWords' tracking and pricing database to improve your results.

More specifically, the chapter covers the AdWords account tree structure—the sets of options that let you specify your campaign target market and budget; the bid for your ad/product group; the text for each ad in your ad group and, finally, the keywords and display options that trigger your ad. It covers the impact, importance and best practices for market targeting, bidding strategies, ad group themes and keywords (or display options) that trigger ad impressions. It also covers advanced features such as Conversion Tracking optimization and Remarketing that make use of AdWords' tracking and pricing database.

AdWords is a computer program that uses various algorithms to determine which ads appear before millions of people online and provides a set of user screens that let you setup and monitor your ads.

The more you understand those algorithms, the more you can leverage them for your own benefit. The more you understand the user screens, the more performance information you can access and the better your advertising decisions can be.

KEY CONCEPT 1: THE ACCOUNT TREE

The *account tree* **is an organizational structure that enables AdWords to find the ads that (1) offer the best customer experience and (2) bring Google the most revenues.** By understanding the account tree, you can structure your advertising to make the best use of your ad budget.

The account tree is composed of five levels of information, each of which controls a set of options. The account, campaign, ad group, ad and audience target options of the account tree offer extraordinary opportunities to pinpoint your market and present your products.

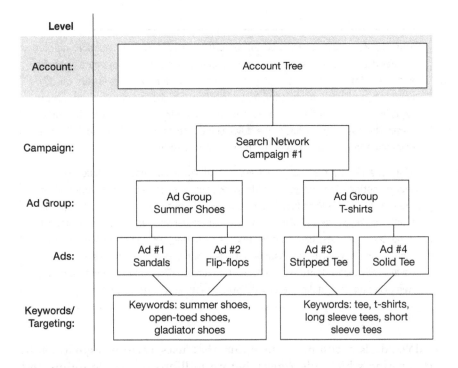

FIGURE 3.1 AdWords account tree

Note the five levels of information for a Search Network Ad

Level 1: The Account

To use AdWords you must have an AdWords account. The account stores basic information about your account, including:

a. *Billing*: where you enter your address, credit card, native currency and time zone and where you view your payment transaction history.

b. *Account access*: where you authorize people to view or administer your account.

c. *Linked accounts*: where you link your account to Google Analytics or to the Google webmaster tools that your webmaster used to add snippets of code required by Google Analytics for certain AdWords features.

d. *Preferences*: where you authorize Google to email you campaign alerts, billing issues, their newsletter, market research and other communications. Also, where you set your currency, time zone preferences and certain other details for special AdWords features.

Level 2: The Campaign

A campaign is a means of organizing all the ads you want to target at a specific market.

At the Campaign Level, you select options related to your market, budget, bidding options and ad extensions, including:

- The Google Network and type of ad you want to use.
- Your market in terms of the geographic area and language(s) you serve.
- The devices (desktop, laptop, tablet, smartphone, etc.) to target; the default is *all*.
- Your bidding strategy; the *basic* options let you (1) enter your own *cost-per-click* bids or (2) let AdWords bid on your behalf beneath your *cost-per-click* limit.
- Your daily budget.
- Ad extension information to include in your ad (i.e., your address, sitelinks, phone number, a callout or a promotional offering).

Most of these options have one or more refinements you can make. The following presents the many choices and their advantages and disadvantages.

1. *Campaign name*: where you can give your campaign a descriptive name. Include the information your management finds important, such as region, market or demographic selection.

2. *Campaign type*: where you specify the advertising network you want to use:

a. *Search Network*: to reach people searching on Google.com, whether on a laptop, tablet or mobile device. Within the Search Network, you have two additional choices that determine the features available to you:

— *All features*: this is the default and the option you want to use. It enables all the features and options available for Search Network ads.

New ads created under this option have the ability to add sitelinks, clickable phone numbers and other *ad extensions* information discussed later in this topic. Because *ad extensions* affect your ad rank, you should use the *all features* option and, at a minimum, set up as many *ad extensions* as appropriate.

If you do not use any of the advanced features in your ad, AdWords may switch your ad to *standard features*. However, you can switch back to *all features* at any time.

— *Standard features*: supports only the most basic text ads on Google's Search Network.

3. **Campaign sub-types:**

a. **Search Network ads**: to reach people using Google Search.
   — *Dynamic Search Ads*: to target searches using the content of your website, instead of keywords. Under this option, AdWords generates ads dynamically with headlines based on your web content. (See Dynamic Search Ads for more about this topic.)
   — *Product listings*: this is a legacy feature for placing ads on the *Google Shopping* network. Google is phasing it out during 2014. You may, however, see such ads or references to the function past that date.
   — *Mobile App Installs*: to reach people interested in downloading your app.
   — *Ads in Mobile App*: to reach people using mobile applications on smart phones (Note: It is *applications*, not websites, this targets).

b. **Display Network ads**: to reach people on Google Display Network partner websites (mostly publishing websites), Gmail and blogs that accept AdWords ads. For the Display Network, the *all features* default gives you access to all options for fine-tuning your ad.

In addition, you can select a subcategory of Display Network ads, including:
   — *Remarketing*: to reach people who have visited your site previously. You must already use the advanced feature, *Conversion Tracking*, to use this option. (See Remarketing Ads for more information.)
   — *Engagement*: to use rich-media, interactive ads.

c. **Search-Ads-with-Display-Select**: to reach people searching on Google, along with people reading content on Google Display Network

Partner websites or viewing YouTube videos that are highly relevant to your ad.

Use the *All Features* options, so you have the option to use text ad, ad gallery (a build-it-yourself tool for creating image and animation ads) and other Display Network ad types. In addition, you can use keywords, placements and *Remarketing Lists* to target your audience.

   d. **Google Shopping**: to easily advertise hundreds of products without writing individual ads. You submit a *feed* (i.e., a file) through the Google Merchant Center.

4. **Load settings**: where you copy the setting from another campaign to quickly setup a new one.

5. **Mobile App**: if *Mobile App Installs* is your campaign sub-type, where you select the App Store (either Google Play or Apple App Store) and enter the name, ID and publisher of the app you want people to download.

6. **Merchant identifier**: if *Google Search Network with Display Select* or *Shopping* is your campaign sub-type, where you enter the *merchant id assigned* to you by Google.

7. **Country of sale**: if *Shopping* is your campaign sub-type, where you enter the country in which you sell your products. Not all countries have access to *Google Shopping*. Currently, most major North American, South American and European countries have it, along with all of Australia.

8. **Shopping setting**: if *Shopping* is your campaign sub-type, where you set this campaign's priority (high, medium, or low) to give one campaign precedence over another campaign even if the other campaign has a higher bid. This is especially useful if you have Search Network ads running for a product, but want a special Shopping promotion to take precedence for a period of time.

9. **Inventory filter**: if *Shopping* is your campaign sub-type, where you identify specific products you want to exclude from *Shopping*. (This is an alternative to marking products in your Ad Group or re-ramping your *Shopping* feed.)

10. **Networks**: if you selected the *Search Network* or the *Search-Network-with-Display-Select* as your campaign sub-type, where you can include or exclude Google's Search Partners, which includes such sites as AOL and Earthlink. Google does not provide a list of Search Partners. If you selected *Display Network* as your campaign sub-type, Google confirms your network as the *Google Display Network*.

11. *Locations*: where you specify the market you want to target. You can
    select:

    - Country.
    - City.
    - State(s).
    - Metro area(s).
    - Postal code(s).
    - Congressional district(s).
    - Radius targets (i.e., a circle you draw on the AdWords map, which
      AdWords translates into the cities or regions covered).
    - Bulk list (up to 1,000 specific locations that you enter via typing or a
      file, using the country codes and 20+ target types [e.g., states, zip
      code, borough, canton, prefecture, TV region, municipality, etc.]
      Google supports. Search in AdWords help for "Geographic targeting"
      for details).
    - Locations groups, including:
      — Place(s) of interest (one or many airports, central commercial
         areas or universities).
      — Locations by demographics (i.e., household income tiers from top
         10 percent down to lowest 50 percent within the specific area you
         designated using the options listed previously. For example, the top
         50 percent of income within postal code 19102 or top 10 percent
         in the United States).
      — Location extension (i.e., a radius around the location in your
         location extension).
      — Location extension upgrade (i.e., a radius around the locations in
         your *location extension feed*. See *Business data* under Step 14: Use the
         Shared Library to Save Time, p. 176, for more information.)

    If you have more than one location, the *advanced search* link lets you
    access a screen for entering multiple options. By entering your market
    as granularly as possible, you can bid more precisely.

    For example, if you enter each of the 50 states, you get performance
    data on each state and can enter a higher or lower bid for a particular
    state. Conversely, if you select "United States" as your choice, you do
    not receive the state-by-state data and cannot make bid adjustments for
    individual states.

    That same screen lets you enter *location exclusions*, where you specify
    areas where you do not want to show your ads. The exclude option is
    useful for companies that do not do business in particular states or
    regions because of regulatory, franchising, licensing or other reasons.

12. **Location options (advanced)**: for Search Network and Display Network ads, where you further target or exclude certain searchers.

Google recommends you target *people in, searching for or viewing pages about your targeted location* and that is the default. However, if you do not sell internationally, you should consider clicking *edit* and selecting *people in your targeted location*.

Your choices are:

a. *People in, searching for or viewing pages about your targeted location.* This includes:
   — People physically in your targeted area.
   — People who include the name of your targeted area in a search query (i.e., your target area is an area of interest)—regardless of where in the world the person is physically; thus, international searchers are included.
   — People viewing content about your targeted area (i.e., people anywhere in the world viewing content (news, articles, etc.) about your targeted area).
   — People selecting your targeted area in their Google search setting (i.e., people anywhere in the world).

b. *People in your targeted location.* These people must be in your targeted area based on the searcher's:
   — IP address: the unique number assigned by an Internet provider to each computer it connects to the internet.
   — Device location: the physical location of the searcher if he/she has authorized location sharing, using GPS, WiFi or cell phone tower location as recorded in Google's database.

   Logically, for desktop searches, Google could obtain the searcher's physical location from his or her Google account; however, Google does not state that.

c. *People searching for or viewing pages about your targeted location.* This includes:
   — People who include the name of your targeted area in a search query (i.e., your target area is an area of interest)—regardless of where in the world the person is physically; thus, international searchers are included.
   — People viewing content about your targeted area (i.e., people anywhere in the world viewing content (news, articles, etc.) about your targeted area.)

   Choose one of the above to exclude. If you selected people in your targeted location to include, you should select people searching for or viewing pages about your targeted location to exclude. (Beware, Google sometimes changes the default and the wording of these questions. Read and choose with care.)

13. **Languages**: where you select the language you want to target from the list of more than 40 languages supported.

- Using the *location* and *language* options, you can fine-tune your audience to target, say, Spanish-speaking people in the U.S. or English-speaking people in Mexico, etc.

14. **Bid strategy**, where you select either basic or advanced bidding options.

Basic options include:

a. *I'll manually set my bids for clicks.* This option is best used after you are familiar with the range of bids that bring you traffic and buyers. You are asked to set a *default bid* to use with any ad or keyword where no override bid exists.

b. *AdWords will set my bids to help maximize clicks within my target budget.* This option is helpful in learning about the bids that bring you traffic and buyers when you first start advertising. It is also a good option for advertisers with little time to monitor ads.

Advanced options include:

a. *Focus on Clicks.* This is the option most people use to bring visitors to their sites. Select either (1) *manual bidding* and set a *default bid* or (2) *automatic bidding* and authorize AdWords to bid on your behalf up to a *CPC bid limit* you specify.

b. *Enhanced CPC option.* The *enhanced CPC* (eCPC) option lets AdWords increase your bid up to 30 percent to help you obtain more traffic.
   — If you use the advanced feature, *Conversion Tracking* (which requires you meet a certain minimum of monthly sales), *enhanced CPC option* (eCPC) is enabled automatically. AdWords then increases your bid automatically up to 30 percent if a searcher fits the profile of your buyers.
   — Using *enhanced CPC* also causes your ad rotation to be set to "optimize for conversions," which means the most productive ad appears the most often.

c. *Focus-on-Conversion.* When you activate *Conversion Tracking*, your bid strategy changes automatically to *Focus-on-Conversion.* Then, AdWords computes a target *cost-per-acquisition* (CPA) amount discerned from data it collects over time.

AdWords then attempts to bring you as many buyers as possible without exceeding that amount. Alternately, you can enter a desired CPA amount. (Note: *cost-per-acquisition* is the same as cost-per-customer).

(See Conversion Tracking (Data Collection), p. 228) for more on this.)

d. *Focus-on-Impressions.* If you select *Focus-on-Impressions,* you pay each time your ad appears, whether or not the searcher clicks it. You set a bid for 1,000 impressions. This option is available for Display Network ads only.

e. *Flexible bid strategy.* AdWords bids automatically on your behalf to meet your specific goal for page-location, ad spend, return on ad spend (ROI), or average cost-per-acquisition.

(See Key Concept 2: Bidding Strategies and Bidding Models, page 88, for more information on bidding options.)

15. **Default bid** (i.e., *maximum cost-per-click* or *max CPC*): where you specify the most you agree to pay to show a Search Network ad. AdWords uses this bid in its auctions if you do not enter an override bid at the Ad Group or Keyword Level for your Search Network ad or a *bid adjustment* for the type of device.

16. **Individual budget**: where you specify the maximum amount of money you agree to spend each day for this campaign. (AdWords may go over this amount occasionally for a single day, but the budget will not go over the total of the daily amount times 30.4 in a single month.)

Alternatively, you can apply a *shared budget*, which you store in the *shared library*, and AdWords divides it among all of your campaigns. The *shared library* command is in the left-hand menu column.

The following advanced features are optional.

1. **Delivery method (advanced)**: where you specify how quickly AdWords spends your budget during the day. The choices are:

   • *Standard:* show ads evenly throughout the day. This is the default.

   • *Accelerated:* show ads as quickly as possible. You must use *manual bidding* or the *focus on impression* bid strategy to use this option. Use this option when you are promoting a sale and want to move merchandise quickly (you must use manual bidding) or you are advertising an event and want as many people as possible to see your ad (usually an Impression Ad) as quickly as possible.

2. *Scheduling*: where you set the days and hours you want your ad to appear:

   a. *Start and stop dates*: where you set a date and time to begin a campaign or to terminate a campaign. This is useful for seasonal promotions and sales.

   b. *Days and hours*: where you set the hours to run your ads each day and the maximum bid to use for each hour of the day. You can exclude specific days and adjust your bid up or down by a specific percentage. This lets you raise your bid during peak shopping hours or in tandem with your sale promotion.

3. *Ad rotation*: where AdWords sets the criteria for selecting an ad from your ad group. AdWords automatically sets this option based on your bidding option.

   a. *Optimize for clicks*: gives preference to the best performing ad. AdWords selects this option automatically when you select *Focus on Clicks* as your bidding option. This is the default.

   b. *Optimize for conversions*: gives preference to the keyword most buyers use. (You must use AdWords' *Conversion Tracking*, an advanced feature, to have this option available.)

   c. Rotate ads equally for 90 days then optimize for clicks, unless *Conversion Tracking* or *enhanced CPC* is being used, then it optimizes for conversion. Use this option to see which of the two ads performs better over 90 days.

   d. *Rotate ads equally* and indefinitely.

4. *Frequency capping*: for Display Network *Impression Ads* only, where you specify the maximum number of times your ad appears to a unique viewer per ad, ad group, campaign, day, week or month.

5. *Devices*: for Display Network campaigns, the default choice for all campaigns is all devices (desktops, laptops, tablets, phablets and mobile smart phones).

   For Display Network campaigns, you can select any, all, or some of the following advanced options for mobile phones and tablet:

   a. *Operating systems to target*: you can target any or all versions of the operating systems supported: Android, BlackBerry, iOS (Apple), WebOS (HP, LG) and Windows Phone (Microsoft).

   b. *Devices to target*: any or all of the tablets, smartphones and/or music devices using the Android or the iOS systems. You can target devices from both operating systems within one campaign.

c. *WiFi and carriers to target*: you can target WiFi users, and you can target all or specific carriers in Canada and/or the U.S.

 — When you use the advanced mobile and tablet option, you cannot have mobile and tablet devices in the same campaign with desktops.

 — To add this option for WAP phones to an existing Display Network campaign, click the *campaigns tab*, select the desired campaign, click the *ad tab* and hover over the ad and the pencil that appears. A panel appears where you can enter your choices.

Note, also, that AdWords lets you specify *bid adjustments* for different *devices* at the Campaign Level or the Ad Group Level. If, after your campaign has run for a few weeks, you see one device is more successful than other devices, you can setup a *bid adjustment* to raise or lower your bids in response to the value of the clicks coming through.

6. *Keyword matching options*: this option is being removed. As of September 2014, your keywords automatically include plurals, misspellings and other close variants for your keywords. This expands your keywords greatly without wasting your time thinking of and entering common typos that people make. However, some close variants may not be appropriate for your ad. For example, a close variant of "hose" is "hoes," but the two are completely different. To eliminate misspelling as possible matches you must enter them into your *negative keyword list*.

7. **IP exclusion**: where you enter your own IP address or that of your ad agency to have AdWords exclude clicks from those IP addresses from inclusion in your ad statistics.

8. **Tracking URL for dynamic links**: if you selected *Shopping* as your campaign sub-type, where you indicate that your product listings file contains the necessary information to enable AdWords to construct a unique URL for each item (and, thus, provide item-by-item performance tracking).

9. **Dynamic Search Ads**: if you selected Dynamic Search Ad as your campaign sub-type, where you opt to have AdWords use your website content to construct Search Network ads for you.

Another important part of campaigns are *ad extensions*, which allow you to add additional information to your campaign. However, *ad extensions* cannot be setup until after your campaign is setup.

The following describe the different ad extensions available.

Ad Extensions **enable you to enter additional information about your business and/or your products.**

- Using *ad extensions* increases your *quality score* and your *ad rank*, so use as many as appropriate for your campaign sub-type.

- You can add *ad extensions* after you setup your campaign, ad group or ads, and you can change them at any time.

- *Ad extensions* added at the Campaign Level apply to all ad groups and ads. In the same manner, *ad extensions* added to an ad group apply to all ads. However, you can change or remove *ad extensions* for individual ad groups and/or ads.

Ad extensions **include:**

a. *Location extensions: where you opt to include your address, phone number and directions in your ad.*

Whether your location extensions show depends on your budget, your targeting settings, *ad rank* or ad approval status. While Google does not specify the rules for showing location extensions, it seems logical to assume your location extensions show if (1) the searcher is near your store locations, (2) your ad appears near the top of the page (i.e., your bid and ad rank are among the highest) and (3) enough space exists to include the location extension.

Your address is taken from your *Google My Business* account. Thus, your information appears the same in all ads and you have only one place to update when something changes. (You can remove the location extension from any individual campaign, ad group or ad.) Google calls this method the *upgraded location extensions* method. It becomes the mandatory method in late 2014.

— Google must approve *location extensions* before they are eligible to show in your ad.

— Both the Search and Display Networks support *location extensions*.

— The Search Network and Display Network, along with the AdMob Network for apps, Mobile Ads and m.google.com (the Google search engine on iPhones) support *location extensions*.

— If you include Google Search Partners in your campaign, an ad that includes a *location extension* is eligible to appear on Google Maps.

— On desktops and laptops, the first 10–15 characters of your headline appear. The entire ad appears if the viewer clicks the map marker. Desktop ads include your phone number and location in the *location extension*.

— On a smartphone, the viewer must tap or swipe upward to see the full ad. This results in a CPC charge, and AdWords charges you a second CPC fee if the viewer uses the click-to-call, share location, save location or navigation features.

— Further, Mobile Ads with *location extensions* show a *get directions* link, which provides instructions for getting to your business and an estimate of how far he or she is from your business.

— You can show multiple addresses. You are eligible to show multiple addresses if your ad includes a location extension and appears in the top ad position on Google.com search results pages. Some large advertisers submit a *location extension feed* of addresses. Contact Google Sales for more information.

Also, your ad is eligible to show multiple addresses if you have more than one location within a given area.

— Some Google Search Partners vary the appearance of your ad depending on the space available. Some show your address with or without a map or omit the location extension altogether.

— Be aware that *sitelinks* override *location extensions*. Ads cannot have both.

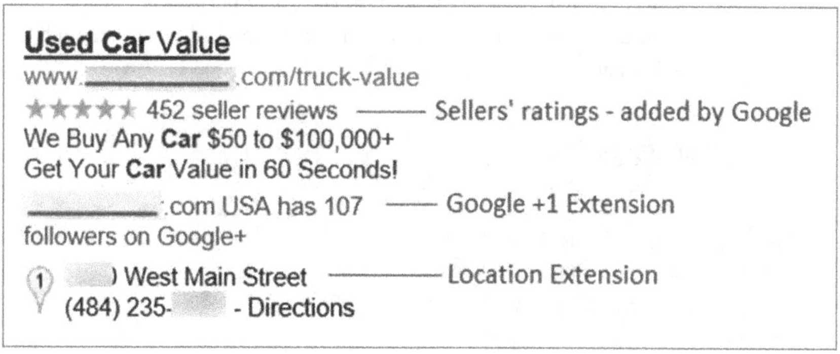

FIGURE 3.2 Sellers' ratings, Google +1 and location extensions

b. Social [extension]: where you associate your ad with your Google+ page. Every +1 click (i.e., a "like") counts as a +1 on your Google Page.

— AdWords does not charge you if a searcher clicks on the +1 extension and goes to your Google+ page.

c. **Sitelinks: where you opt to show links to different sections or pages on your website as part of your Search Network ads.**

— Using sitelinks helps your *quality score* and *ad rank*, so use them!

— Sitelinks for Mobile Ads are invaluable for moving viewers quickly to a specific webpage, a major convenience for small screen users.

— Sitelinks are limited to 25 characters.

71

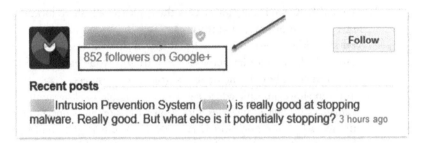

FIGURE 3.3 Social extension

— You can use sitelinks in several different ways:

(1) To highlight major sections within your website (e.g., "About us," "Products," etc.)

(2) To direct searchers to specific pages within your website for deals, discounts and coupons and faster service (e.g., "Order Online Here," "Discount Coupon Here," etc.)

(3) To highlight time-sensitive offers by combining sitelinks with an ad schedule (e.g., a sitelink of "$8 Lunch Buffet" as part of an ad running from 11.30 a.m. to 2 p.m., Monday through Friday).

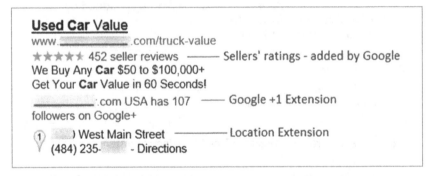

FIGURE 3.4 An example of sitelinks

Notice that these sitelinks include promotional offers. Sitelinks are useful for taking viewers quickly to sale pages.

d. *Call [extension]:* **where you opt to show a clickable phone number in your ad when viewed on a smartphone.**

— You can also rent a phone line from Google for your ad. Search, Display and AdMob Networks support call extension.

— Mobile Ads include a phone icon, which takes space away from the ad. Keep Mobile Ads to 60 characters or less to avoid truncation of your message.

FIGURE 3.5 Mobile Ad with a call extension

e. *Callout extensions*: where you add up to four 25-character messages about your business services, such as "24/7 availability," "Free shipping," "Free returns" or "Lowest prices guaranteed." Callouts are not clickable.

— Best practices recommend using 12–15 characters and capitalizing sparingly.

— Only Search Network ads can use callouts, and callouts show only on ads at the top and bottom of the search results page.

— Callouts impact your ad rank in a positive way, so use them!

— You can apply callouts at the Account Level to show a generic message on all campaigns and ad groups, and/or at the Campaign Level to apply to underlying ad group ads, and/or at the Ad Groups Level for all ads. (Callouts at a high level apply to all underlying levels.)
Callouts at the lowest level in the account tree take priority over callouts at a higher level, if space is limited.

— You can add callouts to Mobile Ads, which offers an especially easy way to provide shoppers with more information about your business before they click your ad. Likewise, you can restrict callouts to desktops/tablets.

— From two to four messages, in total, are permitted per ad, regardless of where the callouts originate.

— Callouts can use start and stop dates and can be used with sitelinks (which send searchers to specific landing pages).

f. *Reviews*: **where you select or enter a customer's comment for use in your Search Network ad.**

— Google recommends using customer reviews that focus on your business and applying them at the Campaign Level.

— The review you add to your ad must meet Google Review Policies and be approved by Google. You must have the legal right to use the review and it must be from a reputable third party.

— Whether a review appears depends on your bid, ad relevance, available space and the other extensions or information associated with your ad.

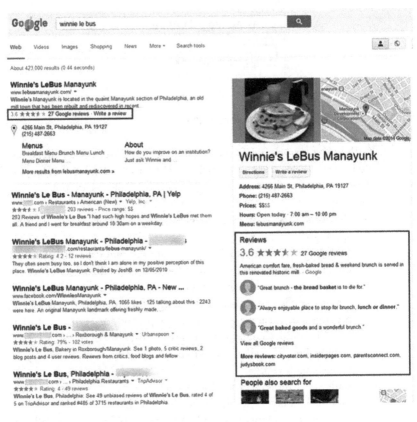

FIGURE 3.6 Google My Business ads with seller's reviews

— Reviews do not show if you use offer extensions.
— To learn more, search in AdWords Help for "Highlight third-party reviews in your ad" and for the policies, "Review extensions."

g. *Sellers Reviews: where Google adds comments made by customers.*
— *Google Shopping* aggregates reviews from such sites as reseller ratings, Bizrate, ReviewCentre.com and Viewpoints, among others and shows ratings automatically if:
(1) Your business has 30 or more unique reviews within the past 12 months.
(2) A composite rating of 3.5 stars or more from buyers using Google Showing.
(3) Ten of the reviews are in the customer's language.
— Zagat's, a rating service since 1979 that Google owns, provides restaurant ratings.

74

(See Add Ad Extensions to Your Search Ads, page 225, for detailed setup instructions for ad extensions.)

Level 3: The Ad Group

An ad group includes one or more ads and focuses on one product (or one product feature). You can run multiple ad groups within a campaign and multiple ads within an ad group.

In each ad group, you specify:

- For your Search Network ads, the keywords to represent your product and, optionally, an override for the *default bid* (max CPC) you entered at the Campaign Level.

- For your Display Network ads, you specify a *default bid* for each ad group, and you specify the *targeting methods* you want AdWords to use to find appropriate websites for advertising your product.

When you create your first ad group for a campaign, you enter the information for the ad group *and* the ad on one screen at the same time. This saves steps and makes sure you do not have an ad group with no ads.

Once your ad group is complete, you can add *ad extension* information if you did not do so at the Campaign Level. Further, you can adjust the default bid for individual keywords, apply a custom bid to items in one of your targeting methods and/or apply bid adjustments to one or more remaining targeting methods.

The following presents your ad group choices and their advantages and disadvantages.

1. *Ad group name*: where you assign a name. It is helpful to include the network (*Search*, *Display* or *Mobile* network) and the product category (shoes, electronics, TVs, etc.) in the title.

2. *Ad Type*: select either Text, App/digital content ad, WAP Mobile Ad, product listing or Dynamic Search Ad.

   If this is the first ad group in a Search Network Campaign:

   - For text ads, you create the ad (see 7a).

   - For Dynamic Search Ads, you enter two lines of generic description, an easy-to-remember URL to display (the *display URL*) and the actual URL of the landing page (the *destination URL*). If you want to track each ad generated by Google, you specify the field in your product feed that contains the unique URL for the product.

3. *Default bid*: for a Search Network or a Search-Network-with-Display-Select campaign, where you enter the maximum amount you agree to pay for an ad (i.e., the *max CPC*).

4. *Keywords*: for a new Search Network campaign, where you enter phrases that describe your product, using AdWords formatting to indicate an exact, partial, board, negative or embedded matching. (More on Keywords to follow.)

5. *Maximum cost-per-click (max CPC)*: for a Display Network ad, where you set the max CPC (also called the *default bid*). The max CPC is used in automated bidding as your highest acceptable bid and in manual bidding it is used if you have not set an overriding bid at the Keyword Level.

   For a Search Network, you can use the *default bid* to override the bid you entered at the Campaign Level. The override applies only to this ad group. You can change the bid again later, and you can override this bid at the Keyword Level.

6. *Targeting method(s)*: for Display Network ads, where you tell AdWords which targeting methods you want to use. Your targeting choices are:

   a. *Keywords*: where you enter words or phrases that a webpage must have within its content for it to be an acceptable site for your ad. All keywords for Display Network ads are *broad-matching*. (More on keywords and keyword matching later in this section.)

   b. *Use different targeting methods*: where you select among these criteria to control where your Display Network ad appears:
   — *Topics* (optional): where you choose from AdWords' predefined list of topics and sub-topics.
   — *Managed placements* (optional): where you enter a list of websites and/or webpages appropriate for your ads. You can also use the display planner tool, under the tools and analytics tab, to find placements.
   — *Interest and Remarketing*: where you specify, from a predefined list, the interests you want your searcher to have. When AdWords knows a searcher is interested in your topic, your ad can compete in the auction. AdWords recognizes a searcher's interests based on previous searches. For example, if you want to reach people interested in environmental issues, people who have visited 10 or more environmental websites would qualify to see your ad.

      Remarketing applies only if you have activated the *Remarketing* feature. This lets you specify which page of your website your visitor must have viewed previously to qualify to see the ads in this campaign. (See Remarketing Ads, p. 282, for more details.)
   — *Age* (optional): where you select one or more age ranges for your desired viewers and include/exclude people whose ages are

unknown to Google. (Not all websites can collect age information. Thus, on many websites the viewer's age is unknown.)

— *Gender* (optional): where you select the sex of the desired viewers for your ad and include/exclude people whose sex is not known to Google. (Not all websites can collect gender information. Thus, on many websites the viewer's gender is unknown.)

— **Exclusions for site categories**: where you can specify the types of websites you *do not want* for your ad. Choices include such things as sensitive topics (crimes, disasters, deaths, etc.), types of sites (forums, parked domains, error pages, etc.), types of videos (rated mature, live streaming, etc.) games and ad locations (below the fold, which requires scrolling).

You can choose more than one of these targeting methods; however, each additional choice narrows the websites that qualify. Thus, targeting requirements are cumulative; a website must meet one criterion or every targeting method you specify.

For example, if you select a gender of female and a managed placement of The Wall Street Journal (WSJ), your ad would qualify to show only if AdWords knows the viewer of the WSJ webpage is female.

7. If this is the first Display Network ad in this ad group, you move automatically to a screen where you enter your ad type and ad copy.

a. For a *text ad*, you enter your ad copy, *display URL* and *destination URL* of the landing page.

You can designate your *device preference* as *mobile* if you want it to show only on smartphones.

b. For an *image ad*, you upload the image—the image constitutes the entire ad, meaning your ad is actually a picture the viewer clicks. You name it and provide a *display URL* and the *destination URL* of the landing page.

You can designate your *device preference* as *mobile* if you want it to show only on smartphones.

c. For an *ad gallery ad,* you setup an ad using a template provided by AdWords. The *ad gallery* makes quick work of creating professional-looking text ads, image ads, animated and interactive ads.

Once you *save* your ad group, you can add additional information, such as:

8. *Ad extensions*: the *ad extensions* you applied at the Campaign Level automatically apply to each Ad Group. However, you can give an Ad Group a different extension or remove the extension altogether.

- For example, the *location ad extension* you apply at the Ad Group Level overrides the location extension you applied at the Campaign Level.

  The *location extension* you apply to a specific ad overrides the *location extensions* you applied at the Ad Group and/or Campaign Levels.

  Programmers call this logic "inheritance," where the code establishes a parent–child relationship. User options flow "down" from parent to child. User options do not flow "up."

  Thus, a child/ad "inherits" its processing options from its parent, the ad group. The ad group inherited processing options from its parent, the Campaign. Conversely, changes applied at the child/Ad Level are *not* inherited by the parent, the ad group, nor are they inherited by the ad group's parent, the Campaign.

To add, change or remove an *ad extension* at the Ad Group Level, use the *all online campaign* menu to go to the ad group you want to affect. Click the *ad extension tab* and the *view: <extensions>* button. Select the appropriate *ad extension* from the drop down menu and enter the new information or remove it.

(See Add Ad Extensions to Your Search Ads, page 225, for detailed setup and override instructions for *ad extensions*.)

9. **Custom bids**: for a *Display Network* ad or a *Search Network with Select Display* ad, you can add *custom bids* to each item in one targeting method at the Ad Group or Ad levels.

    Custom Bids are most often used for Keywords on the Display Network (since you do not have a way to override keyword bids as you do for Search Network ads).

    Select the ad or ad group you want to have *custom bids*. Click the *Display Network tab* and the *view: <choice>* submenu to select the targeting method you want. Above the *statistics table*, click the button beside *bidding:* and select *enable custom bids*. Enter a new Max CPC beside any or all of the items in that targeting method.

    (See Key Concept 2: Bidding Strategies and Bidding Models, page 88, for more information on bidding options. See Add Custom Bids for detailed instructions for implementing custom bids.)

10. **Bid adjustments**: you can apply a bid adjustment (i.e., an increased or decreased percentage of the max CPC) for items within one or more of your targeting methods for an ad group. You cannot apply bid adjustments to keywords (you should use default bid overrides instead) or to a targeting method already using custom bids.

(See Key Concept 2: Bidding Strategies and Bidding Models, p. 88, for an overview of bid adjustments. See Add Custom Bids, p. 275, for detailed instructions for implementing bid adjustments.)

Level 4: The Ad

Every ad resides within an Ad Group within a Campaign. Each Ad should provide a different advertising message for a searcher.

You can run multiple ads within an ad group and, as a best practice, you should run a desktop ad and a Mobile Ad in each ad group. Another best practice is to run experiments to test different ad messages (often referred to as A/B testing).

At the Ad Level, the setup questions asked depend on the type of ad you are creating. In general, you input:

- The advertising message.
- A *display URL* and a *destination URL*.
- Whether you prefer your ad appears only on *mobile* devices (i.e., smartphones).
  (As this book goes to press, Google added *Upgraded URLs* that permit you to add pre-defined codes to a URL to capture additional data about your customer. Search in AdWords Help for "Using *Upgraded URLs*" for the latest information.)

As mentioned previously, when you create your first ad group for a campaign, you enter information for both the ad group and the first ad at that time, on one screen. This saves steps and ensures you do not have an empty ad group.

The components of your ad include:

1. *Heading*: limited to 25 characters, where you state a problem or offer a solution. For example, "Tired of squinting" or "Blaxglass blocks UV rays."

2. *Description line 1*: limited to 35 characters, where you state a solution or tout product features. This line can continue onto the Description Line 2.

3. *Description line 2*: limited to 35 characters, a continuation of the previous line or additional details.

4. *Display URL*: the URL you want customers to remember.

5. *Destination URL*: the actual URL of the landing page you want a prospect to visit.

At the Ad Level, you can enter exceptions to your Ad Group Level choices for:

6. *Keyword default bid(s)* **(override)**: where you can set a specific maximum bid (*Max CPC*) for a keyword in a Search Network ad. This overrides any bid at the ad group or Campaign Levels.

7. *Negative keywords*: where you specify words and phrases you do not want to trigger your ad.

8. *Device preference*: where you check a box to indicate you want your ad to appear primarily on *mobile* devices (i.e., smartphones).

Once you *save* an ad, you can add additional information, such as:

9. *Ad extensions*: an *ad extension* you applied at the Campaign or the Ad Group Level automatically applies to each underlying ad. However, at the Ad Level, you can add, change or remove an extension applied at the Ad Group Level or the Campaign Level.

   • For example, the *location extension* you apply to a specific ad overrides the *location extensions* you applied at the ad group or the Campaign Levels. In short, ads "inherit" options from Ad Groups or Campaigns as explained previously.

   Use the *All Online Campaign* menu to go to the ad you want to change. Click the *ad extension tab* and the *view: <extension>* button. Select the appropriate *ad extension* from the drop down menu and follow AdWords' instructions.

   (See Add Bid Adjustments for Devices, Locations, Ad Schedules and Targeting Methods, p. 276, for more detailed setup and override instructions for *ad extensions*.)

10. **Custom bids**: for a *Display Network* ad, you can add *custom bids* (dollar amounts) to items in one (and only one) targeting method for an ad.

    Select the ad group or ad you want to have custom bids. Click the *Display Network tab* and the *view: <targeting method>* submenu to select the targeting method you want. Above the *statistics table*, click the button next to *bidding* and select *enable custom bids*. Enter a new *max CPC* beside any or all of the items in that targeting method.

    (See Add Bid Adjustments for Devices, Locations, Ad Schedules and Targeting Methods, p. 276, for detailed instructions for implementing bid adjustments.)

11. **Bid adjustments**: you can apply a *bid adjustment* (i.e., a percentage increase or decrease of the max CPC) for items within one or more of your targeting methods for an ad group or ad. You cannot apply *bid adjustments* to keywords or to a targeting method that uses a custom bid.

Use the *all online campaign* menu to go to the ad group or the ad where you want to apply *bid adjustments*. Click on the *Display Network tab* and the *view: <targeting methods>* submenu to select the desired targeting method. Set the button next to *bidding* to *enable bid adjustments* to select bid adjustment. Input your adjustment percentage.

(See Add Bid Adjustments for Devices, Locations, Ad Schedules and Targeting Methods, p. 276, for detailed instructions for implementing bid adjustments.)

Level 5: Keywords, Targeting Methods, and Targeting Groups

Depending on the type of ad, AdWords offers different ways to specify the *audience* and *placements* (i.e., websites) for your ad.

- For Search Network ads, *keywords* describe your product, and AdWords uses them to determine whether your ad is relevant to the searcher.
- For Display Network ads, you have two choices:
  — Authorize AdWords to find relevant web pages for your ad (called, *automatic placement*). AdWords uses the *keywords* you entered to determine whether your ad is relevant to a particular webpage that someone is viewing.
  — Use *targeting methods* to qualify web pages and visitors for your ad. AdWords uses (1) the *keywords* you entered and (2) any *placements* (i.e., websites) and *site categories* you entered to determine whether a website is appropriate for your ad and uses (3) any *topics, interests, age or gender* requirements you set for the viewer of your ad.
- For Video Ads on the Display Network, you have two choices:
  — Authorize AdWords to find relevant web pages for your video (*automatic placements*).
  — Use *target groups* to describe (1) the web pages and audience you want to see your ad and/or (2) the *words* you want to use to trigger your ad on YouTube (e.g., YouTube keywords).

The following describes the functions of *keywords, targeting methods,* and *target groups.*

Keywords

Today, a *keyword* **is seldom a single word.** If you use a single-word *keyword*, AdWords could overrun you with clicks that bring few sales and create many disappointed visitors.

Usually a *keyword* **is a multi-word phrase.** Google and this document use the term keyword to mean any words or phrases you enter in the keyword list for your ad. Essentially, keyword is both singular and plural for AdWords purposes.

Keyword-matching **is a major feature for Search Network ads.** Using keyword matching logic, AdWords evaluates how closely your keyword matches the search term and whether the match is close enough to include your ad in the auction.

You control how precisely your keyword must match the search term. Your choices are:

- **[Exact]** (i.e., a keyword in brackets): means a match occurs if the searcher uses your keyword or keyword phrase exactly as you specify it. Generally, an exact match results in fewer ad impressions and clicks.
- **"Phrase"** (i.e., a keyword in quotation marks): means a match occurs if the searcher uses a keyword phrase in the exact order you specified, even if the searcher's phrase has other words before or after it.
- **Broad** (i.e., a keyword with no punctuation): means a match occurs if the search term uses your keywords in any order, a grammatical equivalent or a synonym.
- **Broad-match**: the most easily matched keyword, and the most expensive, is the default.
- **+Broad match modifier** (i.e., a keyword with a + sign in front of one word): means a match occurs only if the word with the +sign appears in the search term.
- **–Negative keywords** (i.e., a keyword preceded by a minus sign): means a match is prevented for that search term. For example, a minus sign before *iron* prevents the phrase *branding iron* from matching to the keyword *branding*.
- **– [Embedded match]** (i.e., a negative sign in front of a keyword in brackets): tells AdWords to prevent a match if the searcher uses the keyword phrase *without* a specific word. For example, if you want to use "iPad" as a keyword only if it appears with the word "cover," you enter it as –[iPad] cover.

Remember, keywords-matching is only for Search Network ads. For Display Network and Video Ads, all *keywords* are considered *broad-match*.

Match type	Special symbol	Example keyword	Ads can compete for showing if the search queries:	Example searches	Rejected
Broad match	none	women's hats	Contains any word in your keyword phrase, or a close variant, in any order, with or without other terms before or after it. Close variations include misspellings, singular and plural forms, acronyms, stemmings (e.g., such as *floor* and *flooring*), abbreviations, and accents, per Google. synonyms, misspellings, related searches, and other relevant variations	buy ladies hats womens caps hats for girls womans hats Buy red hats for women	
Broad match modifier Increase relevancy, but you may get less ad traffic than a broad match keyword.	+keyword + sign before the specific keyword, with no space between the + and keyword. You can add a + sign to more than one word in a keyword phrase.	+women's +hats	Shows only when the search query contains the modified term(s), or close variations of the modified terms, in any order, with or without other words before or after it. No synonyms No related searches	Buy woman's hats Women's hats	Caps for women (uses a synonym) Hats for women (word in middle) Girl's hats (no related searches)

Match type	Special symbol	Example keyword	Ads can compete for showing if the search queries:	Example searches	Rejected
Phrase match Increase relevancy but you may get less ad traffic than a broad match keyword.	"keyword" Enclose the entire phrase in quote marks.	"women's hats"	Your exact keyword, or close variations, with additional words before or after it. To exclude close variants, go to your Campaign Setting-Advance Features-Keyword option and exclude them.	buy women's hats	
Exact match It brings less traffic, but it brings prospects looking for exactly what you are selling.	[keyword] Enclose the entire phrase in brackets:	[women's hats]	Contains the exact keyword, or close variants, with no other words before or after it. To exclude close variants, go to your Campaign Setting-Advance Features-Keyword option and exclude them.	women's hats	Women's hats on sale
Negative match Filters out irrelevant search queries to prevent unwanted clicks	Put a – sign immediately before the word: -keyword	-baseball	Your ad will not appear if the search query contains that word. Note that a negative keyword works with all the other match types. It prevents your ad from showing regardless of whether your match type is exact, partial, modified broad or regular broad.		baseball hats
Embedded match Filters out an irrelevant term unless a specific, relevant term accompanies it.	Put a – sign immediately before the unacceptable word and include the required word.	-[iPad] cover	Your ad will not appear if the search query contains the unacceptable word without the acceptable word immediately beside it.		

FIGURE 3.7 A recap of keyword matching characteristics

83

Targeting Methods

Targeting methods **provide criteria that tell AdWords where you want your ad to run and who you want to see it.** *Targeting methods* are available only for ads on the Display Network.

As mentioned previously, for Display Network ads you can (1) authorize AdWords to use your *keywords* to find relevant web pages for your ad (*automatic placements*) or (2) use *keywords* and *targeting methods* to specify webpages and viewers criteria for your ad.

If you use *automatic placements***, you enter** *keywords* **to guide AdWords in placing your ad.** *Keywords* are words or phrases describing content of interest to a large number of your prospects.

- For example, on the Display Network an ad for a math software package might have such keywords as: teaching resources for math, teaching math, new math, etc.

If you do not use *automatic placements***, you enter criteria for one or more of the following targeting methods:**

- **Keywords**: where AdWords lets you specify words or phrases describing content of interest to a large number of your prospects. For Display Network ads, all keywords are considered broad match.

- *[Managed] placements*: where AdWords lets you specify the websites where you want your ad to appear. This lets you precisely target prospects and make more cost-effective bids.

  In traditional advertising, specifying where an ad is to appear is a "placement." When you buy a *placement,* you specify a page or section of the magazine. If you pay more money you can get a *managed placement*, which lets you specify an inside column, outside column, top of page, etc. within a page.

  In AdWords, a *placement* refers only to the website or the webpage where your ad appears. The website owner determines where on the page an ad appears. If you let AdWords find the best websites for your ad (based on your *keywords*) it is called *automatic placements*.

  When you tell AdWords the websites where you want your ad to appear—that is you enter actual websites using URLs—you are using a targeting method called *placements*. In the recent past, Google called these *managed placements*, since you manage them rather than AdWords. Increasingly, Google is using the more succinct term *placements*, rather than *managed placements*.

84

Regardless of the term, the difference between selecting websites yourself and letting AdWords select the website for you is major, and when you are talking about placements, you need to know who is in control, you or AdWords.

To find desirable *placements* for your ad, use the *display planner tool* (under the *tools* menu). Be aware that thousands of websites exist in the Display Network and selecting your own placements severely limits your advertising. Using a set list of websites as your only placements can be a powerful strategy if you pick the right sites, otherwise it is a major constraint.

- **Topics**: where you specify, from AdWords' predefined list of topics and sub-topics, the topics that a webpage must show to be appropriate for your ad.

- **Demographics:**
  - — **Age**: where you select the age group(s) of the desired viewers for your ad. (Not all websites can accommodate this criterion.)
  - — **Gender**: where you select the sex of the desired viewers for your ad. (Not all websites can accommodate this criterion.)

- **Interests**: where you select interests that you want searchers to have exhibited, using AdWords' predefined list of interests and sub-interests. AdWords determines peoples' interests from their search histories.

- *Remarketing Lists*: where you select the *Remarketing Lists* you want AdWords to use to recognize previous visitors to your site. (*Remarketing Lists* are part of the advanced AdWords feature, Remarketing, discussed later.)

- **Site categories**: where you can specify the types of websites you *do not want* for your ad. Choices on the pre-defined lists include such things as sensitive topics (crimes, disasters, deaths, etc.), types of sites (forums, parked domains, error pages, etc.), types of videos (rated mature, living streaming, etc.) games and ad locations (below the fold, which requires scrolling).

- **Exclusions**: where you can specify *keywords, placements* (websites), *topics, interests, ages* and *gender* to specifically exclude.

Targeting methods are cumulative. If you use two targeting methods, a website must meet criteria for both methods; if you use three targeting methods, a website must meet criteria for all three targeting methods, etc.

You can change your keywords and targeting methods at any time.

Further, you can set different bids for your *targeting method* criteria. This lets you bid aggressively for your most successful methods and/or lower bids for your less successful methods.

- To do this you must use *manual bidding*. You adjust bids using *custom bids* and/or *bid adjustments*. These topics are explained later. (See Add Bid Adjustments for Devices, Locations, Ad Schedules and Targeting Methods, p. 276, for more information on bidding options.)

Targeting Groups for Video Ads

By default, your Video Ad shows to all viewers unless you define a specific audience(s), called *targeting groups*.

You define a targeting group using:

1. *Viewer demographics*: where you indicate the people you want to see your ad (i.e., namely age, gender and/or parental status).

2. *Targeting*: where you define the subject matter using the same methods available for Display ads, namely topics, interest, managed placements, *Remarketing Lists* and keywords.

Once you setup a *targeting group*, you can assign it to any of your Video Ads. This is a great time saver.

As with other Display Network ads, *targeting groups* are cumulative. That is, a viewer must match *all* your criteria in order to see your ad.

A Well-Crafted Campaign Makes Monitoring and Reporting Faster and Easier

AdWords has rules that govern how you setup campaigns, ad groups and ads. Know that:

- Your Campaign *always* defines your market (i.e., the geographic location where your ad appears and language used).

- You *must have* separate campaigns for Search ads versus Display Network ad types.

- You *always* want one ad group for each product. (*Never* mix products within one ad group. All the keywords for an ad group apply to all the ads. For example, people searching for refrigerators generally do not respond to ads for vacuum cleaners.)

- You *always* want a *device preference: mobile* ad and a regular ad in an ad group.

Aligning your AdWords hierarchy with your company's marketing goals lets you provide performance data in the way your management wants it.

- If your management sets sales goals by geographic market region (think, cell phone services), you may need a campaign for each region or market.
- If management sets sales goals by product (think, cars), you may need a campaign for each product (model of car).
- When in doubt, structure your AdWords campaign in the same way your website is structured.

Thinking about your business and campaign needs before you start building ads lets you create a more intuitive hierarchy.

1. Think about the types of campaigns you want to run. Do they vary by language? Do you plan to use the Search Network or the Display Network or both? Will you need a separate campaign for each of those elements? A separate campaign can make it easier to track performance for an individual element.

2. For each campaign, how many ad groups do you need? One per product? One per brand? One per season?

3. What is the theme of each ad group? All your keywords should relate to one common attribute. For example, it is unwise to put hiking boots and ballet slippers in the same ad group, even if you use separate ads.

4. For each ad group, determine the different versions or these of the message you want to use. Consider whether people decide to buy hiking boots because of warmth, comfort or ruggedness.

5. Name your campaigns carefully to make the different goals of each campaign obvious. For example:

   Search—Desktops—Shoes—Summer Sale

   Display—Mobiles—MBA program—Finish Degree

   U.S.—Search—Desktops—Coffee—Dark Roast

   France—Search—Desktop—AutoBid—Café—Torréfié Foncé

   Germany—Search—Desktop—AutoBid—Kaffee—Dunkel Geröstete

AdWords' labeling capability lets you regroup keywords by categories you devise. This lets you construct and report on different groupings long after the initial campaign structure is established. You can assign multiple labels to a keyword.

Your overall AdWords success depends on monitoring each of the many components that comprise a campaign and making adjustments when needed:

- Campaign options (markets, demographics, device types, ad types and delivery methods).
- Ad group(s).
- Landing page(s).
- Product offer(s).
- Ad message(s).
- Keywords.
- Bidding options.
- Bids.

In addition, you must understand the AdWords software, and you must stay abreast of new features.

KEY CONCEPT 2: BIDDING STRATEGIES AND BIDDING MODELS

Your bidding strategy, bidding model and maximum bid play an important role in determining whether your ad appears online, the ad position it occupies and how much it costs you.

In the following pages, we discuss the several different ways of meeting your marketing goals using bidding models and associated options.

Focus-on-Clicks (CPC)

The most commonly used bidding model in AdWords is *Focus on Clicks*. A *click* represents one visitor to your landing page. The *Focus on Clicks* strategy assumes that you want more visitors and that more visitors ultimately mean more sales. You pay Google each time someone clicks on your ad. You set a *maximum cost-per-click* (also called a *max CPC* or default CPC) for your campaign.

AdWords calls this type of bidding model *cost-per-click* (CPC). Marketers also refer to this as pay-per-click (PPC).

You normally use this bidding model for Search Network campaigns where you want people to click on your ad, come to your website and take a specific action (i.e., buy something).

To support this strategy, AdWords offers its *cost-per-click* bidding model in several different variations:

a. *Cost-per-click* **(CPC) with automatic bidding**

Under CPC and *automatic bidding*, AdWords bids on your behalf when an auction takes place and attempts to maximize your ad exposure and, in turn, your clicks.

- This CPC bidding model is available for the Search Network or the Display Network but not the Google Ad/Mob network.

- If your landing page is converting visitors into buyers at a nice rate, this is an easy way to sell. Conversely, this is a costly option if your landing page is not converting visitors to customers—every click costs you money but does not bring you revenue.

- Use this option if you are a novice and want to learn how your keywords and ads perform or if you are too busy to manage your ads closely.

- With *automatic bidding*, you can enter a *limit bid* below which AdWords must keep your bids. The *limit bid* prevents high bids that erode your profit margin.

- With *automatic bidding*, you cannot set a *default bid* at the Ad Group, Ad or Keyword Levels, and you cannot use the Campaign Level *ad scheduling* features.

b. *Cost-per-click* **(CPC) with** *manual bidding.*

With CPC and *manual bidding*, you can set a bid for each individual keyword, so you have maximum control over your costs.

- This option is available for campaigns using the Search Network or the Display Network, but not the Google Ad/Mob Network.

- If your landing page is converting visitors into buyers at a nice rate, this bidding model can be a cost-saver, because you can often find a lower bid that wins as many auctions as a higher one.

- Use *manual bidding* if you have the time and skill to watch your performance data carefully and adjust your keyword bids, as needed, to maximize traffic while minimizing *cost-per-click*.

Manual bidding gives you flexibility to set bids for your Search Network ads in either or both of two ways. You can:

- Set the max CPC at the Campaign Level. Later, if needed, you can override the setting at the Ad group, Ad or Keyword Levels to more aggressively or more conservatively pursue impressions.

- Set *bid adjustments* at the Campaign Level to increase or decrease your bid by a specified percentage for:
  — Devices (desktops, mobile phones and tablets).
  — Locations (as defined by countries, cities, radius from your store, etc.).
  — Ad schedules (day, hour, etc.).

You can use these two ways independently or together. Thus, you can set a bid of 75¢ for all *keywords*, then set a bid of $1 for a special keyword and have that $1 bid bumped up by 10 percent if the keyword is searched from a smartphone.

Warning: This type of multi-dimensional bidding can become complicated, confusing and time-consuming. Use it judiciously. Keep careful notes on your strategy so you remember why you set the bids that you did.

For Display Network ads, manual bidding gives you several layers of flexibility. You can:
  — Set the *max CPC* at the Ad Group Level, but with the ability to override it at the Ad Level or at the *target method* level.
  — Set *bid adjustments* at the Campaign Level to increase or decrease your bid by a specified percentage for:
    (1) *Devices* (desktops, mobile phones and tablets).
    (2) *Locations* (as defined by countries, cities, radius from your store, etc.).
    (3) *Ad schedules* (day, hour, etc.).
  — Set *Custom bids* for any item in one of your *targeting methods* (keywords, topic, managed placement, interest, Remarketing list, gender or age) at the ad group or Ad Level.

AdWords applies *custom bids* and *bid adjustments* in addition to the Ad Group Level max CPC bid and on top of each other. For example, in an ad group with a default bid of $1, a 10 percent *bid adjustment* increase for smartphones adds $0.10 to the max CPC, resulting in a new max CPC of $1.10. Next, the custom bid of 10 percent for a particular managed placement increases the new max CPC of $1.10 by $0.11, for a final max CPC of $1.21.

Warning: This type of multi-dimensional bidding can become complicated, confusing and time-consuming, so use it judiciously, and keep careful notes on your strategy so you remember why you set the bids that you did.

c. **Manual bidding with *enhanced cost-per-click* (eCPC)**

With *enhanced cost-per-click (eCPC)*, AdWords bids on your behalf and increases your bid for previously successful keywords up to 30 percent above your max CPC to give your ad its best chance of winning an auction.

(See Key Concept 5: Power Features That Drive Success, p. 125, for information about *Conversion Tracking*.)

- Use this option if your landing page is converting well, you want to maximize traffic and you want an aggressive effort to use your entire budget.

- Consider using it also when you are testing ads and landing pages over a short time period to ensure maximum exposure for your ads.

- This option is available for campaigns using the Search Network or the Display Network but not the Google Ad/Mob network.

- Use *manual bidding* with *enhanced CPC* to avoid the tedious task of setting and resetting override bids for high-performing keywords.

Focus-on-Impressions (Cost-per-Thousand (CPM)) for Display Network Impression Ads

The *Focus-on-Impressions* option lets you set a fixed cost for 1,000 impressions (CPM). (In the abbreviation CPM, the M represents the Roman numeral for 1,000; thus, you read CPM as "cost per thousand.")

Focus-on-Impressions is a traditional advertising bidding model used for decades in other advertising channels. Historically, magazines charged for advertising in "1,000 readers" increments.

Only ads using the Display Network can use the *Focus-on-Impressions* options. Ads using this option are called *impression ads.*

- This type of advertising works well for brand awareness and for spreading the word about an event, new product, etc.

- Impression ads do not require a landing page, which makes them very easy and quick to deploy.

- This option makes it easy to compare online advertising costs and results with other advertising channels.

- Be aware that some online publications and social media networks may have cheaper CPM ad rates than you pay AdWords for its network of publishers. Do some comparisons.

- Google recommends a CPM bid be somewhat higher than the CPC bid for text ads (with the same targeting).

- Sometimes CPM text ads are given the entire ad space, rather than sharing the space with other text ads, which increases their visibility. Google does not explain the circumstances under which a CPM text ad monopolizes an ad space.

Focus-on-Conversions (Cost-per-Acquisition, (CPA))

The *Focus-on-Conversions* bidding model works with AdWords' *Conversion Tracking* and *Conversion Optimization* features to bring the best prospects to your landing page at the lowest *cost-per-acquisition* (CPA) or, in other words, the lowest cost-per-*buyer*.

- *Conversion Tracking* captures the search and buying behavior of your visitors and buyers. It uses that information to create a profile of the best prospects for your website.

- *Conversion Optimization* uses the Conversion Tracking data to calculate a weighted-average CPA for your customers. AdWords then uses the CPA as the benchmark to determine how much leeway it has for increasing bids.

- AdWords uses its *Conversion Optimization* logic to bid aggressively on your behalf to secure impressions before searchers who more closely match the behaviors of buyers (rather than visitors). Conversely, AdWords bids less aggressively on impressions for less likely prospects. By paying more for visitors likely to buy and less for visitors unlikely to buy, AdWords attempts to keep your costs as close to your desired cost-per-acquisition as possible while bringing you more paying customers.

- AdWords requires a consistent history of 15 conversions a month before you can deploy *Conversion Tracking*, and the more *Conversion Tracking* history available, the better your results.

  (See Key Concept 5: Power Features That Drive Success for a more full discussion of these powerful features.)

Focus-on-Engagement (CPC)

The *Focus-on-Engagement* pricing method works with Display Network —Engagement Ads. It works in the same manner as the *cost-per-click* bidding model.

- You are charged each time a viewer activates your ad by hovering, tapping, swiping, etc., it (rather than just clicking your ad as with the *Focus on Clicks* pricing method).

- Engagement ads attract and hold a viewer's attention by using rich media capabilities to do such things as expand the ad, run video, show animation, etc. A viewer must hover over, tap, swipe, click or take some other action to activate the ad.

- Performance data for Engagement Ads appears in the *statistics table* under the same columns used for *cost-per-click* (CPC) ads.

Cost-Per-View (CPV)

As this book goes to press, Google has merged its functions for video ads (*AllVideo Campaigns*) into the *All Online Campaigns* menu. *Cost-per-view* (CPV) bidding is used with all Video Ads created on the *all video campaign* screen. (Google calls this function AdWords for Videos in some of its help documentation.) Video Ads created on the *all online campaign* screen use *cost-per-click*.

With CPV bidding, you do not pay for impressions; rather, you pay for each viewer. Thus, you are charged only if:

- The viewer selects your video to watch (as in the case of an ad promoting your video on YouTube)

- The viewers continue to watch your video to the end or for 30 seconds, whichever comes first. This applies to videos that start automatically, such as *in-stream Video Ads* that run before a YouTube video.

Flexible Bid Strategies (CPC)

The *Flexible Bid Strategies* let you fine-tune AdWords' *automatic bidding* feature to help you meet your marketing goals while saving you time.

- You set a *flexible bid strategy* at the Campaign or Ad Group Level and it applies to the level where it is set and to all underlying levels. That is to say, setting a *flexible bid strategy* at the Campaign Level applies it to all the underlying ad groups. Setting it at the Ad Group Level applies it to that Ad Group.

- You can apply a single *flexible bid strategy* to multiple campaigns, and you can establish multiple *flexible bid strategies*. Be sure to give your strategies unique names.

  For example, you can set a "Maximize Click Strategy for Holiday Products" for $500 to share between Campaigns 1 and 2, and you can set a separate "Maximize Click Strategy for Winter Sports Products" for $250 to share between Campaigns 6 and 10.

- Strategies are setup in the *Shared Library* for your account, so they are available to all your campaigns, ad groups and ads.

The different types of *flexible bid strategies* include:

1. *Maximize clicks*, which tells AdWords to obtain as many impressions as possible within the *target ad spend* you specify (or within your daily budget if you do not specify an ad

spend). ("Ad spend" is marketing jargon for the amount of money you spend on an ad or campaign.)

- This option is a timesaver. It is useful for controlling multiple campaigns or ad groups that involve low priority or long-tail keywords, where you do not want to spend time monitoring infrequently searched keywords.

- The *maximize clicks* strategy requires you to establish a *CPC limit bid* and a *target ad spend*, which you can then apply to the campaign(s), ad group(s) or keyword(s) you want to use for that strategy.

- **Under the *maximize clicks* option, AdWords does not override your daily budgets, max CPC bids, manual bids or any other bid restriction you have set.** To give the strategy the ability to act, you need to remove your budget and/or manual bids from the campaigns, ad groups and keywords. (Leave the bid field empty. Do not enter a bid of zero.)

- If you do not specify a *target ad spend*, AdWords uses your daily budget(s). If your *target ad spend* is higher than your daily budget, AdWords still caps your total spend at the daily budget level.

2. ***Enhanced CPC***, which tells AdWords to raise your bids up to 30 percent if a conversion is likely or lower it up to 100 percent if a conversion is unlikely. AdWords considers device, browser, location and time of day when adjusting a bid.

    - Use this option if your landing page is converting well, you want to maximize traffic and you want an aggressive effort to use your entire budget.

    - Consider using it also when you are testing ads and landing pages over a short period to ensure maximum exposure for your ads.

    - This option does not require the use of *Conversion Tracking* (as the *manual bidding* with *enhance CPC* option does).

3. ***Return on ad spend (ROAS)***, which tells AdWords to try to achieve the return on investment (ROI) you set.

    (Your ROI is the value of your sales divided by the cost of your AdWords. For example, if you receive $1,000 in sales revenue for $200 in AdWords costs, your ROI is 400 percent. You received $4 for every $1 you spent.)

    You must use *Conversion Tracking* to use this option. Campaigns and ad groups assigned to this strategy must have at least 30 conversions with consistent conversion values in the last 30 days.

Your ROAS should be realistic. Set it slightly above your current conversion value/cost ratio.

- For Search Network ads, AdWords uses the average conversion value of the campaigns, ad groups or keywords you assign to this strategy as the benchmark for raising your bids to achieve more clicks.

- For the Display Network, AdWords uses the average conversion value of the campaigns or ad groups assigned to this strategy. Either way, AdWords works to achieve the conversion average within the ROAS you set. It considers device, browser, location and ad schedule when adjusting a bid, so it offers a great deal of precision.

- For the Search Network, two advanced bidding options are available— setting a *max bid limit* and/or a *minimum bid limit*—but each defeats the purpose of targeting ROAS. Google recommends not setting this limit.

- AdWords recalculates your performance every day, so check it day-by-day to see if your campaign is close to the goal and improving.

4. **Target search page location**, which tells AdWords to increase bids for Search Network ads to obtain an ad position on the top of the first page or, alternatively, anywhere on the first page of results. Note that this strategy does not guarantee top of page or first-page placement.

You have several options within the *target search page location* strategy, including:

a. **Ad position**, which tells AdWords to aim for a top-of-first-page position or, alternatively, a position anywhere on the first page.

b. **Bid automation**, which tells AdWords how to raise bids to match the competition's first page and top-of-page bids. You can do this in two ways:
   — *Automatically raise and lower bids* to match first page and top-of-page bids.
   — *Set bids yourself, but automatically adjust bids.* With this setting, you'll allow AdWords to automatically raise an existing bid to the estimated top-of-page bid if it drops below the estimate.

c. **Bid adjustment**, which tells AdWords to raise or lower your bid by as much as a certain percentage of the top-of-page bid. You specify the percentage.

d. **Max CPC**, which tells AdWords the highest bid you ever want to make. This sets an absolute ceiling for bids (above which a bid or adjusted bid cannot go). A Max CPC Bid Limit is optional.

e. **Limited budget**, which tells AdWords what to do when your budget is within a few clicks of running out. You can raise your bid even if it means you run out of budget sooner. This brings in clicks faster. Alternatively, you can stretch your budget by not raising your bid and, hopefully, get more clicks at a lower rate.

    f. **Low quality keywords**, which tells AdWords whether to raise bids on keywords with *quality scores* of 4 or less.

5. **Target CPA**, which tells AdWords to try to keep the *average cost-per-acquisition* (avgCPA) equal to your Target CPA.

    • You can apply this strategy across a specified set of campaigns, ad groups, ads or keywords in either the Search Network or Display Network or both.

    • Campaigns and ad groups assigned to this strategy must have at least 15 conversions in the last 30 days and must have similar rates of conversion for the last few days.

    • This bid strategy overrides any *bid adjustment* you have made for devices, locations, browsers or time of day for the campaigns, ad groups or ads.

Bidding Options	Ad Type	Automatic Bidding by AdWords	Manual Bidding
Focus on Clicks (Cost-per-Click (CPC))	Search, Display	√	√
Sub-option: Use Enhanced CPC	Search, Display		√
Focus on Conversions (CPA) Cost-per-Acquisition	Search, Display	√	√
Focus on Impressions (Cost-per-1000-Impressions (CPM))	Display Only		√
Flexible Bid Strategy			
Maximize Clicks	Search, Display	√	
Enhanced CPC	Search, Display	√	
Return on Ad Spend	Search, Display	√	
Target Search Page Location	Search, Display	√	
Target CPA	Search, Display	√	
Cost-per-View (CPV)	Videos Only		√

FIGURE 3.8 A recap of bidding models

KEY CONCEPT 3: AD RANK AND QUALITY SCORE

During an auction, AdWords determines which ads get the top ad positions by computing an *ad rank* for each ad. The ad rank represents the competitiveness of the ads.

The ad with the highest rank gets the top ad position, the ad with the second highest ranking gets the second ad position, and so on.

Ads with low ad ranks fall to lower positions. For Display Network ads, ads with low ad ranks may not secure a position at all because of the limited number of spaces available on the average website.

Your *ad rank* is the product of your *quality scores* times your *bid*.

The *quality score* represents how well the buying experience you offer meets the need of the searcher or, in the case of Display Network ads, the webpage viewer. The "buying experience" includes virtually everything that might affect the searcher/viewer, including:

1. How well an ad's keyword matches the search term or, in the case of Display Network ads, the content on the webpage. An exact match trumps a partial match, and a partial match trumps a broad match. (See Keywords, p. 81, for more details about fine-tuning keywords.)

2. Whether your keyword appears in your ad and your display URL. If your ad does not mention your keyword, AdWords considers it less relevant than someone else's ad that does mention the keyword.

3. Whether your ad has a clear call to action. Google knows that you must tell the viewer what to do or else he or she generally does nothing, so words such as "learn more," and "buy now," etc. add to your *quality score.*

4. Whether your ad was successful in the past. Google assumes success breeds success, so your previous click-through rate is a heavy factor.

5. Whether your AdWords account as a whole is making money. If you do not attract visitors to your landing pages for any of your products, your *quality score* is very low.

6. Whether your landing page relates to your ad. The more times your keywords appear on your landing page, the more relevant the content is to the viewer, and the higher your quality score.

7. Whether your landing page is effective. (The longer a visitor stays on your site, the higher AdWords rates the site, and the higher your *quality score.*)

97

To compute the *quality score,* **AdWords weighs some 200 factors.** In addition to the items just mentioned, AdWords assesses dozens of other factors. The formula for determining a *quality score* is one of the biggest mysteries surrounding AdWords. Many articles online attempt to explain it.

Current wisdom says an advertiser's click-through rate is the biggest determinant of a *quality score.* That theory makes sense. If searchers are clicking on your ad more often than they click your competitors' ads, your *quality score* should be higher. In short, if you make money for Google, Google helps you make money.

A *quality score* **of 5 is average (in 2013), according to one large Boston agency that has access to over $100MM in AdWords advertising.** They claim that AdWords discounts the costs for ad with *quality scores* above average. Higher-than-average scores brought the following discounts:

Score of 6 = 16.7 percent discount

Score of 7 = 28.6 percent discount

Score of 8 = 37.5 percent discount

Score of 9 = 44.4 percent discount

Score of 10 = 50 percent discount

Based on this data, increasing your *quality score* nets big cost savings—and potentially an even bigger increase in revenues if you use those savings to gain more buyers.

The *quality score* **is stored with the advertiser's keyword that triggered participation in the auction.** AdWords computes a new *quality score* for the keyword each time the keyword participates in an auction. You can

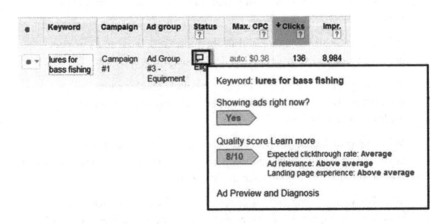

FIGURE 3.9 Quality score icon in status column

view the *quality score* for your keywords as part of the performance data on the *statistics table*. Hover over the speech bubble.

Click on the icon near a keyword to see its *quality score*.

You set a Max CPC when you create a campaign.

- For Search Network ads, you set the *Max CPC* at the Campaign Level but can override it at the Ad Group Level, the Ad Level or the Keyword Level.

- For Display Network ads, you set the *Max CPC* at the Ad Group Level but you can set *custom bids* to increase or lower it for items in one (and only one) targeting method and/or you can set *bid adjustments* for different devices.

AdWords respects your maximum CPC, unless you use one of the following pricing method options:

- *Enhanced cost-per-click* (eCPC) **pricing method**: where you authorize AdWords to increase your Max CPC bid up to 30 percent in order to win a better ad position. You can set a *limit bid* to prevent AdWords from bidding so high it depletes your profit margin.

- *Conversion Tracking* **feature:** where you authorize AdWords to maximize your bid to secure more impressions while maintaining—or lowering—your *average cost per customer acquired* (CPA). You can set a *limit bid* to prevent AdWords from bidding so high it compromises your profit margin.

AdWords does not tell you the bid amount it used for you during the auction.

Ad rank **uses the** *quality score* **for your keyword along with the maximum bid you set (or the maximum bid calculated by AdWords under an automated bidding option) to determine which ads take the top ad positions.** Google does not disclose the *ad rank* formula, but some researchers believe it is a simple multiplication of the maximum bid times the *quality score*. AdWords uses the ad rank to sort ads, highest rank to lowest, and to assign each an ad position.

Ad rank also determines the actual CPC that AdWords charges you when someone clicks your ad. AdWords uses the *ad rank* to determine the lowest bid that would preserve your ad position. AdWords adds 1¢ to that amount and uses that amount as the fee to charge you if your ad is clicked by the viewer.

- Note that the eCPC and CPA bidding options can skew auction results in favor of the advertisers that use those options, since it gives AdWords the authority to outbid other advertisers.

Advertiser	Max CPC Bid	Quality Score	Ad rank (Max CPC x Quality Score)	Ad Position
Advertiser A	$0.45	8	$3.60	1
Advertiser C	$0.80	3	$2.40	2
Advertiser D	$0.75	3	$2.25	3
Advertiser B	$0.30	5	$1.50	4
Advertiser E	$0.25	2	$0.50	5

FIGURE 3.10 Advertiser order after sorting by (quality score x max CPC)
After sorting by Ad Rank, Advertiser B is two positions lower.

In the following example, the "could-have-bid" for Advertiser A is $0.30. Had Advertiser A bid $0.30 (rather than $.45) his/her *ad rank* would be $2.40 (8 x $0.30), which is as high as the ad rank of Advertiser B. Adding 1¢ to that amount ensures a clear auction winner. It eliminates the possibility that rounding to the nearest dollar would cause the two Advertisers to tie.

Advertiser	Max CPC Bid	Quality Score	Ad rank (Max CPC x Quality Score)	Ad Position	Could have bid	Actual CPC charged, if ad is clicked
Advertiser A	$0.45	8	$3.60	1	$ .30	$ .31
Advertiser C	$0.80	3	$2.40	2	$ .75	$ .76
Advertiser D	$0.75	3	$2.25	3	$ .50	$ .51
Advertiser B	$0.30	5	$1.50	4	$ .10	$ .11
Advertiser E	$0.25	2	$0.50	5	*	*

FIGURE 3.11 Ads after actual cost calculation

The eCPC and CPA bidding options give advertisers a competitive advantage because they give AdWords the authority to outbid other advertisers. However, other advertisers can compete using these strategies:

1. **Determine if you can succeed with your ads in lower ad positions.** Note that Advertiser B paid only $0.11 per click for the top position in the right-hand column (as opposed to the top three ads which took the three positions above the search results). If this position brings you visitors and, ultimately, sales, you can bid lower and still generate revenues.

2. **Raise your bid.** The quickest and easiest way to improve your ad position is to simply offer Google more money to show your ad. In the previous example, a *quality score* of two with a maximum CPC of $1.81 could buy you the top ad position.

3. **Improve your *quality score* by improving the buying experience your ad offers.** Use AdWords' *experiment* feature to tweak different aspects of your ad campaign. You can pit one ad against another to see which messages draw more visitors or one landing page against another to see which produces more buyers.

(See Step 13: Use AdWords Experiments to Improve Your Ads and Save Money, p. 170, for details about running experiments).

KEY CONCEPT 4: AD MANAGEMENT SCREENS

Two screens provide the major management functions for your AdWords ads. The *all online campaigns* screen is the major screen for tracking performance and for editing options for all campaigns except video campaigns. The *all video campaigns* screen performs the same functions for Video Ads.

Note: as this book goes to press, Google has merged the All Online Campaign and All Video Campaign menus into a single menu.

All Online Campaigns

The *all online campaigns* management screen functions as a multi-dimensional spreadsheet. It lets you select a campaign or ad group and view information about that campaign or ad group or, alternatively, drill down to the underlying ad group or ads and view the same data for those levels. In addition, it lets you view data unique to a specific level.

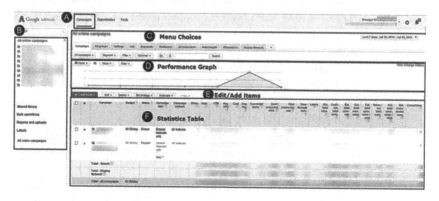

FIGURE 3.12 All online campaigns screen

You use the *All Online Campaigns* screen for all ads except videos ads. Note that the data in the *Statistics Table* (5) changes based on the campaign or ad group you select (2), the tabs you select (3) and the sub-menu choices you select (the buttons under the tabs).

Because of its many options and views, *all online campaigns* **is extremely flexible, and it takes some time to master.** As a novice, you need to review your data carefully to confirm that you are looking at the correct data.

Note the following major functions within this screen:

1. **Main menu**: the menu across the upper-most left of the screen presents the major tabs for AdWords:

   - **Home**: where a dashboard of all your AdWords data appears. Learn more on this in The Dashboard, p. 121.

   - **Campaign** (showing in the image above): where you monitor and manage your campaigns. This is the main screen for running campaigns.

   - **Opportunities**: where AdWords offers you suggestions for improving your ad (a discussion follows below).

   - **Tools**: where AdWords offers you a list of tools to help you analyze your ads. Solutions and tools to use for improving your ads are in Tools and Reports.

   - **Gear icon (⚙)** (at far right):
     — **Billing profile**: where you enter the name, address, tax status (business or individual), and language. Google assigns you a Billing ID, which shows on your invoices. Note that the Billing ID is not the same as your Google Account ID.
     — **Billing settings**: where you enter the name of the company paying for AdWords and how the bill is paid (automatically) and where you enter the credit card information for the payer.
     — **Transaction history**: where you can view the "debits and credits" to your account in detail for:
       (1) Costs: the total costs of your clicks.
       (2) Earnings: if you use Conversion Tracking and include transaction amounts.
       (3) Payments: charges to your credit card.
       (4) Adjustments: such as a promotional coupon from Google
       (5) Taxes: state taxes required by the account owner's state of incorporation.
     Note that the data is from Google's accounting perspective. Thus, credits is the amount of money Google will invoice, debits is the amount of money you have paid Google and the balance is either (1) the amount you owe Google if the number is positive, or (2) the amount Google has received from you that has not yet been spent on ads if the number is negative.

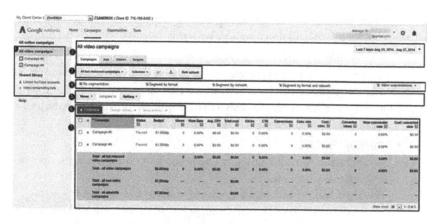

FIGURE 3.13 Google billing transactions

For this new account, the company used a $100 promotional coupon, received 23 clicks worth $100.81 for a balance-owed of $8.81. The balance owed trigged an automatic payment of $50.00, leaving a balance-available for ad purchases of $41.19.

Transaction history also lets you look at the volume of clicks for each ad in a time period, information that the *statistics table* does not provide. This can be an added source of information about how your ad is performing and when bids started to rise.

- **Bell (🔔):** where AdWords alerts appear. An alert may advise you of opportunities found by AdWords that could refine or expand your advertising.
- **Send feedback:** where you can send Google an email about a problem with AdWords.
- **Help:** where you access the help menu for AdWords.

2. **Navigation menu:** this menu lets you see all your campaigns and ad groups as well as input certain information accessible by all campaigns.

- *All online campaigns* **menu:** provides a directory of all your non-video campaigns.
   — Click the *all online campaigns* link to expand the list to show all campaigns. Note that the information in the *statistics table* changes as you move from campaign to campaign.
   — Click a campaign listed under the *all online campaign* heading to see the ad groups listed under the campaign. The performance data for each ad group then appear in the *statistics table*.
   — Click an ad group listed under the *all online campaign* heading and the performance data for each ad in that ad group appears in the *statistics table*.

103

After you select a campaign and/or ad group, you use the main menu choices to see drill down to ads, keywords, etc.

- *Shared library*: provides an input screen for ads, audiences, budget, negative keywords and placement exclusions that you want to use in multiple campaigns. This is where you also can enter a budget and have it apply to a list of campaigns you enter. (See Step 14: Use the Shared Library to Save Time, p. 176, for more information.)

- *Bulk operations*
  — **Scripts**: provides an input screen for Java programming scripts to control your bids.
  — **Bulk edits**: provides a means of viewing the mass changes you made across one or more campaigns, ad groups, ads or keywords.

- *Reports and uploads*: provides a screen where you review reports you ran previously or have scheduled to run in the future and where you upload bulk changes to your campaigns. (See Tools and Reports, p. 327, for more information on Reports.)

- *Labels*: provides a screen where you maintain a list of labels that you want to use on reports and where you view reports of labels used at the Campaign, Ad Group, Ad or Keyword Levels.

- *All video campaigns*: where you setup, monitor and refine Video Ads. This screen is discussed later in this section.

3. **Tabs**: where you can view settings or performance data about one or all campaigns, ad groups, ads, keywords or display ad targeting methods.

Tabs work with the navigation list to lets you see information about:

- All your campaigns: select either *all online campaigns* or *all video campaigns* in the hierarchy navigation.

- A specific campaign: select a campaign under *all online campaigns* or *all video campaigns*.

- A specific ad group: select an ad group under *all online campaigns* or *all video campaigns*.

In addition, each menu choice has a sub-menu to let you drill-down to specific details for the hierarchy level you selected.

The *statistics table* changes each time you click a different level in the hierarchy menu and each time you click a different tab.

- **Campaigns**: appears only when you select *all online campaigns*, it shows a list of your campaigns and the performance data for each. Check the box next to a campaign and one of the tabs (for example, the Ads tab) and a list of the ads within that campaign—across all ad groups—appears, along with their performance information.

- **Ad groups**: for the campaign you selected under *all online campaigns*, it shows each ad group and the performance data for each ad group. It brings up a sub-menu from which you can select:

  — *All, all enabled* **or** *all but removed* **ad groups**: to limit your view to the ad groups most relevant to you. *All* shows all campaigns whether they are running or not. *All enabled* shows all active campaigns (i.e., paused campaigns are excluded). *All But Removed* shows all actively running and paused campaigns.

  — *Segments*: let you show and thus, compare, performance data for the following data elements at the Campaign, Ad Group, Ad or Keyword/Targeting Levels:

    (1) Time: tells you what time of day, day of the week and hour of the day your ad does best and how many clicks you received by week, month or quarter.

    (2) Conversions by name: tells you how many conversions you received for each type of action (purchase, signup, etc.).

    (3) Conversions by category: tells you how many conversions you received by category of actions.

    (4) Network: shows clicks for the Search Network and Display Network.

    (5) Network Search Partner (with, without): shows clicks on Google Search Partner webpages (AOL, EarthLink).

    (6) Click type: whether visitors clicked your headline or your sitelinks.

    (7) Devices: shows clicks by people using mobile phones, tablets and desktops.

    (8) Top of page vs. other ad positions: shows clicks by ad position. **Segments let you compare the performance of the different choices you made for your campaigns.** For example, which keywords within an Ad Group perform best, which ad position performs best, which day of the week gets the most clicks?

- *Filters*: let you find ads that are greater than, less than or equal to an amount you specify for any of the performance data elements on the *Statistics Table*. The major elements include:

  — Bidding strategy (name, strategy).

  — Performance (active view).

  — Impression share.

  — Search funnels.

  — Analytics.

- — Conversions.
- — Performance.
- — Default max CPC.
- — Max CPM.
- — Status.
- — Ad group.
- — Ad group name.
- — Auction insights.
- — Labels.

(See the discussion on the *statistics table* for data elements definitions.)

Filters **let you find the best and worst performers within your campaigns, ad groups, ads and keywords.** For example, you can find ads with a click-through rate below 1 percent, ads with a click-through rate over 2 percent, keywords costing more than $5 and keywords costing less than $5.

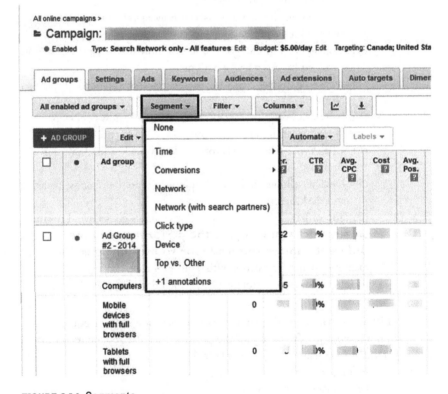

FIGURE 3.14 Segments

Segments breakout ad impression characteristics by time of day, day, week, month, quarter, network, type of click, device, top vs other [top of page vs other ad slots], and Google Plus annotation.

You can use multiple *filters* **to narrow your criteria.** For example, you can find ads with a click-through rate over 10 percent and a max CPC below $1.

- *Columns—customize columns*: lets you add and remove columns of information on the *Statistics Table*. (The *Statistics Table* is discussed later in this section.)
- *Graph icon* (⌐☑): lets you show or hide the graph.
- *Download icon* (⌐⬇): lets you download the currently shown data as a spreadsheet or, alternatively, schedule that view for automatic production on a regular basis. You can email scheduled reports to yourself or management, and you can modify and upload spreadsheet as bulk changes.
  — **Settings**: for the campaign you selected under *all online campaigns*, it shows all options you choose for that campaign. (If you did not select a specific campaign, it shows a list of campaigns.)
  — **All settings**: if you selected one campaign under *all online campaigns*, you automatically see the choices you selected for that campaign. If you did not select a campaign under *all online campaigns*, you see a list of campaigns. Check the box next to a campaign and click the *all settings* button to see its settings.
  — **Locations**: if you selected one campaign under *all online campaigns*, you see the location(s) you specified for that campaign. If you did not select a campaign under *all online campaigns*, you see the locations for every campaign. Check the box next to a specific campaign and click the *locations* button to see the details for that campaign.
  — **Ad schedules**: if you selected one campaign under *all online campaigns*, you see the ad schedule(s) you specified for that campaign. If you did not select a campaign under *all online campaigns*, you see the *ad schedules* you specified for every campaign. Check the box next to a specific campaign and click the *ad schedule* button to see the details for that campaign.
  — **Devices**: if you selected one campaign under *all online campaigns*, you see a breakout of data by device (i.e., by computers, smartphones and tablets). If you did not select a campaign under *all online campaigns*, you see a breakout of data by device for every campaign. Check the box next to a specific campaign and click the *device* button to see the details for that campaign.
  (1) **Ads**: for the campaign or the ad group you selected under *All Online Campaigns,* it shows each ad.

107

(2) **Keywords**: for Search Network ads only, it shows the keywords associated with the campaign, ad group or ad you selected under *all online campaigns.*

(3) **Audiences**: for Search Network Ads only, it shows data for your *Remarketing Lists* (i.e., list of people who visited your site previously if you use the Remarketing feature). You can use the *segment* button to breakout the data by device, time frame, etc. This tab can be suppressed by clicking the down-arrow (⬇) button.

(4) **Ad extensions**: for all campaigns if you do not select a specific campaign or for a specific campaign, you can view and edit *ad extension* information (i.e., locations, phone numbers, sitelinks, offers, product extension, dynamic search information, Google +1 social extension or app extension). Click the button marked *view: <option>* to view a drop-down menu and select a specific *ad extension* type.

— **Auto targets**: brings up a drop-down menu for more information about product listing targets (a feature that is being deprecated in 2014) or Dynamic Search Ads. This tab can be suppressed by clicking the down-arrow (⬇) button.

From the drop-down menu entitled *view*, you can select:

(1) **Product targets**: to enter, view or change the criteria you want AdWords to use to select products to advertise. Criteria include *product ID, product type, brand, conditions, labels* or *group*, each of which corresponds to a field in the feed you upload to Google.

(2) **Dynamic Search Ads**: to enter, view or change the pages in your website you want AdWords to use for your *Dynamic Search Ads.* You can specify pages by category, URL, page title (as set by the page_title field in the HTML) and page content (as set in the page_content field in the HTML).

— **Dimensions**: brings up the performance data (in the *statistics table*) for your campaigns by *label, time* (day of week, week, month, quarter, year, hour of day), *destination URL, geographic areas, user location, search terms* that trigger your ad, *automatic placements, free clicks* or *call details.*

Dimensions offer a wealth of information that helps you fine-tune your ads.

— **Display Network**: for Display Network ads, a sub-menu appears to let you:

(1) *Change display targeting*: a pop-up screen lets you make your changes.

(2) *View* (or change) *display keywords, managed placements, topics, interests and Remarketing lists, gender* or *age*, depending on which button you select.

— **Drop-down menu**: where you can suppress the *Audiences* and *Auto Targets* buttons -- buttons you do not intend to use for the moment.

— **Date selector**: where you enter the time period for the data you want to review. You can select today, yesterday, this week, last week, etc., or you can enter a *custom date* range.

(1) The date selector also includes the option to compare the performance during your selected date range with that of either (1) the previous period, (2) the same period last year, or (3) a time period you specify. The comparison appears on the graph. You can select any two elements and compare them against each other and against a previous period.

For example, you can easily compare this December with this November; this December with last December, or your Holiday sales between November 25th and December 25th with your Summer Festival sales between July 4th and August 4th.

FIGURE 3.15 Dimensions

Dimension breakout performance by various campaign options, such as location, language, top movers among all your campaigns, etc.

(2) The comparison also appears within the *Statistics Table*. A +
sign (⊞) appears above the individual metrics in the *Statistic
Table*. Click the +sign beside each metric to see the data for
the two periods.

(3) For example, you can compare the impressions for last month
against this month. Use this capability at the *all online
campaigns* to quickly determine which campaigns are
decreasing in impressions, clicks or conversions and, thus,
need attention.

Note that *custom dates* must be full months or the comparison is
inaccurate. For example, a comparison of custom dates of
9/1/14–9/15/14 (a partial month) are matched by AdWords
against the previous period of 9/1/13–9/30/14 (a full month).

4. *The performance graph*

**The graph in the middle of the screen lets you compare two
dimensions, such as *clicks* and *impressions* (as shown as follows),
to see how one corresponds to the other across the time period
you select.** You can select a time period from the drop-down menu in
the *date selector*.

Daily, weekly, monthly interval: lets you control the interval between
points on the graph.

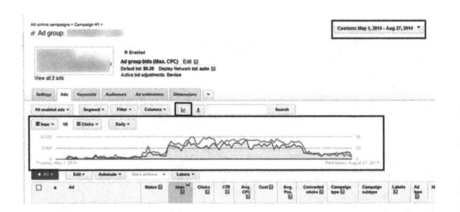

FIGURE 3.16 The performance graph

The performance graph shows data visually for a specific date range, making trends
more obvious. Above, the graph indicates the more *impressions* the ad received, the
more *clicks* it gets. Note the small icon above the graph. Click it to remove the
graph from view.

110

5. *Add, edit, details and automate*: this menu line lets you perform four different functions.

- + *<item level>*: the text on the button varies depending on your level in the hierarchy. For example, if you are viewing campaigns, the button reads +*campaign*. Click the +*campaign* button and AdWords starts asking questions to establish a new campaign. The button works the same way at for every item on the main menu.

- *Edit*: lets you change options quickly, as well as copy and paste options from one campaign to another, one ad group to another, etc.

  Check the box next to a line item and click *edit* to change any of the following: the budget set at the Campaign Level; a bid at the Ad Group Level; the text of an ad or to copy an ad at the Ad Level or the *bid*, text, *match type* or *destination URL* at the Keyword Level. Also, you can create a spreadsheet when you need to make large numbers of changes quickly.

  — Note: AdWords also offers an Editor that lets you download your account, make changes and upload the results into AdWords. Using it, you can run searches across campaigns, make mass changes and email your proposed changes to your management for approval before you make the changes. Download the AdWords Editor at google.com/adwordseditor.

- *Details*: check the box next to a keyword and click the *details* button to see: (1) the *search query* report, which shows the search terms your keyword wins, (2) the *auction insights* report, which shows a list of advertisers competing against your ad or (3) the *keyword diagnostic* tool, which lets you see which of your keywords are not triggering ads and why. Not all choices appear for all hierarchy level. (See Tools and Reports, p. 327, for more information about these reports.)

- **Bid strategies**: for Search Network ad group, select:
  — Use flexible bid strategy: lets you select (or preview) an existing Ad Group Level flexible bid strategy.
  — Use campaign bid strategy: lets you select (or preview) an existing Campaign Level flexible bid strategy.
  — Use manual CPC bidding: lets you switch to the manual CPC bidding option and set a Max CPC for the ad group.
  — Manage flexible bid strategies: lets you setup a new flexible bid strategy or change an existing one.

- *Automate [rules]*: the *Automate* button lets you define a rule or rules to apply to whichever element is showing (i.e., ad group, ad or keyword). Based on the conditions you specify, you can change the

111

daily budget, start a campaign, pause a campaign or change the *Max CPC* for a campaign. (See Step 12: Use Automatic Rules to Maintain Ad Performance, p. 167, for more on creating rules.)

- *Labels*: the *label* button lets you create a label for, or add an existing one to, a keyword.

6. ***Statistics table***: the *statistics table* shows statistics for a campaign(s), ad group(s,) ad(s), etc. depending on your choice on the *all online campaigns* or the *all video campaigns*.

- The data on the *statistics table* changes depending on the date range you select, using the *date selector*. You can also request data for a second period of time.

  When comparison data is requested, you must click the + sign in the title row for the comparison data to appear.

- For the *all online campaigns* hierarchy, the *statistics table* shows the basic data fields, along with any extra *sets of data* that you add using the *column* and *customize columns* buttons.

  To add sets of data, click the *column* and *customize columns* buttons and select the category of data you want to add. Include as many items as you want. You must click the save button to add the elements.

For *all online campaigns* (i.e., non-video campaigns), use the following as a reference list for all the data items available, organized by *columns*.

Attributes. Different elements are available at different hierarchical levels.

- Campaign elements include:
  — **Campaign type**: the network on which the campaign runs, either the Search Network, the Display Network or the Search Network with Select Display sites.
  — **Campaign sub-type**: whether the campaign includes a special capability.
    For Search Network campaigns, sub-capabilities include using (1) *standard features* or *all features* and (2) *Google Shopping listing* or *Dynamic Search* Ads.
    For Display Network campaigns, sub-capabilities include (1) *all features* and (2) *Mobile Apps, Remarketing* or *Engagement* Ads.
  — **Labels**: names you apply to ad groups, ads and keywords to group them together for reporting purposes.
  — **Bid strategy type**: the bidding model used in the campaign, either CPC, CPM, CPA or eCPC. (See Key Concept 2: AdWords Supports Several Bidding models to Maximize Your Budget, p. 88, for more information on bidding options.)

— **Bid strategy**: the strategy used by the campaign to maximize clicks, target a page location, meet a targeted spend amount, meet a return on investment percentage or meet a cost per acquisition. (See Key Concept 2: AdWords Supports Several Bidding Models to Maximize Your Budget, p. 88, for more information on bidding options.)

- At the Ad Group Level only, all of the campaign elements plus:
  — **Active bid adjustment**: the percentage by which you have adjusted a targeting method, such as topics, placements or *Remarketing Lists*.

- At the Ad Level only:
  — **Ad type**: the format for your ad, such as text, image, mobile or video.
  — **ID**: a unique number assigned by Google to identify an ad
  — **Device preference**: whether the ad runs on all devices or only on mobile devices.
  — **Policy details**: whether Google has approved, is reviewing, or has disapproved your ad.
  — **Image URL**: the website where your ad images are stored.
  — **List name**: the group of ads shared across multiple campaigns that includes this ad. (See Step 14: Use the Shared Library to Save Time, p. 176, for more information.)

- At the Keyword Level only:
  — **Dest. URL**: the actual URL your customer visits after he or she clicks an ad.
  — **Qual. score**: the score computed by AdWords representing the relevance of your ad, keywords, landing page, etc., to the searcher's query.
  — **Est. first page bid**: AdWords' estimate of the bid you need to achieve a first page ad position.
  — **Est. top page bid**: AdWords' estimate of the bid you need to achieve an ad position above the organic search engine results.
  — **Match type**: whether you specified your keyword to match the searcher's query exactly, partially, broadly, with another word or modified broadly.
  — **Ad group**: the name of the ad group(s) you are viewing (appears automatically).
  — **Status**: whether your campaign, ad group, ad or keyword. (depending on your level in the hierarchy) is *pending approval* from Google, *disapproved* by Google, *enabled* and either running or *paused* by you or *removed* by you.

Bidding information.

- **Default Max CPC**: the most you are willing to pay if a viewer clicks your ad on this network. If you see *auto.*, it means AdWords is automatically bidding for you. If you see *enhanced*, it means AdWords is automatically bidding for you and using the Enhanced CPC bidding model.

- **Display Network Max CPC**: the highest amount you set as the most you are willing to pay if a viewer clicks your ad on the Display Network.

- **Max CPC**: at the Keyword Level, the highest amount you set as the most you will pay if a viewer clicks your ad.

Performance data—for the period you selected

- **Clicks**: the number of times a viewer clicked your ad and viewed your landing page.

- **Impr. (impressions)**: the number of times your ad appeared.

- **CTR (click-through rate)**: the total clicks received divided by Impressions.

- **Avg. CPC (Average Cost-per-Click)**: the total cost of clicks divided by number of clicks received.

- **Avg. CPM (average cost-per-thousand)**: the total cost of your CPM, flat-fee ad divided by the number of clicks received.

- **Cost**: the total cost of clicks (CPCs) and flat-fee impressions (CPMs).

- **Avg. pos.**: the position your ad received, on average, for the period.

- **Total cost**: the total cost of Impressions.

- **Invalid clicks**: clicks AdWords deems to be accidental (as when someone double clicks an ad). AdWords reimburses you for these ads.

Performance metrics (active view).

- **Active view viewable impr.**: the number of impressions considered viewable (i.e., in an ad slot where a viewer is highly likely to see it and with 50 percent of the ad viewable for one second or longer).

- **Active view viewable CTR**: the number of times a viewer clicked your ad after it was viewable.

- **Active view avg. CPM**: the average cost per 1,000 viewable impressions.

As this book goes to press, Google is moving toward counting a click ONLY if it is 50% for one second or longer.

Conversion Tracking (See Conversion Tracking (Data Collection), p. 228, for details about the data elements supporting this function).

Call metrics (Use *Segment—Clicks* to see the source of your calls).

- **Phone impressions**: the number of times AdWords showed your ad with your clickable phone number.

- **Phone calls**: the number of phone calls to your Google-provided, 800-number that forwards calls to your business phone.

- **PTR (phone-through rate)**: the number of times your phone was called divided by the number of times your ad showed with your phone number.

- **Avg. CPP** (average cost-per-phone call): the cost of manually-dialed calls to your Google phone number divided by the number of calls dialed.

Competitive metrics (for the period you selected, for the network running your ad)

- **Search impr. share**: your *share of impressions* on the Search Network.

- **Search exact-match IS**: your *share of impressions* using exact-match keywords divided by the total number of exact-match keyword *impressions* available. (Low *quality score* and budget are two reasons you lose exact-match keyword impressions.)

- **Search lost IS (budget)**: at the Campaign Level, the percentage of *impressions* you did not receive on the Search Network because your budget was too low.

- **Display impr. share (budget)**: at the Campaign Level, your share of *impressions* on the Display Network.

- **Search lost IS (rank)**: the percentage of *impressions* you did not receive on the Search Network because of poor *ad rank*.

- **Display lost IS (rank)**: the percentage of *impressions* you did not receive on the Display Network because of poor ad rank.

Search funnel (See Conversion Tracking (Data Collection), p. 228, for details about data elements on the search funnel reports).

The buttons just above the *statistics table* include *add new, edit, change status, automate* and *labels*. The items you can add or change differ depending on the level of the hierarchy you select.

- *Add new*: click the *add new* button and AdWords starts asking questions to establish a new campaign, ad group or ad, depending on your level in the hierarchy.

- *Edit*: lets you make changes quickly. Check the box next to a line item and click *edit* to change any of the following: the budget set at the Campaign Level, the bid at the Ad Group Level, the text of an ad or to copy an ad at the Ad Level or the bid, text, match type or destination URL at the Keyword Level. Also, you can create a spreadsheet when you need to make large numbers of changes quickly.

  Note: AdWords also offers an editor that lets you download your account, make changes and upload the results into AdWords. You can run searches across campaigns, make mass changes and email your proposed changes to your management for approval before you make the changes. Download the AdWords Editor at www.google.com/adwordseditor.

- *Automate* (**rules**): the Automate button lets you define a rule or rules to apply to whichever element is showing (i.e., ad group, ad or keyword). Based on the conditions you specify, you can change the daily budget, start a campaign, pause a campaign or change the max CPC for a campaign. (See Step 12: Use Automatic Rules to Maintain Ad Performance, p. 167, for more on creating rules).

- *Labels*: the *label* button lets you create a label for, or add an existing one to, a keyword.

All Video Campaigns

The *All Video Campaigns* **management screen is a multi-dimensional spreadsheet that functions similarly to the all online campaign management screen.** However, videos have different metrics than static ads, which makes a separate screen for video campaigns necessary.

To move to the *all video campaigns* management screen, click the command at the bottom of the navigation menu on the *all online campaigns* described previously.

1. **The navigation menu works as it does on the *all online campaign* screen.** Click the *all video campaigns* link to expand your list of video campaigns. Note that the information in the *Statistics Table* changes as you move from campaign to campaign.

   (If *all video campaigns* does not appear as a choice in the left-hand menu, go to the *all online campaign* in the left-hand menu and click the red +*campaign* button. At the bottom of the options, click *online video*.)

2. **The tabs on the *all video campaigns* screen function just like the tabs on the *All Online Campaigns* screen discussed previously.**

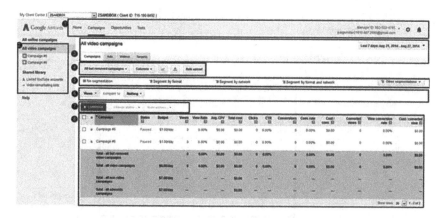

FIGURE 3.17 All video campaigns screen

- Click *all video campaigns* on the left menu and click the *campaign tab* to show data for all your video campaigns in the *statistics table*. Likewise, the *ad*, *video* and *targets* tabs also show information for all your campaigns.

- Click a single campaign on the *all video campaigns* menu on the left and select the *campaign tab* to show data for that campaign. Likewise, the *ad*, *video* and *targets* tabs also show information for all your campaigns.

- Note that the *statistics table* changes each time you click a different campaign or tab.

3. **The *all but removed campaigns, graph* icon, *download* icon and *bulk upload* buttons work the same as on the *all online campaign* screen; however, the *columns* button has pre-set screens, rather than lists of data elements you can select.**

   The following describes the data elements that appear on the *statistics table* of the *all video campaigns*.

   These items appear on every column-set:
   - **Campaign name**: the name you assigned to identify this campaign.
   - **Status**: indicates the ad is *eligible* to run, *paused* by you, *deleted* by you (but you can re-enable it), *pending* but scheduled for the future, *ended* (i.e., passed the end date you set), *suspended* for lack of budget or *limited by budget* so it shows infrequently (click the graph icon for a recommended budget).
   - **Budget**: the maximum amount you agree to spend each day.

117

FIGURE 3.18 All video campaigns screen with column choices
The columns button offers a menu of screens, pre-set for specific purposes.

- **Views**: the number of times someone watched your video. AdWords counts a person each time he or she watches your video. If someone views your ad repeatedly, AdWords counts him or her repeatedly.
- **View rate**: the number of times someone clicked your Video Ad divided by the number of times your Video Ad showed.
- **Average CPV**: the total cost you paid for all the views of your ad divided by the number of views.
- **Total cost**: the total amount you paid for all views for your video.

Views: where you monitor your views and the interest value of your video.

- *Campaign* or *ad, status, budget, views, view rate, average CPV and total costs* as mentioned previously.
- **Earned views**: the number of times someone watched another of your videos (not the advertised one) within seven days of watching your Video Ad.
- **Video played to**: the number of visitors who watched 25 percent, 50 percent, 75 percent or 100 percent of your video.

Audience: where you track the engagement of your viewers.

- *Campaign* or *ad, status, budget, views, view rate, average CPV and total costs* as mentioned previously.
- **Earned views**: the number of times someone watched another of your videos (not the advertised one) within seven days of watching your Video Ad.

- **Earned subscribers**: the number of subscribers your YouTube channel received from people watching your paid Video Ad.

- **Earned shares**: the number of viewers who clicked the share button for your video within seven days of watching it.

- **Earned likes**: the number of viewers who clicked the like button for your video within seven days of watching it.

(Note: To protect the privacy of the viewer AdWords does not report a number if it is less than three.)

Branding: where you track the number of viewers and their interest in your ad.

- *Campaign* or *ad, status, budget, views, view rate, average CPV and total costs* as mentioned previously.

- **Unique viewers**: the number of people who viewed your ad (with no one counted twice).

- **Avg. view frequency**: the total number of times your ad was watched divided by the number of unique viewers. A rate of 1.0 means everyone viewed your ad once. A number above 1.0 means some people watched the ad more than once.

- **Impressions**: the number of times AdWords showed your ad. Click the plus icon (⊞) to see more details, namely:
  — **Impressions (thumbnail)**: for in-display, in-slate and in-search Video Ads, the number of times AdWords showed a thumbnail of your ad or video
  — **Impressions (videos)**: for *in-stream ads* (which run automatically), the number of times AdWords showed the video.

- **Average impression frequency**: the number of times most people were exposed to your Video Ad. The number is determined by dividing the total number of impressions by the total number of people.

- **Reach per frequency**: the number of people who saw your ad one-though-seven times.

Note that Video Ad-counts on AdWords may not match view-counts on your YouTube account. AdWords does not include views of your video by people who find your video in ways other than clicking on your ad (e.g., a search on Google, an email link from a friend, etc.). Thus, your YouTube view-counts are often higher than AdWords website clicks.

Conversions: where you monitor activity on your website or app resulting from your Video Ad.

- *Campaign* or *ad, status, budget, views, view rate, average CPV and total costs* as mentioned previously.

- **Clicks**: the number of viewers who clicked through to your website (the same as click-throughs for Search Network and Display Network ads).

- **CTR**: the number of people who clicked your ad and moved to your site divided by the number of times your video showed. The site can be your website, YouTube channel, a designated URL or landing page for your video.

- **Conversions**: if you use *Conversion Tracking*, the total number of *conversions* (leads, sales, etc.) resulting from your Video Ad. (Note: if you track leads *and* sales, this is the aggregate.)

- **View-through conversions**: the number of times someone bought something after seeing a thumbnail of your ad but not viewing your video.

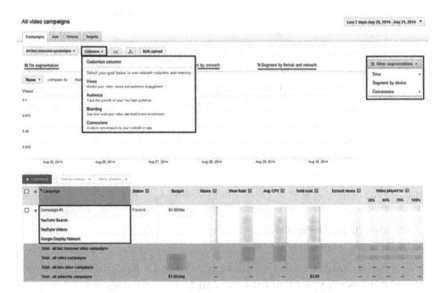

FIGURE 3.19 All video campaigns with format and network segmentation

The above shows branding statistics segmented by format and network. Click the plus sign (+) beside Impressions to show the segmentation by thumbnails and videos. Click the plus sign beside *Avg. Impr. Freq.* to see the *Reach per Frequency* (i.e., number of people saw your ad for 1, 2, 3, etc. time up to 7 times). The *Statistics Table* shows data for each video type (*In-Slate, In-Display* and *In-Stream*) for the Display Network, YouTube Search and YouTube Video pages.

120

- *Conv. Rate* (conversion rate): the number of clicks divided by the number of conversions that could be tracked to your ad. It tells you how often, on average, a visitor becomes a cuctomer.

- *Cost/Conv.* **(Cost per conversion): the total cost of your video clicks divided by the total number of conversions.**

4. **Like the** *all online campaign* **screen, the** *all video campaigns* **also lets you segment (i.e., breakdown) data by** *format, network, format-within-network, time* **and** *devices.*

   Segmentation options appear as blue text on the *all video campaign screen*. *Segmentation by format/network, time* and *device* appear under the *other segmentations* button.

5. **The** *performance graph* **works the same as it does on the** *all online campaign.*

   The red +*video* **button lets you add a new video campaign.** (Each video is its own campaign.)

6. **The** *statistics table* **works as it does for the all online campaign screen.** At the bottom of the table, totals appear for your segments along with totals for *all, enabled* or *all but removed* videos.

Dashboard

The AdWords homepage is a *dashboard* that you can configure to show an overview of your campaigns, ad groups and keywords results.

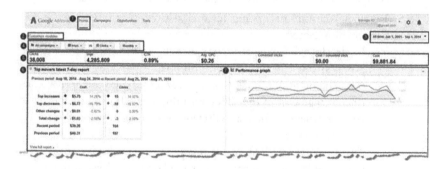

FIGURE 3.20 AdWords dashboard (top)
The dashboard provides a quick overview of your campaigns.
It also alerts you to troubled keywords.

121

Note the following choices and capabilities:

1. **Home**: the top level menu choice that brings up the Dashboard.

2. **Customize modules**: where you select the hierarchical level and tables you want to access on your dashboard. You can select any number of these:
   - **Hierarchy level:**
     — All campaigns.
     — All enabled campaigns.
     — All non-active campaigns.
     — All enabled ad groups.
     — All non-active ad groups.
   - **Tables:**
     — Good quality, but low traffic keywords—keywords infrequently used by searchers.
     — Keywords below first page bid—keywords with CPCs below that required to appear on the first page of results.
     — All enabled keywords—all keywords that are active (not paused).
     — All non-active keywords—all paused and removed keywords.

3. **Date selector**: where you select the time period for the data on the dashboard. (Select This Month or This Week to keep your data current.)

4. **Hierarchy and performance graph filters**: where you select:
   - The campaigns or ad groups you want to view (only the types you selected in 2 previously will appear).
   - The type of data you want to see or the data elements you want to compare on the Performance Graph (discussed in point 7 as follows).
   - Whether you want data points for each day, week or month in the time period you selected.
     — **Basic data**: a bar of basic, pre-set data for the campaign(s) or ad group(s) you selected as a filter (in point 4 previously). *Conversions* (i.e., the number of sales/leads you received) and *cost of conversions* (the average cost of each click resulting in a sale) appear only if you use *Conversion Tracking*. (Previously, *conversions* was called *converted clicks*.)
     — **Top movers for last seven days**: a snapshot display of the level of change in your campaigns over the last seven days. In the left panel, it shows the total cost for campaigns that have increased the most and decreased the most, followed by the total for all the other campaigns that have not experienced a major shift and the total change for all campaigns. The total costs for ads for this week and last week are shown. The same information is presented in the second panel for clicks.

⊕ Top movers latest 7-day report

Previous period: **Aug 19, 2014 - Aug 25, 2014** vs Recent period: **Aug 26, 2014 - Sep 1, 2014**

	Cost		Clicks	
Top increases	⬆ $5.75	14.46%	⬆ 13	12.38%
Top decreases	⬇ - $6.64	-16.70%	⬇ -16	-15.24%
Other changes	⬆ $0.24	0.60%	⬆ 2	1.90%
Total change	⬇ - $0.65	-1.63%	⬇ -1	-0.95%
Recent period	$39.11		104	
Previous period	$39.76		105	

View full report »

FIGURE 3.21 Top mover report

Based on the data in the cost column, this report indicates some campaigns have experienced increases in CPC while others have not. If you recently increased the CPC for good keywords in one campaign but decreased the CPCs of some keywords in another campaign to maintain your budget, this shift is not surprising.

The closeness of the percentage increases in cost and clicks (14.46% and 12.38%, respectively) indicates that greater costs are resulting in more clicks, while the closeness of the percentage decreases in costs and clicks indicate that lower costs are resulting in few clicks.

This could be exactly the results you expected from your CPC modifications. If not, click the view full report to see exact which campaigns have experienced shifts.

Click on the *view full report* link to see which campaigns have experienced the most increase/decrease in costs or clicks.

You must rely on your knowledge of the changes you have made and the influences in the marketplace to determine if the shifts are reasonable, were expected or are a surprise. In most instances, the closer the numbers are within a panel, the less dramatic the shift in performance. The closer the numbers are between costs and clicks, the less dramatic the shift.

- **Performance graph for the period**: a bar graph presenting information for one data element for the period or, alternatively, presenting the relationship between two data elements for the period. A plethora of data elements are available for comparison.

The bottom half of the dashboard shows tables of data for the campaigns and/or ad groups you selected using the *customized modules* options. You can arrange the page to be most useful to you.

123

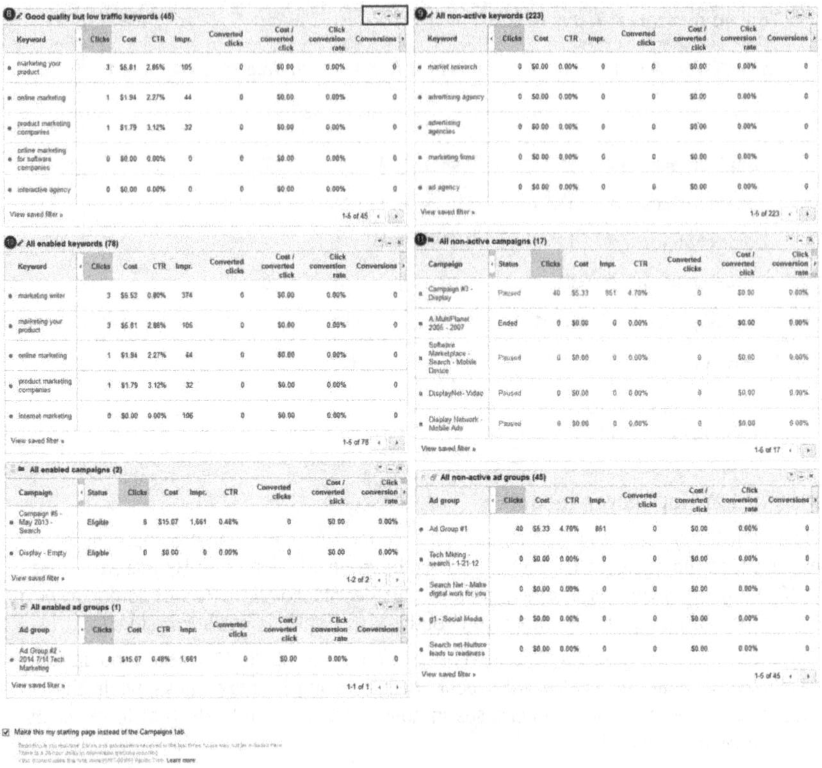

FIGURE 3.22 AdWords dashboard (bottom)

The lower half of the dashboard shows information about the different aspects of your campaigns and ad groups you selected using the Customize Modules options. You can close any of the tables to simplify the page.

- You can move the boxes around to put the ones most important to you at the top. Mouse over the title line until the cross arrows (✛) appear, then hold down the mouse key and move the table to a new location.
- Click the arrow at the side of the row of data to scroll through additional data elements.
- Click the down arrow to see options for refining the table.
- To re-open the box, return to the *customize modules* menu.

The dashboard can be overwhelming at first. Review it after your ads have run for a week or two, and it should make more sense. In a short time, you will find the dashboard provides a quick update on your ads and progress.

KEY CONCEPT 5: POWER FEATURES THAT DRIVE SUCCESS

AdWords has a number of advanced features that puts the full power of AdWords logic to work for your campaigns.

These features require that your campaign reach a certain level of proficiency (often 15 clicks per month) before you can activate the feature. Also, some require changes to your webpages.

Nevertheless, using these features should be the goal of every AdWords user. The features are:

1. *Conversion Tracking*: Conversion Tracking works to show your ad to your best prospects and increase traffic to your website without increasing your costs. This greatly increases your return on investment (ROI). Google claims double-digit increases in conversion are not unusual with Conversion Tracking.

    *   In AdWords terminology, a *conversion* occurs when a visitor to your landing page takes whatever action you request—for example, buying an item, signing up for a newsletter, downloading an app or downloading a white paper.

    *   *Conversion Tracking* is an advanced feature that captures data about the conversions on your site, such as the search term(s) the searcher used before clicking your ad, the competing sites they visited and the dollar amount of purchases. The data helps you determine which keywords introduce your product along with which keywords entice visitors to return. It also helps you define the stages people go through before buying your product (i.e., your sales funnel).

    (See Conversion Tracking (Data Collection), p. 228, for more information.)

2. *Conversion Optimizer*: one of the major benefits of using *Conversion Tracking* is the opportunity to add the *Conversion Optimizer* feature.

    Once you achieve 15 clicks a month for a Search Network campaign using the Conversion Tracking feature, you have the option to use Conversion Optimizer.

    The *Conversion Optimizer* calculates an estimated *cost-per-acquisition* (CPA) for your campaign using Conversion Tracking data and adjusts your bid up or down to secure more impressions before people with search profiles similar to your buyers while maintaining the CPA.

3. *Conversion Tracking with the Conversion Optimizer*: this combo puts two of AdWords' most powerful impression-generating technologies

125

together to work for you: *Conversion Tracking* to identify likely buyers and *Focus-on-Conversions* to automatically adjust your bids. Using them together you (1) garner more ad impressions before likely buyers and (2) maintain your average cost-per-acquisition.

(See Conversion Optimization [Bidding], p. 238, for information on these topics.)

4. **Remarketing**: *Remarketing* enables you to reach people who previously visited your site, your YouTube channel or YouTube video. You can coax them back for a second look or a second purchase using different copy and/or offers of coupons, discounts, additional information, etc.

    *   *Remarketing* requires you to add a tag to your landing page (or multiple tags on your e-commerce site). It also requires you to associate the tag with a list that you name and set up.

        When someone visits your landing page, AdWords places a file called a cookie on his/her computer. The cookie contains a unique ID number. AdWords also records the ID in the list you established.

        As the person visits Display Network Partner sites across the Internet, your ad appears, reminding them of your product or offering them an incentive to return.

    *   With *Remarketing*, you can construct sophisticated strategies to bring prospects back to your site regardless of where they are in their buying process. For example, you can use Search ads with keywords generally used by not-ready-to-buy prospects to bring those prospects to your website to learn about your product. Then you can use Display Network-*Remarketing* Ads using keywords associated with more sales-ready prospects to entice visitors to return and buy. This messaging strategy lets you use inexpensive ads to bring people to your site and use more expensive ads as they move toward conversion.

    *   *Remarketing* lets you advertise to visitors based on (1) the webpages they visited or did not visit, (2) when they visited and (3) what actions they took. For example, you can target a person who visited a certain page within the last 30 days and signed up for your newsletter.

        Further, you can target people who visited this page *and* that page; visited this page *or* that page; this page *but not* that page; visited these *two* pages, etc. You can use *targeting methods* with Display Network ads to fine-tune your *Remarketing Lists*. For example, you can target previous visitors to your site who are female between the ages of 18 and 24.

        In addition, you can target people with interests similar to your existing visitors and customers (called *Interest-Based Remarketing*).

This lets you greatly expand your marketing beyond your current buyers; however, you must have 100 or more visitors to your site after activating *Remarketing* before you can activate this feature.

Finally, you can use *Remarketing* with *Google Shopping* (called *Dynamic Remarketing*) to target previous visitors with ads created dynamically by AdWords from data you submit to Google in a feed (file).

Together, these targeting strategies let you create highly segmented ad campaigns with different calls-to-action for each segment.

- You must use *Conversion Tracking* and you should use the *Conversion Optimizer* with *Remarketing*. These capabilities in conjunction with Remarketing let you put AdWords' extensive trend analysis logic to work for you—showing your ad to the best prospects at the best possible price.

5. *Conversion Tracking, Conversion Optimizer and Remarketing Together*: using Conversion Tracking and Conversion Optimizer with any of the Remarketing features puts a "triple threat" on your side, to further heighten your opportunities for increasing buys and lowering costs. Recall that:

- *Remarketing* Ads follow previous buyers to give you a second chance at selling to them.

- *Conversion Tracking* identifies likely buyers for whom you should bid more.

- *Focus-on-Conversions* adjusts your bids so you win more ad impressions before previous and likely buyers.

To garner this advantage, implement *Conversion Tracking*, followed by the *Conversion Optimizer*, and followed by one of the *Remarketing* Ad types. The three features work together without special adaption.

Building your campaign(s) to the point where you can use *Conversion Tracking, Conversion Optimizer, Remarketing* **and** *Interest-Based Remarketing* **is a savvy strategy.**

(See Activate Conversion Tracking, p. 228, and Conversion Optimization, p. 238, and Remarketing Ads, p. 282, for information on these topics.)

6. *Display target optimizer*: with targeting optimization, AdWords shows your Display Network ad in places and to people outside your *targeting methods* when the AdWords algorithm indicates they could be advantageous to you. (See Display Targeting Optimization, p. 282, for more information.)

7. *Experimenting*: **experiments let you pit one ad element against another to see which one wins the most auctions and, ultimately, which one generates the most conversions.** AdWords Experiments are a great way to test your ideas and prove their effectiveness before investing more money. They are especially valuable when Sales, Marketing and Management have different ideas about what customers want, where they gather or what engages them.

Experiments are valuable because they:

- Show objectively what works and what does not.

- Take the emotion out of decision-making.

- Let you find good ads and bids quickly, as well as quickly remove poor ads and bids.

- Save you money.

(See Step 13: Use AdWords Experiments to Improve Your Ads and Save Money, p. 170, for information on these topics.)

KEY CONCEPT 6: ADWORDS CONSTANTLY CHANGES

Google releases a steady stream of new AdWords capabilities. Google previews, announces and discusses new capabilities through these mechanisms:

1. **Ad innovations**: on this website, Google provides overviews and demos of newly introduced capabilities, capabilities moving into beta or in

FIGURE 3.23 Google Ad Innovations news site

limited release and future offerings. Check this page from time to time if you want more details about a new feature or want to know about an upcoming feature.

- **Beta means one or more users are testing an item.** When the item works consistently, predictably and without faults (bugs), Google releases it on a limited basis or to all users. (The software development world gives a nod to the Greek alphabet by calling in-house testing "alpha testing" and subsequent testing by actual users "beta testing.")

- **Limited release means one or more selected users are using the new feature.** Often, large, sophisticated clients require features that are confusing and/or unproductive to smaller users. Consequently, Google may or may not release items to all users. Further, they may or may not announce the release.

- **Rollout refers to the process by which Google releases a new feature to users.** Everyone may not receive the new feature at once. Google may or may not announce how long the rollout will take. New features that require users to change items or learn new features usually take longer.

- **Legacy refers to any option that is still in use but for which an improved or upgraded option is available.** The new option usually provides an easier, more useful or more robust function, and Google usually recommends upgrading to the new function as well as implementing the new option in all new campaigns.

Some legacy options continue to work indefinitely, and you may encounter them in older campaigns. Conversely, Google sometimes requires you to upgrade to the new option within a certain period of time, after which Google deprecates (removes) the old option.

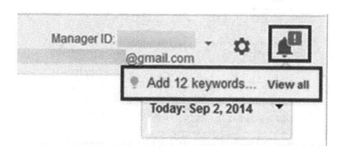

FIGURE 3.24 Google Alert

2. **Google alerts**: sometimes Google places an exclamation point over the alert bell on the right-hand AdWords border (beside your customer ID) to announce a new feature and opportunities for improving your ads. Announcements stay visible until you click the message, read it and click the *dismiss* button.

3. **Banner notice**: Google makes many changes to screen prompts without prior warning. Generally the changes do not impact your use of AdWords. The change may be a new feature moving into beta testing, a change to behind-the-scenes processes (such as the auction), a code correction (bug fix) or a minor change to a screen or report.

> A new version of the AdWords interface is available. Please refresh this page to try again.

FIGURE 3.25 Banner notice

Banner notices require immediate action before the application continues.

4. **Inside AdWords**: Google's official blog provides lengthy posts about AdWords features, both new and old. It also has two links, which bring new features to your attention.

   • **Major updates on our blog**: links you to posts, in reverse chronological order, about updated AdWords capabilities. Posts bear the label "updates."

FIGURE 3.26 Google Inside AdWords blog

FIGURE 3.27 Google research blog

- **All updates on Google+**: links you to real-time news about AdWords on the Google Ads Google+ page. Posts bear the tag #adwords #updates. Follow this page to have updates hit your Google+ stream as Google issues them.

5. **Google's Research Blog**: this website offers research results and insights, along with an interactive infographics tool for presenting the data to your management or to your clients. The site stores facts and figures curated by Google from its own research, research conducted by AdWords users and research conducted jointly by Google and users. Use this site to construct compelling arguments for deploying a particular feature at your company or on behalf of your clients.

Google works to accommodate their sophisticated clients, while supporting their small clients. It is not an easy thing to balance.

Large clients use lots of options and capabilities and want quick, easy ways to apply those options in as few keystrokes as possible. Conversely, small clients need straightforward, intuitively obvious screens. Finally, Google wants to present data as consistently as possible, as "live" as possible and with as few codes as possible.

To a large extent, Google has succeeded in meeting the demands of its diverse client base.

    a. Input screens ask for essential information only and provide content-sensitive help (i.e., those little blue question marks).

131

    b. Non-essential options reside in separate tabs such as ad extension, dimensions, auto targets and Display Network.

    c. The *statistics table* serves as the single place to do many functions—to view your campaign (all hierarchy levels), update options, view performance data and download reports. Once you learn the mechanics of the *statistics table* for one hierarchical level, you have the working knowledge to manage, monitor and report all levels. Further, Google has only one place to make changes. It's an ingenious approach.

Less successful is the use of inheritance. Setting options at the Campaign Level and letting the lower hierarchical levels "inherit" them works well for simple campaigns. However, companies running sophisticated campaigns want to fine-tune their campaigns at every hierarchical level, as they become savvier about their buyers. Consequently, Google now provides overrides for inherited options at nearly every hierarchical level (e.g., like max CPC and *bid adjustments*). This is confusing for smaller clients who rightfully ask if they are *supposed* to change an option because the option appears again.

Once you understand the client needs and the application's pathways, AdWords screens make more sense, as do the enhancements Google makes.

KEY CONCEPT 7: ADWORDS—A GOLDMINE OF MARKETING INFORMATION

Because of the data it collects about customer behavior, AdWords is one of the best tools for understanding people in your market.

More specifically, the power of a search engine marketing program is threefold:

1. **Product research**: AdWords provides accurate and current insights into the products and attributes people want. AdWords search statistics show:
   - The products people want (e.g., shoes, pumps, stilettos, etc.).
   - The features, capabilities and attributes people want (e.g., soft soled shoes, black pumps, 5″ stilettos).
   - The popularity (trending) of a product or feature over time (through the Google Insights report).

   Compared to other product research techniques such as surveys, focus groups, etc., AdWords provides an extremely low-cost means of collecting highly-relevant and up-to-date data.

2. **Market research**: smart marketers research keywords for online advertising, but they also use those keywords to optimize their website

and develop more lucrative positioning and messages across all their advertising channels.

AdWords provides a mechanism for finding websites popular with your prospects. By running ads on the Google Display Network, you can:

- Identify websites popular with your prospects.
- Test various messages on popular websites to determine which message(s) works best.

Compared to other market research techniques such as surveys, focus groups, etc., AdWords provides an extremely low-cost means of collecting data.

3. **Advertising**: AdWords provides ways to find and test the best market, messages and offers for your product.

AdWords lets you:

- Provide different messages based on the different words people use to search.
- Show your ad to thousands of people in well-defined regions (by country, city, region, state and zip codes) and at specific times of the day, night or weekend.
- Pay for the advertising only if the viewer clicks on your ad and visits your website (called a click-through).
- Pay less for an ad than any other advertising medium.
- Tailor ads to the item sought by the searcher.
- Run as many ads as you want.
- Change your ads as often as you want.
- Rotate ads to test which messages work best.
- Obtain statistics that show which messages work best, so you can improve your ad and increase results over time.

Compared to other advertising channels such as TV commercials, info-mercials, magazines and newspapers, this is a low-cost advertising option.

Chapter 4

Getting Started

This chapter provides detailed instructions for setting up a basic Search Network campaign so you make money from the very beginning. It lays out the tiny details and tricks-of-the-trade across the campaign, ad group, ads, keywords and landing pages that spell the difference between mediocre performance and success. It shows you the specific steps and metrics to use to evaluate your results and provides a strategy for prioritizing your next steps to achieve higher results faster.

More specifically, it covers the key goals and strategy you need as a foundation for your campaign, and it shows you how to construct your campaign, find affordable keywords and ad themes, devise a productive landing page and align your ad with your landing page to turn visitors into customers. It walks you through the setup of your first ad and evaluating your performance, cost, business value and ROI. Finally, it discusses strategies for growing and expanding campaigns, the built-in A/B testing capabilities of AdWords and provides a number of time-saving procedures.

Now that you know the basic principles driving AdWords, it's time to dip your toe into the AdWords river of advertising!

The master strategy for success is:

1. **Learn about your prospects, your market and AdWords by using Search ads first.** Search Ads are usually the cheapest ads available.

2. **Fine-tune your ads and keywords until visitors are buying (called *converting*).** Introduce Display Network ads to gain more visibility. Use AdWords experiments to fine-tune your ads and AdWords rules to keep campaigns selling.

3. **Once you achieve 15 sales a month, activate the** *Conversion Tracking* **option.** This option puts the power of AdWords on your side to help you gain as many impressions as possible without raising your costs.

4. **Activate the** *Remarketing* **feature as soon as possible after** *Conversion Tracking.* This keeps you in touch with your best prospects—your previous customers and people like them.

Executing an AdWords campaign requires forethought. The following pages walk you through an efficient scenario to ensure you learn as you go and conserve your budget while you learn. The major steps are:

1. Devise your goals and strategy.

2. Prepare your ads and landing page.

3. Setup your campaign.

4. Run a couple of ads.

5. Learn how to monitor and manage your ads.

6. Expand your efforts.

The more steps you skip the more money it costs you! When done well, an AdWords budget can bring newfound revenue. When done poorly, an AdWords budget can disappear quickly.

Step 1: Determine Your Business Goals

Before you advertise on Google, you must decide what you want to accomplish. Setting your business goals beforehand helps you construct the right advertising offering, develop the right message, aim it at the right audience and achieve the right results.

The following questions help you identify your business goals.

1. Do you want to sell a product, sell a never-existed-before revolutionary product, generate leads, get people to sign-up for a newsletter or get people to download an app?

2. What product(s) are you selling?

3. Where is your market (local, regional, national, international)?

4. What are the dollar goals for sales? Or, alternatively, how many newsletter sign-ups do you want (or how many impressions do you want)?

Without goals—even if they are very low—you will not know if you have succeeded and neither will your management. Having a goal keeps you on your toes.

5. What is your AdWords budget?

6. How many units must you sell to break even (will you have enough new revenues to cover your ad budget)?

7. How many units must you sell to reach the monetary goal? You will need to know the profit margin for each unit.

8. What need is the buyer trying to fill with your product? What distinguishes your product from that of other companies? How does your price compare to other sellers?

   • If it is a product, what are the features and logistical details (transaction processing, shipping, returns, etc.) that attract buyers?

   • If it is a service, how do the customers or clients contact you (sign up, call, live chat, etc.)?

Keep your business goals in mind as you move through the next steps.

Step 2: Review the AdWords Landscape

Your ignorance makes money for Google. You can spend a great deal of money throwing ads online and seeing what "sticks." Alternatively, you can explore and learn your market and make profitable decisions.

Before you spend significant cash on AdWords, you should verify your market. By running a few searches in Google using your most obvious, ordinary keywords, you can determine if your product can sell successfully online.

To verify your market, determine the following:

   • If more than three AdWords ads appear at the top of the page and at least four appear at the right side, a viable market exists for your product.

   • If fewer than three AdWords appear at the top of the page and fewer than four appear at the right side, you should consider Display Network ads for your marketing effort.

   • If 10–20 keywords pass these tests, you have a valid market for your product. Move on to the next step.

Be aware that Google prohibits the advertising of certain products. To see the list, go to AdWords Help and search for "AdWords policies."

Step 3: Identify Lucrative Keywords

Finding the most lucrative keywords is one of the most important factors in determining your AdWords success.

- **In AdWords, two- and three-word phrases work best.** They often have less competition and succeed with lower bids. As the competition for AdWords increases, multiple word phrases often make the best keywords—and, often, are the only affordable keywords.

- **The more specific the keyword, the better it works to attract an interested prospect and set his or her expectations.** "Dog" is an expensive keyword. "Micro Teacup Yorkie" is much cheaper. Vague, generic keywords cost money.

- Use longer, less competitive keywords (long-tails, as they are called) to be visible to highly qualified customers and to obtain as high a position as possible on a SERP.

Google recommends you use no more than 15–20 keywords per ad group.

To find your most lucrative keywords, follow these steps:

1. **Generate keyword ideas.**
   - **Think about your customers' needs.** A keyword can meet one of many different needs. For example, a searcher for shoes usually wants more than just any ol' pair of shoes. They may want:
     — A certain aesthetic, e.g., strapless, peau de soie.
     — A certain subcategory of product, e.g., narrow heel, extra-wide.
     — A certain capability, e.g., a comfortable, durable or water-resistant pair of shoes.
     — A low price, e.g., discount, sale.
     — Fulfillment of a psychological or emotional need, e.g., a sexy, fashion-forward or expensive shoe.
     — A certain brand, e.g., Prada shoes or Frye boots.
     — A certain business credential, e.g., shoes from a brand-name company or brick-and-mortar stores.
     — A certain business policy, e.g., shoes from a company with easy returns, free shipping, overnight delivery, etc.
     — For Display Network ads (when you're ready to use them), think about the topics your prospects are likely to read, such as news items, industry topics, upcoming conferences, interest categories (AdWords has a predefined list), along with specific websites.
     — For Display Network ads, keywords are broad-match only and usually cost more than Search Network ads. Use the *display planner*

tool, under the *tools* tab at the top of the page, to identify websites your audience reads.

— Learn how Google categorizes each keyword. Use the *searches related* suggestions Google offers at the bottom of the SERP.

Include the name of competing brands in your list of keywords if you are in an especially competitive market.

• **Use the *keyword planner* tool, under the *tools* tab at the top of the page, to get AdWords' suggested keywords for Search Network ads.** Use the *search for new keywords and ad group ideas* option.

• **Think about the keywords your competitors use.** Use the *keyword planner* tool, under the *tools* tab at the top of the page, to get AdWords' suggested keywords for your competitors' websites. Enter their web page into the *keyword planner*.

2. **Review the search engine results for each keyword you are considering to see what type of website the keyword evokes.**

• If a keyword evokes shopping sites, your ad should relate to shopping.

• If a keyword evokes informational sites, your ad should offer information, such as white papers or e-books.

• If a keyword evokes a video site, you want to link to a video from your Search ad.

3. **Review the *searches related to* phrases that Google provides at the bottom of the SERP page and decide if any of those terms could work for you.**

4. **Review the expected traffic and cost for your keywords.**

• Use the *Keyword Planner* tool, under the *tools* tab at the top of the page, to get an idea of the potential traffic, average CPC and cost-per-day for your keywords. Use the *get traffic forecasts for a list of keywords* options. The *keyword planner* tool provides useful—but highly imprecise—data about keyword search volumes and costs-per-click. Once you run an ad, AdWords will show you better, more accurate, data.

• Do not let the high *cost-per-click* for a keyword scare you away from a keyword just yet. Try it for yourself. Many ads never pay the max CPC for an impression.

5. **Identify negative keywords to save money and protect your *quality score.***

• Negative keywords prevent AdWords from showing your ad to people who are *not* looking to buy your exact product. This protects your *quality score* and saves you money.

- Build a list of negative keywords for your product. For example, "stiletto knife" is not relevant to your ad for "stiletto heels."

  Make "knife" a negative keyword—but *not* the word *stiletto*! If you include "stiletto," AdWords stops running your ad because your keyword is negative!

- Filter out keywords such as "review," "rate," "rating," "compare," "comparing" and "comparison" (i.e., make them negative keywords) to eliminate people researching for a product or just window shopping. This focuses your budget on serious buyers.

6. **Select your best 10–20 keywords.**

Step 4: Create a Compelling Landing Page

Your landing page should *not* be your homepage. Nothing kills an ad's success faster than sending visitors to your homepage where they have to search for information about the item or service you sell. This scenario costs you money for the clicks, does not result in a sale or a sign-up, frustrates the searcher and, ultimately, causes AdWords to lower your *quality score*.

Always send your visitor to the exact webpage for the product you advertise.

By creating your landing page before you create your ads, you remain focused on your product and the sales pitch appropriate for your audience. Your ad copy should come naturally and easily from your landing page.

The process for creating a good landing page is:

1. **Determine your ad offering and your value proposition before you begin working on the landing page.**

2. **Do your keyword investigation and select the keywords most appropriate for your product.**

3. **Write your landing page *after* you select your affordable keywords and *before* you write your ad.**

4. **Your landing page must use the keywords that searchers use.** Describing your product or service in the terms people actually use sets the foundation for a better customer experience. However, do not sacrifice your value proposition to make a keyword fit. It just frustrates your visitor.

5. **Your landing page should complement your keywords and ad.** Google checks that landing page keywords match with the keywords in your ad. If they do not, Google may not approve your ad.

6. **For Search Network ads, create a landing page that compels your prospect to buy your product(s).** Your landing page must help the visitor overcome his or her objections to buying—and visitors have many objections, including fears, questions and risks.

To overcome fears, use:

- Testimonials, endorsements, interviews and reviews from satisfied customers, or show professional association memberships and endorsements.
- If you sell multiple products on your landing page, keep your list of products short; do not let people be overwhelmed.
- Free trial usage of the product or a limited version of the product.
- Video demonstration of the product.
- Detailed product specifications.

To stimulate their interest and educate them, give them something of value, such as:

- A free trial of the product or a limited version of the product.
- A webinar.
- A video demonstration of the product.
- A free white paper, e-book, case studies, etc.

To overcome questions, use:

- Live chat capabilities.
- An 800 phone number.
- Instant Messaging capabilities.

To overcome the fear of loss, provide (preferably close to the Buy/Sign-up button):

- A money-back guarantee.
- Free returns, in-store returns, etc.
- Free shipping, free return shipping.
- A privacy policy.
- VeriSign$^{(r)}$ or some other type of payment verification authority.
- An email address.
- The physical address of your company.
- Your photo.

7. **Keep your landing page simple.**

8. **Provide a call to action.** Whether it is "sign up," "buy" or "call," you must have a call to action. Do not assume a prospect acts without some nudging.

9. **Make sure people can see the order form without scrolling.**

10. **An effective landing page *must* have a button telling your visitor what to do.**

    • Keep your "buy" button simple.

    • Make it a contrasting color.

    • Repeat your call to action on the button itself.

11. **For Display Network ads, create a landing page that interests and intrigues visitors enough that they willingly provide their email, phone number or social media name.**

    • To encourage sign-ups, keep the opt-in form short!

    • Ask for as little information as possible—name and email address only.

    • Show a privacy policy.

12. **Use a keyword in your *display URL* and *destination URL!*** This ensures your ad relates to the product you sell.

13. **Use Google Analytics.** It has the capability to test up to five variations of your landing page (each with its own URL so tracking results is easy) with a random sampling of your visitors. (See Content Experiments on GoogleAnalytics.com.)

14. **Your landing page must meet AdWords' policies and standards.** Your ad and landing page must satisfy the AdWords reviewer so that the visitor will not be disappointed.

    Read and comply with the standards. For AdWords policies, search on "AdWords policy center" in AdWords Help.

Step 5: Write Attention-Grabbing Ad Copy

AdWords ads are some of the most difficult ads to write because they are so short.

Every word must move your viewer toward action. Thus, an ad must address the specific problem, issue, need or interest of the user at that very moment.

1. **Your ad should capture your unique value proposition, i.e., how your product and its attributes solve a specific problem for a specific client.**

   - Do not contradict your value proposition. Even if AdWords' *keyword planner tool* indicates a million women search for stylish shoes each month, do not write ads that emphasize style if you do not sell stylish shoes.

   - If you do not know your prospect's problems, issues or needs, you do not know your value proposition; find out. Ignorance costs money when you use AdWords.

   Talk with people inside your company (sales people, customer service representatives, etc.) about your products and the competitors' products. Read the trade publications and e-zines, read the blogs of industry leaders and talk to some customers.

   - Continually research your market. Things change quickly in the business world today, and you cannot afford to be asleep at the switch when they do.

   - Do not get so carried away with writing a great ad that you drift from your value proposition.

   - Obviously, write your ad and keywords in the language you specified for your campaign.

2. **Write your headline using your best keyword in the headline!**

   - Ads that use keywords in their copy get more clicks. Many advertisers do not realize this, so doing it gives you an advantage.

   - Grab all the attention you can! Write your headline like the title of a magazine article—with emotion and urgency. Look at the cover of any magazine for ideas on headline construction. Write "Stunning Spring Fashions," rather than "Dresses for Spring."

   - Do not be afraid to use bold or emotional ads, even if your competition does not. Such ads have worked for years in magazines. You can always test the ad or change it later.

3. **Follow AdWords' rules for grammar, capitalization, etc.** AdWords does not accept your ad until it complies with all the rules. AdWords requires:

   - Correct grammar, verb tense and spelling

   - No funny business, such as repeated punctuation (!!! or . . .), O D D S P A C I N G, bullet points, or ALL CAPS unless it is part of a trademark or legal name

- Non-standard usage of symbols, characters, numbers, superscripts, intra-word capitalization unless it is part of a trademark or legal name

- No exclamation mark in the headline, thoughelsewhere is ok.

For the rest of the rules search in AdWords Help for "Editorial standards" for a full listing of rules.

4. **Write your headline to address the specific need of a specific prospect.**

   - Be savvy. "Expensive Shoes, Cheap" brings many lookers, while "Prada Pumps 30% Off" brings buyers. Simple, enticing ads work best.

   - Check out the competition. Look at the competing ads and make yours better.

   - Do not try to cover multiple needs with one ad. Write ads that use the just-right keywords for a particular need. Trying to appeal to everyone usually appeals to no one.

   - If a keyword fits with multiple ads, that keyword may be too general. The more specific the keyword, the more economical your advertising.

   - If your prospects have multiple motivations for buying (and most prospects do), write multiple ads.

   - Fortunately, Google does not care how many ads you run. Write as many ads as you require to address the customer needs you can meet. Just make sure you have the right keywords for each ad.

5. **Write your *description lines* to pique customer interest and tout your unique benefit.**

   - Make your description dance!

   - Include important benefits or features in your description lines.

   - Benefits and features are often confused. A benefit solves a problem and evokes a feeling, while a feature describes what something can do or how something works. A talented marketer can make every feature a benefit. For example, a pair of shoes can make a woman feel sexy (a benefit), but a soft sole (a feature) can keep her dancing all night (a benefit).

   Use descriptive words to attract the type of viewer you want. Words such as "luxury" and "premium" entice high-end buyers and dissuade discount shoppers. Words such as "buy online" dissuade people who only buy in retail stores.

   - Help your prospect come to the right decision—mention benefits that reduce risk.

- Every buyer has the adage "buyer beware" etched in his or her mind. By reducing the buyer's fear, doubt and apprehension, you increase his or her willingness to take action.

- The words "free shipping" and "free returns" are major risk reducers for online buyers.

- Offer a "satisfaction guarantee" if you can.

6. **Include a call to action.** Ask your prospect to "Learn more," "Buy now" or "Order today."

7. **Write your *display URL* using a primary keyword and capital/lower case letters**.

   - Use hyphens if it makes the *display URL* easier to read and remember.

   - Be aware that your ad must meet Google's standards and policies, which revolve around trust, accuracy and positive user experience. To see all the policies, go to AdWords Help and search on "Advertising policies help."

8. **Verify your ad.** Once you complete an ad, check that it still works with all your keywords, accurately represents the product you sell and meets AdWords' advertising principles.

Figure 4.1 shows examples of ads created for different value propositions. Note that AdWords shows the keywords from the searcher's query in boldface.

Step 6: Determine Your Bids

Bidding is the most intimidating part when you begin using AdWords.

The following suggestions help guide you to a reasonable bid.

1. **Bid less than one-hundredth of your profit margin.** According to Google, for many ads only one of every 100 (1 percent) visitors to a website buys something. Thus, your profit from one sale must cover the cost of 100 clicks to break even. Divide your profit by 100 to obtain your absolute maximum bid.

   Until you have some experience with your ads, you will not know if one buyer in every 100 visitors is typical for your site. Further, you will not know the typical transaction amount, especially if your website sells many products. Watch your ad's statistics carefully during the first few months to make sure you are not spending too much on keywords or ads.

Style:

> Dress **Pumps** that Say Wow
> www.xxxxxxxxxx.com/pumps
> See New Spring Shoe Trends
> Great Selection & Prices

Keywords: pumps, heels, dress shoes

Brand:

> **Prada Shoes**
> www.xxxxxxxxxx.com/shoes
> Shop the New Collection
> Get Instant Sale Alerts

Keywords: Prada Shoes, Prada collection

Product Feature:

> **Water Proof** Shoes
> www.xxxxxxxxxx.com/shoes
> Keep Your Feet Dry
> Huge Selection, Free Shipping

Keywords: waterproof shoes, water proof shoes

Policy:

> **Shoes, Shoes, Shoes**
> www.xxxxxxxxxx.com/shoes
> 240,000 shoes. EZ Return
> Free Shipping 8/15/13

Keywords: shoes, shoes with free shipping, shoe selection, shoe returns

Psychological Need:

> **Sexy** Sinful **Shoes**
> www.xxxxxxxxxx.com/shoes
> Erotic Heels & Platforms
> Sinful Shoes at Sinful Prices

Keywords: sexy shoes, sinful shoes, erotic shoes, stiletto shoes

Price:

> Closeout **Shoe Deals**
> www.xxxxxxxxxx.com/shoes
> Big Discounts. Name Brands
> Up to 75% Off

Keywords: discount shoes, closeout shoes, shoe sale

Credentials:

> **Shoes** at Macy's
> www.xxxxxxxxxx.com/shoes
> Free Shipping Today Only!
> On $99 Orders

Keywords: Macy's, Macy's shoes

Convenience:

> **Shoes** Overnight
> www.xxxxxxxxxx.com/shoes
> Explore 3,000+ Shoes
> Overnight Delivery

Keywords: shoes overnight, overnight shoes, shoes fast delivery

FIGURE 4.1 Examples of ads

Each example is aimed at a different buying criterion and set of keywords.

2. **Use the *bid simulator / traffic estimator* to see what various keyword costs.** As part of the *keyword planner*, Google provides a tool that displays the average cost per keyword and the number of clicks you can expect at different CPCs. See the discussion for the bid simulator, part of the *keyword planner*, under Tools and Reports, p. 327.

3. **Compare the number of clicks you are likely to receive at your benchmark bid and decide if that level of traffic is worthwhile.**

   Consider:

   - **Are your best keywords too expensive? (You must define "too expensive" in terms of your goals.)**
   - **Could you use less expensive keywords and receive adequate traffic? (You must definite "adequate" based on your business goals.)**

4. **Over time keep viable keywords and increase your bid for these keywords in small increments (8 to 10 percent) if necessary to maintain your desired ad position.** Check the Avg CPC often on these keywords and drop keywords that fail your profit threshold.

Step 7: Run a Campaign to Activate Your Account

The following steps enable you to establish an AdWords account, verify that it is active and gather a small amount of data.

To verify your account, you *must run an ad*. This costs you a few dollars.

To run an ad, you need a valid landing page. This is why you created the landing page in a previous step.

Once you start setting up a campaign, ad group or ad, you must complete it. Google does not save incomplete campaigns, ad groups or ads.

Be aware that AdWords dialogue changes often and the options provided here may not appear in the same way—or may not be available—when you read this. That said, do the following:

1. **Login to AdWords and create an account.** Login to AdWords at www.Google.com/AdWords. If you already have a Google account, you must use that account. An account can be associated with only one business.

   (Ad agencies can become Google Partners and run multiple accounts through the "My Client Center." Sign up for a My Client Center account online at www.google.com/adwords/myclientcenter/.)

2. **Under** *billing,* **activate your account by answering the questions under** *billing setting* **and** *billing profile.* You need a credit or debit card to initiate an account.

3. **Setup a campaign for the Search Network only, using these parameters** (AdWords terminology is in italics):

    • *Campaign name*: Use something like "Test—Search Network."

    • *Campaign type* should be *Search Network only.* Click the circle beside *all features.*

    • Ignore *load settings from existing campaign* for now.

    • Under *network,* unclick *include search partners* for now. Once you are converting visitors you can include Search Partners.

    • Under *location,* use the *advanced option* to specify your desired location. (Rather than use U.S., enter each of the states. This lets you get performance information by state and, later, adjust bids by state as you learn more about your audience.)

    • Under *location options,* use *people in your targeted areas* if you do not want to advertise internationally.

    • Under *language,* leave *English* as a default (or select your own language).

    • Set your *bid strategy* as *Focus on Clicks* and *AdWords will set my bids to help maximize clicks within my target budget.* This lets you gather data about your *costs-per-click* before taking on the responsibility of manual bidding.

    • Under *budget,* enter $5 *per day.*

    • Keep the *delivery method* default of *standard: show ads evenly over time.*

    • Ignore the *advanced options* for now.

    • Click *save and continue.* Your Campaign Level options are now complete.

4. **Add your** *ad extensions.* Click the *ad extension tab* and then the *view: call extension* button. Click *eExtension* to add a phone number to your ad.

    • Repeat these steps for as many *ad extensions* as appropriate.

5. **Next, create an Ad Group.** When you complete your Campaign Level options, AdWords moves you automatically to the ad group setup screen where you setup an ad group and your first ad.

    For this exercise, your ad runs only once, just to verify your account setup. Do not worry about writing perfect copy at this point. Similarly, use your homepage URL if you do not have a separate landing page yet.

6. **If AdWords does not take you to the ad group setup screen, click on the *ad group tab.***

   Enter the following:

   a. *Ad group* name. Enter *Search Network test ad* as the name.

   b. Under *create an ad,* click the circle beside *text.*

   c. Write your ad by entering:
      — A headline hawking your product.
      — Two description lines.
      — A fictitious or real display URL using your domain, and a real destination URL using your domain name.

   For example:

   ## Mastering AdWords
   www.multiplanetmarketing.com
   AdWords Are Harder Than You Think!
   Buy It Today & Make More Money.

   ---

   d. In the *keyword* section, put your best keyword in brackets (for an exact match) in the input box.

   e. Under the *ad group bids* section, input a *default bid* of $1.

   f. Click *save ad group.*

7. **Verify your ad.** Go to the *tools* tab and click *ad preview* (or use www.Google.com/AdPreview). If your ad appears, your account is setup.

   • If it does not appear, Google may not have given editorial approval yet. Go to the *ad tab* and check the ad for an AdWords message, in red letters. You may need to wait 24 to 48 hours for Google to approve your ad and prepare it to show.

   • For details on gaining Google ad approval, search on "Advertising principles" in AdWords Help. Correct any problems and repeat this task if necessary to gain Google approval.

8. **Test your ads.** Never debate what works; test and determine what works.

   AdWords provides the ability to rotate ads within an ad group, so you can write two or three ads for the same theme, rotate them and determine which message generates the most profit. Run each test for at least 30 days.

9. **When your ad appears, you know your account is active.**

10. **Return to AdWords and *pause* the campaign.**

PRACTICING BEFORE SPENDING

Thus far, you have your AdWords account setup, your first campaign is setup, and you have an ad group with the ad you ran to test your account.

Now you need to run a few ads to learn what works for your business.

Unless you like to give your money to Google, you need to (1) run a round of ads using *manual bidding* and a small budget and (2) learn how to measure your results *before* initiating an extensive advertising effort!

A preliminary campaign test tells you:

- That people actually search your specific product online.
- The specific keywords people use most often.
- The different messages and value propositions that work (and the ones that don't).
- More precisely, the cost and availability of ad space.
- How to bid frugally.
- The messages and keywords that bring buyers.
- How to control your budget and use it wisely.
- The ins-and-outs of AdWords.

Be aware that AdWords dialogue changes often and the options suggested here may not appear in the same way or in the same order—and may not be available at all—when you read this.

To gain experience with your ads and keywords without killing your budget, follow Steps 7 through 13 before you launch an expensive campaign.

Step 8: Run and Evaluate a Preliminary Campaign

To gain experience without killing the budget, setup a campaign that follows these guidelines:

1. **Revise your test campaign from Step 6, or setup a new campaign.** Click the *campaign tab* and select *Search Network only* and *all features*. Uncheck *include search partners*. (Exclude search partners until your ads are drawing buyers and more clicks mean more sales.)

2. **Run Search Network ads until your landing page starts to have visitors and buyers.** Then, when you know what keywords and messages work, you can add Display Network ads.

   a. Name your campaign to reflect the network, geographic area and main keyword. For example: Search-National-Labradors

   b. Select *Focus on Clicks.*

   c. Enter a default bid of $1.

   d. Set a *daily budget* of between $2 and $5. This exercise calls for you to stop your ad in a few days, but be aware that you are liable for your daily budget times 30.4 days if you do not stop your ad.

   Click on the *ad group tab* if AdWords does not move you to the ad group setup screen automatically.

   e. Name your ad group. For example: Search-National-Labradors-Cuddly

   f. Enter your ad. (See Step 5: Write Attention-Grabbing Ad Copy, p. 142, for more information.)

   g. In the keyword input box below your ad, enter your list of 10–12 keywords (created in Step 3: Identify Lucrative Keywords, p. 138) putting each keyword in a bracket for an exact match.

   h. Save your ad group and ad.

3. **After one week, review your performance results to make sure you are not spending money aimlessly, with lots of impressions and no clicks or no sales.** If you are not seeing results, give the campaign more time—another week or perhaps two.

   Click on the *campaign tab* to see your performance data. To see competitive data, you need to customize the columns. On the small submenu under the campaign tab, click on *columns—customized columns—competitive metrics—all columns.*

   • Which keywords made sales?
     — For now, focus on the keywords that made sales—that is, the keywords where the conversion rate (*conv. rate*) is not zero.
     — Keep these keywords active.

   • Which keywords are too expensive?
     — To determine the amount that is "too expensive" consider this: as a rule, one out of every 500 (i.e., 0.0025 percent) of visitors buy on an e-commerce site. Thus, your profit from one sale must cover the cost of 500 clicks. (Note that it is the *profit* from one sale, not the retail price of the item sold.)

If you multiply the Avg CPC for a keyword by 500, and the result is *lower than the profit* on your product, that keyword is a viable revenue-generator for your product. Mark all such keywords as GOOD.

If a keyword had a sale but the avg. CPC is greater than your profit, pause the keyword. You have lost money. The bidding game is too rich or too risky for this keyword. If all your keywords fall into this category, AdWords is not the right channel for selling your product.

Beware! It takes approximately 500 click-throughs to get a statistically significant (i.e., mathematically reliable) average cost-per-click. You need to review Avg CPC periodically until you see a definite, sustained pattern.

- Of the keywords that did not have sales, which ones are viable?
  — A keyword is presumed to be viable if the Avg CPC is less than one-hundredth of the profit on the item you are selling *and* your ad appeared at least once in every 10 times it was eligible—that is, the *percentage served* is at least 10 percent.
  — In other words, the profit on your product is high enough to cover the cost of more than 100 clicks. A click-through rate of 1–2 percent is typical of AdWords ads.
  — Keep viable keywords and increase your bid for these keywords in small increments until you get 10% Served. Check the Avg CPC often on these keywords and drop keywords that fail your profit threshold.

4. **Pause any keywords with an Avg CPC higher than one-hundredth of your profit and less than 10 percent of the eligible impressions.**

   - Until you make money with your best keywords, do not expand your traffic—do not add more keywords, ads or ad groups for the product. Nothing is gained by paying for more clicks if your ad and landing page do not convert visitors to clients.

Step 9: Measure Your Results and Profit

The only way to know if AdWords is a good advertising medium for your company is to set a goal, run a campaign and measure the results.

When measuring your results, you need to have a measuring stick! Ask your management which definition of success you must meet:

1. First degree: a campaign generates more revenue than AdWords costs or, better yet, the campaign generates more revenue than AdWords and your time costs.

2. Second degree: the wholesale cost of the product plus the cost of the AdWords ads is 20–30 percent less than the retail value of the product. That is, the product has a 20–30 percent profit margin, which is acceptable in most businesses. Alternatively, use some other, lower, percentage acceptable to your management.

3. Third degree: the profit margin on the AdWords ad is greater than the profit margin for the same product sold through other marketing channels. That is, the product sells better online than through other channels. This requires knowledge of the costs and success of other channels.

Once you know your goal, you can measure the success of your AdWords campaigns. Keep the following principles in mind.

1. **Three types of metrics exist: performance, cost and value.**

   - **Performance metrics help you operate AdWords.** They tell you if your efforts are going in the right direction. Impressions, clicks, CTR and conversion metrics relate to your operation of the campaigns.

   - **Cost metrics help you evaluate whether you are making the most of your budget.** They tell you if you are spending your money effectively. Average cost-per-click is a cost metric.

   - **Value metrics are the most important because they help you evaluate your profits.** AdWords does not calculate value metrics for you.

   Profit is the money left after all costs are covered. Despite its simple definition, profit is often difficult to determine (primarily because products share so many resources, such as managers, factory space, equipment, bulk shipping, etc.). Do not be surprised if your management cannot give you the profit margin on company products.

   If profit margins are not available ask your management to give a theoretical profit margin to use in measuring your results. If no profit margin is available, use 30 percent of the retail price for your own measurement.

   Many AdWords managers forget about profitability as they run their campaigns and spend too much time on generating clicks or focusing on low profit (aka low margin) products.

2. **Each metric tells you something important.**
   - Impressions indicate how well your keywords relate to search terms.
   - Clicks indicate how well your ad draws visitors.
   - Conversions indicate how well your landing page works.
   - Profit indicates whether your ads are worth running. Profit is the goal.
   - Return on investment (ROI) lets you compare your AdWords investment with other marketing channels.

3. **Not all metrics are equally important, and the importance of a metric changes depending where you are in the maturity of your campaign.**
   - When your campaign is new, the priority statistics are: the right keywords, impressions, clicks, conversions and profit. (Without good keywords, you cannot get impressions; without impressions, you cannot get clicks, etc.)
   - Once you have enough impressions and traffic that you should be getting conversions, the priority of the statistics change to: profits, conversions, clicks, impressions and keywords. (Without profit, you are wasting your money on conversions; without clicks, you cannot get conversions, etc.)

4. **AdWords does *not* tell you if you are succeeding.** You must determine for yourself:
   - If your ad is working well.
   - If your landing page is working well.
   - If you paid too much for your keywords.
   - Whether you made money.

The following section presents information to help you determine which ads and keywords are best, using the performance and cost metrics AdWords provides.

Performance Metrics

Performance metrics tell you the level of traffic and the number of buyers your campaigns, ad groups, ads and keywords secured.

Performance metrics do not tell you if your campaign, ad group, etc. is "doing well," and they do not tell you if you are making money.

The four most important performance metrics are (1) clicks, (2) click-through rate, (3) conversion rate and (4) return on investment.

1. *Clicks* **indicate how well your keywords are performing.** If users do not use your keywords, you have no chance to sell your product. Each time a viewer clicks your ad, AdWords records a click.

2. *Click-through rate (CTR)* **indicates how appealing your ad is to viewers.** CTR shows what percentage of viewers came to visit your website out of all the people who viewed a SERP where your ad appeared. AdWords computes the CTR for you, by dividing the number of visitors to your landing page by the number of times your ad appeared (i.e., the number of impressions).

3. *Conversion rate (conv. rate)* **indicates how appealing your landing page and your promotional offer are to your website visitors.** It shows the percentage of people who bought something out of all the people who visited your website. (AdWords computes this for you only if you use the *Conversion Tracking* option.)

   - To compute the *conversion rate*, divide the number of buyers by the total number of visitors.
   - The higher the *conversion rate*, the better. You want as many buyers as possible.
   - Your *click-through rate* (CTR) drives your conversion rate.

4. **Return on investment indicates how valuable AdWords is in comparison to other marketing channels.**

   - To compute return on investment, subtract costs from revenues (this is your net profit) and then divide that by your costs to get your percentage growth (or loss).
   - A position ROI represents growth. The higher the better. A negative ROI represents loss. The lower the better—though having a loss is never desirable.
   - To raise your ROI, you need to lower your advertising costs or raise your product's price.

Cost Metrics

Cost metrics help you compare different keywords, ads within the ad groups and campaigns to determine which ones are too expensive to continue.

1. **The most important cost metric is average *cost-per-click* (avg. CPC).** It indicates what you are paying, *on average*, to bring one individual visitor to your website. AdWords does not provide the CPC for each visitor; it provides only the average.

- Average *cost-per-click* highlights high cost keywords and ads. (*Average cost-per-impression, average cost-per-view and average cost-per-acquisition* metrics work the same way as the *average cost-per-click.*)

- AdWords provides the *average cost-per-click* for each level of the AdWords hierarchy—campaign, ad group(s), ads and keywords. This enables you to compare campaigns, ad groups, ads and keywords.

- **The lower the avg. CPC, the better—*if you are getting buyers!*** That is, your *avg. CPC* is low, but your conversion rate is high. Cheap ads that do not bring buyers are a drain on your marketing budget.

2. ***Avg. CPC* is useful at the Ad group and Campaign Levels of the AdWords hierarchy to determine whether to eliminate entire product lines and campaigns.**

3. **Cost is important, but you must balance cost against opportunity and profit.**

   - *Avg. CPC* for each *keyword* lets you identity inexpensive keywords. This is powerful information. Improving the *conversion rate* for an inexpensive keyword is a double winner—low cost and higher volume of traffic.

   - *Avg. CPC* for each *ad* (i.e., the average for all the keywords) lets you compare ads to see which is cheaper to run and, perhaps, find a niche with few competitors.

   - *Avg. CPC* for each *ad group* (i.e., all the keywords across all the underlying ads) lets you compare products. (Recall that different products should be in different ad groups.)

   - If you use different ad groups for *features* of a product, a low *avg. CPC* tells you which product feature has less competition in the marketplace. Perhaps a market opportunity exists for that feature.

   - If you use ad groups to represent different *products*, a low *avg. CPC* tells you which products are cheaper to sell online. You may want to drop some expensive products.

4. **Many other names exist for *average cost-per-click*, such as *average cost-per-visitor* (*Avg. CPV*) or *average cost-per-buyer*.** Your management may prefer these. It is always acceptable to ask for a precise definition of a metric, and it is prudent to do so. It is better to define your metrics clearly than misrepresent your results.

Value Metrics

While an ad can attract visitors to your website and prompt them to buy something, it may or may not bring in enough revenue to satisfy your revenue goals. The same goes for a keyword, an ad group, a campaign or AdWords overall. The following metrics help you compare dollars to dollars and find your most lucrative opportunities.

These value metrics help you determine (1) which keywords, ads, ad groups or campaigns bring in the most revenue for the money spent and (2) how AdWords revenues compare to those of other advertising media, such as TV, radio, magazines, etc.

You must calculate your own value metrics. AdWords cannot do it for you.

Important value metrics include:

1. **Average revenue-per-*sale* (ARS)**: this indicates the revenue, on average, generated by each sale. This metric is essential for comparing ads, campaigns and marketing channels.

    *   If you need to meet a revenue goal, this number tells you approximately how many sales you need.

    *   When you know the number of sales you need, you can calculate the number of visitors you need based on your conversion rate and the number of impressions you need based on your click-through rate (i.e., the approximate budget you need).

    *   Remember, these numbers are "on average," so be sure to pad your estimates to give yourself some breathing room.

2. **Average revenue-per-*customer* (ARC)**: this indicates how much revenue, on average, a customer (i.e., a buyer) brings in.

    *   This metric compares the value of online buyers with offline buyers to determine if AdWords is a competitive channel for advertising.

3. **Average value-per-*lead* (AVL)**: this indicates how much revenue on average is generated by someone who came to the website via your ad and later became a customer.

    *   This metric is difficult to obtain. It requires that you match signups from your website against purchases made by customers over a defined period. Customers, especially retail customers, often respond to online ads, offline ads, in-store promotions and face-to-face discussions with sales people before they buy. That makes it virtually impossible to say which channel drove the purchase. Usually the channel that processes

the sales transaction takes credit, even if the customer learned of the product online.

- Nevertheless, knowing this metric is very useful in projecting future revenues.

The ability to calculate value metrics and manage a campaign against them is the difference between" running a campaign" and "managing sales and profitability" for your company.

Step 10: Track Your Bills

AdWords bills your credit card or debit card at the end of 30 days, provided you do not go over your *billing threshold*.

AdWords sets a billing threshold for your account of either $50, $200, $350 or $500 (whichever is the first amount higher than your daily budget times 30.4). To see your threshold, go to the *billing tab*. It appears in the section *How you pay*.

- For example, if your daily budget is $5, your threshold is $200, since $200 is the nearest higher number to your monthly budget of $152 ($5 × 30.4 = $152).

AdWords may exceed your daily budget on some days of high traffic. In no case, however, are you charged more than 20 percent over your daily budget on any given day, nor is your monthly budget ever exceeded during a billing period.

Your bill may vary a small amount if billing takes place during the thirtieth day. If you maintain your daily budget of $5 throughout the month, on the thirtieth day after your account starts you are billed. If your costs are under the maximum allowed per day, your bill will be less than you expect. If costs are over, you are billed the exact amount (30.4 x daily budget), and the overage rolls to the next month (to be offset during that month).

If you raise your daily budget during the month, your account could reach its threshold and, thus, (1) trigger immediate billing, (2) a higher threshold and (3) a new monthly billing day.

- For example, if you increase your budget from $5 a day ($152 a month) to $7 a day ($218 a month) on the first day of October, you reach your threshold on October 29th (29 x $7 = $203). AdWords (1) bills you immediately for $203, (2) sets your threshold to $300 and (3) sets your next billing date as 30 days from this billing date.

(In the United States, Google has discontinued pre-payment accounts where you put money into your AdWords account and AdWords debited the account during the month. Pre-payment accounts were prone to run out of funds and ads sat idle until the account was replenished.)

For more information about billing, search in AdWords Help for "Understanding why you've been charged."

MAKING MONEY

An unmonitored AdWords campaign is expensive. You must monitor your campaigns frequently to prevent a torrent of clicks that do not convert visitors to customers.

Keep the following principles in mind.

1. **Monitor your AdWords campaigns from the top down to meet the demands of your company's management.**

   - Business managers in your company want information about revenues, costs and products sold and whether those amounts are increasing or decreasing.

   - AdWords operational data (clicks, click-throughs and conversions) are of little interest to most managers.

2. **Monitor the direction of revenues, costs and sales over time.**

   - AdWords currently does not provide trend information on the performance of campaigns, ad groups, ads or keywords. Consequently, you must compile the information yourself or deploy a third-party software application.

3. **It is imperative to keep periodic reports (at least monthly) to use in compiling management reports and for tracking campaign performance over time**.

Step 11: Evaluate Your Profitability

You must evaluate your campaigns from the top down. Do not start by delving into the success or failure of each ad and keyword or the impressions or clicks each received.

Review the hierarchy as follows:

1. **Campaigns, to verify you are addressing the right markets.**

2. **Ad groups, to verify you are promoting the right products.**

3. **Ads, to verify you are using the best message.**

4. **Keywords, to verify you are speaking your prospect's language.**

That sequence lets you compare regional sales and products. The discussion below assumes you use that hierarchy.

First, Evaluate AdWords as a Whole

Compile the high-level information your manager and senior management want to know, using a format like the one shown in Figure 4.2.

1. **Be sure you are reviewing the correct time period.**
   - Click the date range menu on the top right corner of the page and select the time period you want to analyze.
   - Be aware that complete data for yesterday is not available until 3 p.m. PT (6 p.m. ET) today.

Total AdWords	Status:		
	Last Period	*This Period*	*% Change*
Total Revenues			
Total Costs			
ROI			

FIGURE 4.2 Sample spreadsheet for evaluating AdWords campaigns as a whole

2. **For AdWords as a whole, note the following statistics:**

   Click *All online campaigns* and then click the *campaign tab*. Review the *total all campaigns* data at the bottom of the statistics table.
   - Total revenues driven by AdWords. Obtain this from your Sales or Accounting Department. (Don't be surprised if it is not available or not discernable.)
   - Total costs. See the bottom line of the statistics table on the campaign tab.
   - Return on investment (ROI). Subtract this period's costs from this period's revenues to see your profit; then divide the difference by this period's cost to see the growth. Multiply by 100 to get the percentage (e.g., 0.20 becomes 20 percent).

- Compare last period's data with this period's data to determine:
  — Total revenues growth. Subtract this period's revenues from last period's revenues to get the difference; then divide the difference by the last period's revenue to get the growth (or loss). Multiply by 100 to get the percentage.
  — Total costs percentage change. Subtract this period's costs from last period's costs to get the difference; then divide the difference by the last period's costs to get the growth (or loss). Multiply by 100 to get the percentage.
  — At this rate of increase, will the current budget cover the cost of AdWords for the rest of the year?
    (1) Project your costs to the end of the current year (multiplying the cost for the period by the number of periods remaining in the year). Compare that number to your budget. At a minimum, you need a budget equal to this amount. If the number of impressions increases each period, you will need a greater amount.
  — Total ROI percentage change. Subtract this period's ROI from last period's ROI to get the difference; then divide the difference by the last period's ROI to get the change in ROI amount. Multiply by 100 to get the percentage.

Once you know the profitability for AdWords as a whole, drill down to the campaigns to check their profitability.

Second, Evaluate Campaigns (Markets)

Create a report like the one in Figure 4.3. Include the name of the campaign and a short description of the market with your data.

- If you are running multiple campaigns for a region, your management may want you to aggregate the data for the region. Similarly, regional managers may want aggregations by product lines for their regions.
- To produce aggregations quickly, click the *all online campaigns* menu in the left-hand menu and then click the *ad groups* tab. Data for all the ad groups appear. Download it to a spreadsheet application and sort it by the regions and/or product lines you need.

1. **For each campaign determine the following to complete the table in Figure 4.3. Use the data on the statistics table on the *campaign tab* and the formula for computing percentage changes as done for your previous evaluation of AdWords overall.**

Campaign: New York Region – English speaking, all age groups	Status:		
	Last Period	*This Period*	*% Change*
Revenues			
Costs			
ROI			

FIGURE 4.3 Sample spreadsheet for regional reviews

    a. Revenues generated and the percentage change.

    b. Costs and the percentage change.

    c. Return on investment (ROI).

2. **Update the status of a campaign to "*under review*" if revenues are static or declining, costs are increasing, costs are higher than revenues and/or ROI is declining.** Pause the campaign online to stop losing money while you research ways to improve your results. You need to review all components of your ads.

    Update the status of the remaining campaigns (all of which should have increasing revenues) as "*growing revenues*."

Third, Evaluate Ad Groups (Products)

1. **At the Ad Group Level, determine which products are selling well.**

    • On the left-hand menu, click your first campaign. Then, click the *Ad group tab* to show data for all ad groups associated with that campaign.

    • Create a report similar to the one for the campaigns, using the table in Figure 4.4.

    • If you have assigned *labels* to your keywords to represent brands, designers or other groupings, you can obtain performance information by clicking *dimensions* and *labels*.

    • Download and aggregate the data by product category.

2. **For each product within each campaign, determine the following (just as you did for campaigns).**

    a. Revenues generated and the percentage change.

    b. Costs and the percentage change.

Campaign: New York Region	Status:		
Product Line: Shoes	*Last period*	*This Period*	*% Change*
Total Revenues			
Total Costs			
ROI			
Product Line: Dresses	*Last period*	*This Period*	*% Change*
Total Revenues			
Total Costs			
ROI			

Figure 4.4. Sample spreadsheet for reviewing ad groups

   c. Return on investment (ROI).

   d. Update the status of a product category to "*under review*" if any of the following conditions exist:

     — **Revenues are static or declining, costs are increasing, costs are higher than revenues and/or ROI is declining.** Pause the campaign online to stop losing money while you research ways to improve your results. You need to review all components of the ads.

     — **Impressions, clicks or click-through rate are declining.** Put "Reviewing keywords and targets" in the Notes column.

     — **Conversions or clicks-to-conversions are declining.** Put "Reviewing landing page" in the Notes column.

3. **Review the underlying ads for the products (ad groups) within each campaign to determine which message or messages resonate best with prospects. Create a report using the table in Figure 4.5.**

   • For the profitable ads (revenues are greater than costs), enter the ad message(s) and destination URL. Put the messages in order of profitability, with the most profitable message first.

   • For the unprofitable ads, list the ad messages and destination URL.

Product Category Messaging	Revenues	Costs	Visitors (click-throughs)	Sales (Conv.)	Destination URL
Most successful messages:					
Unsuccessful messages:					

FIGURE 4.5 Sample spreadsheet for reviewing ads

At this point, your management should assign priorities for reviewing and working to improve campaigns and ads, based on corporate strategy and revenue goals.

At a minimum, you need to know which products are or should be major revenue generators and, thus, most important to review and work to improve.

Step 12: Plan Your AdWords Maintenance Work

Without a disciplined approach and diligent review, managing a large number of AdWords campaigns can be overwhelming and fraught with errors and missed opportunities. It is reasonable to ask your management to set priorities concerning the campaigns and products to review and tweak first.

Using the data compiled previously and the priorities set by management, set your plan for reviewing ads and keywords.

Consider the best practices that follow and, as you do, write a to-do list. This ensures your review is systematic, follows corporate priorities and covers all the campaigns.

Priority 1: Stop losing money. Preserve your budget to use on successful campaigns.

    a. Pause campaigns that are losing money.

    b. For profitable campaigns, within the ad groups that are losing money, pause the unprofitable ads.

    c. For profitable ad groups, pause any ads that are losing money.

Priority 2: Nurture your profitable campaigns in the priority order management assigned.

Usually it is better to use the bulk of your time building on your success, rather than fixing poor-performing ads and keywords.

    a. Work the top priority and profitable product lines (ad groups) first.

b. Review the profitable ads and their keywords and work to optimize and expand them.

(See Step 13: Use AdWords Experiments to Improve Your Ads and Save Money, p. 170, for tips on how to expand your campaign while protecting your *quality score* and minimizing the impact on your current revenues.)

(See Growing Your Campaign sections of Chapter 5, p. 216, for the particular type of ad you are using to find suggestions for expanding your campaigns.)

Once you review all your product lines (ad groups), move to the next campaign.

Priority 3: Estimate the work required to refine poor-performing campaigns, ad groups, ads and keywords, and set a schedule for completing your work. Recognize the following:

- Ads with few conversions require work on the landing page, which can take days to refine, program and release.
- Ads with low click-through rates require changes to ad text, which take only a few hours.
- Ads with few impressions require higher bids or tweaks to keywords, which takes a few minutes or a couple hours to complete.

Your longer-term strategy from here is to:

1. **Use AdWords rules to monitor your ads and save time.**
   - Use *automated rules* to monitor and adjust your good ads so you have time to experiment with new advertising ideas and expand your campaigns. (See Step 12: Use Automatic Rules to Maintain Ad Performance, p. 167.)
   - Use a *Flexible Bid* strategy to monitor low performing campaigns or ad groups.

2. **Use AdWords experiments to improve your ads and save money.** (See Step 13: Use AdWords Experiments to Improve Your Ads and Save Money, page 170, for details about running experiments.)
   - Unless you keep learning about your keywords, you can overpay for AdWords ads.
   - AdWords *experiments* lets you:
     — Test different value propositions, messages, placements, topics, interests, geographic areas, ages and genders to find your market demographic and sales sweet spot.
     — Find more effective keywords and messages to attract more visitors.
     — Improve your landing page.

— Identify better promotional offers (or content to generate more sign-ups).

— Generate more revenue for Search ads.

— Reduce your costs for Display Network ads.

3. **Expand your campaigns and achieve consistent sales.**

   - To achieve your sales goals, you may need to expand your campaign using other networks (the Display Network or the Google AdMob Network) and ad types. (See the discussion in Step 13: Use AdWords Experiments to Improve Your Ads and Save Money, p. 170.)

   - Keep reviewing performance metrics and profits, and keep experimenting with different bids (and CPM, CPV pricing) to reduce your *cost-per-click* as much as possible. (See Chapter 5, p. 180, for monitoring steps for each type of ad.)

4. **Activate *Conversion Tracking and Conversion Optimization* as soon as possible after you achieve consistent sales**.

   - Activating *Conversion Tracking* and *Conversion Optimization* puts the power of AdWords rules for showing ads and identifying potential buyers to work for you. This is a definite advantage.

     (See the discussion in Activate Conversion Tracking, p. 228, and Conversion Optimization, p. 238, for more information.)

   - You must achieve consistent sales each month before you can activate Conversion Tracking (usually 15 sales or more).

5. **Implement *Remarketing* as soon as possible after *Optimizing for Conversions*.** *Remarketing* lets you stay in touch with your buyers and gives you the opportunity to coax them back to your site for repeat sales. *Conversion Tracking* must be in use before you can use *Remarketing*.

   - *Remarketing* uses the power of AdWords to present ads to your previous buyers and people who share characteristics with your buyers. This is a powerful way to expand your market. (See the discussion in Chapter 5 on Activating Remarketing.)

SAVING MONEY AND TIME

AdWords offers a number of features that make running ad campaigns easier. Two in particular are extremely important: (1) *automated rules* and (2) experiments.

The following explains the *rules* and *experiment* features, along with the shared library and several time-savers.

Step 13: Use Automatic Rules to Maintain Ad Performance

AdWords lets you establish rules to manage your campaigns, ads and keywords automatically based on conditions that you set up. *Automated rules* give you a level of control over events when your attention is not on AdWords.

Automated rules are established at the Campaign, Ad Group, Ad and Keyword Levels. In essence, *automated rules* let you:

- Set rules for (1) keywords, ads or ad groups within a specific campaign, (2) all entities in a specific campaign or (3) all entities in *all online campaigns*. Further, options exist to apply rules based on an ad's *display URL*, *destination URL*, type (text, image, etc.) and label.
- Set Start/stop date for campaigns:
  — Raise/lower bids (within the minimum and maximum you set) under certain conditions. If you want, AdWords can email you when it invokes a rule.
  — Consider whether *automatic bidding* or *Conversion Optimization*, which puts AdWords' massive amount of data to work for you, would serve your purpose just as well as a rule can.

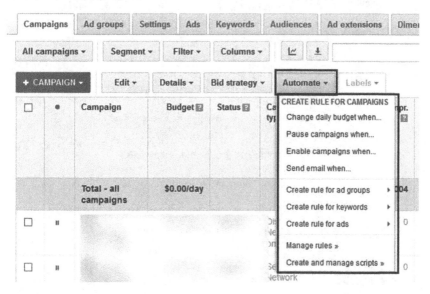

FIGURE 4.6 Automated rules menu

- Raise/lower your daily budget under certain conditions. Again, if you want, AdWords can email you when it invokes a rule. You can set a maximum and minimum.
  — Consider whether a *flexible bidding strategy*, which can maximize your existing budget, would serve your purpose just as well as a rule can.
- Specify the frequency and/or conditions under which your rules run. (For example, run the rule *Frequently* to check that this ad is in the *top of page* position.)
- Pause or delete rules as needed.

To setup an *automated rule,* click the desired campaign, ad group, ad or keyword and then click the *automate* button above the *statistics table* as shown in Figure 4.6. Figure 4.7 shows the subsequent screen.

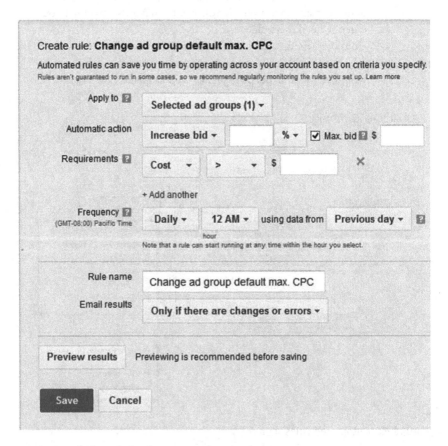

FIGURE 4.7 Automated rules screen for an ad group

AdWords maintains a list of rules in effect, along with a log of changes made to the rules.

AdWords Rules lets you respond immediately to changing competition and business conditions. You can establish rules to:

1. **Pause a campaign, when an ad group or ad meets a certain conversion or performance metric.** Use this to:

   * Stop an ad before you deplete your inventory.

   * Stop an ad if performance rates are unacceptably low over a specific period of time. Use a reasonable period of time since conversion rates take weeks or months to build.

2. **Enable or pause a campaign, ad group or ad on a specific date or for a specific timeframe.** Options exist to designate ads by *display URL*, *destination URL*, type (text, image, etc.) and label. For bids, you can set a maximum and minimum. Use this to:

   * Run limited-time promotions and sales (e.g., Fourth of July sale or first anniversary sale).

   * Run a weekday or weekend special repeatedly every week (e.g., 10 percent discount every Monday, free shipping on weekends).

   * Increase your bid after 5 p.m., if your ads draw more buyers during the evenings.

   * Pause all ads containing a specific word, such as "holiday," "fall" or "sale."

3. **Raise or lower the max CPC bid for a keyword or pause the keyword.** Use this to:

   * Raise your bid to maintain your ad position (e.g., it falls below the top of page, it falls off the first page or your average position falls).

   * Pause a keyword if performance falls below a certain point.

   Note that lowering your bid can result in a downward spiral of performance, as when the lower bid results in a lower ad position, which results in fewer clicks and a lower click-through rate and, subsequently, in a lower *quality score*, still lower ad position and a repeat of the cycle.

4. **Raise or lower your daily budget.**

   * Raise your daily budget when traffic is heavy and many click-throughs are occurring.

   * Raise your daily budget when ads are performing well (e.g., the number of conversions is high and the *cost-per-conversion* is low).

5. **Pause a campaign that hits a certain cost.** Use this to preserve your budget when business conditions inside your company change.

   Warning: Set a ceiling amount that is about 20 percent less than the amount you really want. For example, if you want your campaign to stop when it reaches $1,000 in costs, set your rule for $800 in costs. AdWords can go over a daily budget by 20 percent and, as luck will have it, that will happen when your account approaches $1,000.

6. **Alert you via email when a certain condition occurs.** Use this to:
   - Alert you when your daily budget runs out during the day.

Rules are more productive if you:

- **Use a parameter, such as** *impression > 1,000* **to control the timing of a rule.** This lets you make sure a trend is solid before the rule goes into effect. For example, a rule stating "if impressions are greater than (>) 1000 and clicks are less than (<) 10, pause keyword." This gives your keyword time to prove it is not succeeding before you turn it off.

- **Set frequency and timeframes carefully.** For example, if you run a rule every day to increase your bid if results for the last 30 days are below a certain level, you are likely to have many bid increases before those 30-day results are significantly higher, which can be a costly mistake.

- **Set a rule to run once, before you set it as recurring.** This lets you verify the setup and results before multiple changes are made.

- **Periodically check your rules to see if they still meet your business need.** While *automated rules* provide a safety net, you are still responsible for the performance of your campaigns.

Step 14: Use AdWords Experiments to Improve Your Ads and Save Money

Experiments let you pit one ad element against another to see which one wins the most auctions and, ultimately, which one generates the most conversions.

- Experiments are a great way to test your ideas and prove their effectiveness before investing more money.

- They are especially valuable when marketing team members have different ideas about what customers want, where they gather or what engages them.

Experiments are valuable because they:

- Show objectively what works and what does not.
- Take the emotion out of decision-making.
- Let you find good ads and bids quickly, as well as quickly remove poor ads and bids.
- Save you money.

Before you plan an experiment, be aware of the following constraints:

- **Experiments affect your** *quality score.* Thus, they should be serious efforts to make better ads and bids, rather than casual efforts to simply try anything.
- **Only campaigns using** *manual bidding* **and either the** *cost-per-click* **(CPC) or the** *cost-per-impressions* **(CPM) option can run experiments.** Campaigns using other bidding models cannot run experiments.
- Running an experiment does not incur any costs above those of your ad's CPC or CPM.
- You can experiment with any element at the *Ad group*, *Ad*, or *Keywords/Target Method Levels*.

The item you elect to test depends on your business goal and whether you are testing a Search Network ad or a Display Network ad, as Figure 4.8 shows:

AdWords does not permit testing of most Campaign Level options, including:

- Targeting at the Campaign Level (geographic, language, network and device targeting).
- Bidding features (Only campaigns using *Focus on Clicks* or *Focus on Impressions* can run tests.)
- *Daily budget.*
- *Ad extensions.*
- *Ad scheduling.*
- *Frequency capping.*
- *Negative keywords* at the Campaign Level.

The best ad experiments follow the rules of scientific methodology.

1. **Document the performance of the current ad you want to test.** Your current ad is your *control* ad, and the performance data is your *baseline* for comparison.

Business Goal:	For Search Ad experiments by:	For Display Ad experiments by:
Increase Impressions	Adding a new Keyword Changing: - a Keyword match type - a Keyword bid - Ad Group *default bids* - the Conversion Optimizer Max CPA - Ad group CPC or CPM default or bid	Adding: - a new Keyword, or - a new placement Changing: - a Keyword bid - Ad Group default bids - a placement bid - the Conversion Tracking Max CPA - Ad group CPC or CPM default, or bid
Increase Clicks	Adding *keyword insertions* Changing: - the ad copy - call-to-action	Adding: - *keyword insertions* - an image - animation - video - a placement Changing: - the ad copy or - call-to-action
Attract More Qualified Prospects	Adding a new Ad with new Keywords Changing: - the ad copy or - call-to-action	Adding a new ad with new Keywords and Target Methods Adding *Remarketing* capabilities Changing: - the ad copy - call-to-action - placement(s) - topic(s) - gender/age - interests
Increase Conversions	Changing: - the landing page design - your product offer - Moving the buy button to the top of the page	Changing: - the landing page design - your product offer - Moving the buy button to the top of the page
Reduce Costs	Changing your bid on an Ad Group, Ad or Keyword	Changing your bid on an Ad Group, Ad or Keyword
Improve ROI	Adding *Negative Keywords*	Excluding Keywords, placements and websites selected by automatic placement Adding *Negative Keywords*

FIGURE 4.8 Experiment goals

2. **Change only one *variable*, i.e., one item, in the ad.** That variable can be the ad text, the landing page, the keywords, the placements, the topic, etc., but it can be only one ad component. If you change two or more variables, you will not know which variable caused the end results.

3. **Give each ad the same opportunities to participate in auctions.**

   * AdWords can select ads evenly (more or less) for participation (i.e., a 50–50 split) or can give preference to the control ad or the experimental ad, if you so specify.

   * **Using something other than a 50–50 split is unscientific. However, this is marketing, not science, and money is at stake. Therefore:**
     — If you have a great ad but want to experiment with a change to the ad copy, you can give your experimental ad 10 percent of the auctions while letting the great ad get 90 percent and continue to bring buyers to your site. Your results are not statistically significant, but you get a sense of whether your experimental ad is worth using or refining with as little impact on revenues as possible.
     — Run your test longer if you do not do a 50–50 split to give the slighted ad enough participation to get reasonable, if not statistically significant results.

4. **Monitor the performance of your ads during the test.** If, after a reasonable time, one ad is clearly outperforming the other ad, stop the test. Don't waste money on a non-performing ad.

   * AdWords provides statistical data to indicate which ad is performing *statistically significantly* better (or worse) than the control ad. Sophisticated mathematical formulas evaluate results to confirm only a small chance exists that the results occurred by chance. If only a small chance exists, the results are statistically significant.

   * The word *significant* means the results meet statistical measures for validity (whether the results are up or down, better or worse). Do not use the word *significant* if your results do not meet that statistical measure.

5. **At the end of the test, compare the results for the control ad and the experimental ad and end the AdWords experiment.**

   * Save a copy of your data at the end of your test period in case someone questions your results.

6. **Decide whether to apply or discard your experimental ad.**

The major steps for executing an experiment involving keywords are:

1. Select an existing campaign to use for your experiment.

2. Go to the campaign *settings*. Near the bottom, under *advanced settings*, click on *experiment*.

3. Enter a descriptive name for your experiment. Include the element you are testing. For example, Ad Copy-Chocolate Labrador Retrievers.

4. Choose how to split the auctions between your control and your experiment.
    *   A 50–50 split renders results fastest.
    *   For risky experiments where you have money at stake, give your experimental ad less exposure (i.e., a lower percentage of the auctions.)
    *   You cannot change your split after you start your experiment.

5. Choose when to start your experiment.
    *   To start your test immediately, enter today's date.
    *   To start your test at midnight on a particular date, enter that date.
    *   Otherwise, make sure the "no start date" button is filled, so your experiment is on hold.

6. Choose when to end your experiment. Leave the input box filled for "30 days from start" or enter a date. You can change your end date later to extend the date up to three months from your start date.

7. Save your input.

8. Go to the *campaign tab*. In the left-hand menu, click on the *campaign* where you entered your experimental options.

9. To test keywords, click the + *new keyword* tab and select the ad group for your test.

10. Enter your keyword(s). Do not forget to set your match types.

11. At the bottom of the input panel, click the box next to "*Add as experimental keywords.*"

12. Save your input.

13. If you use Google Analytics, you can add a *ValueTrack tag* to your ad's *destination URL* to tell Google Analytics whether a click comes from the control keywords or the experimental keywords.

- Add ?type={aceid} to the end of the URL, as in www.example.com/chocolate-labradors?type={aceid}. With this in place, AdWords assigns an ID number to your control group and your experimental group, and each click bears the ID number of the group responsible for the click.

- *My change history* in Google Analytics stores your control and experimental ID numbers.

14. If you have not set a start date for your test, return to the *campaign settings* and enter the appropriate date.

15. Monitor your experiment weekly. Do the following:

   a. Setup reports that run on a regular basis. You can email reports to yourself and others. A trail of reports is essential when unexpected results suddenly emerge.

   b. During your experiment, view the performance data for the experimental item and compare it to your control item.
      — Evaluate your test from the top down, i.e., Campaign, Ad Group, Ad and Keyword Levels.
      — Determine if your ad group *click-throughs*, *CPCs* and *conversions* are higher with the experimental item running. Again, the experimental item may have stopped keywords from competing with each other, which can make a campaign more successful.
      — Determine if your *click-throughs*, *CPCs* and *conversions* for the experimental ad are higher than for the control ad and whether the performance of either is statistically significant.
      — Only statistically significant data gives you a fair evaluation of an ad's performance. However, statistically significant results are not enough. The better ad is the one with results that are (1) statistically significant *and* (2) better than the other ad.
      — At the Campaign Level, click on the *segment* tab and then *experiment* on the drop-down menu. The "experiment" row shows data for your experimental item, and the "control" row shows data for your control item.
      — The *statistics table* uses icons to indicate the performance of your test:
         Blue arrows indicate statistically significant data.
         (1) An up arrow (⧻) shows performance increased and a down arrow (⧼) means performance decreased.
         (2) One arrow indicates 95 percent certainty performance is not due to chance, two arrows mean 99 percent certainty and three arrows mean 99.9 percent certainty.

175

(3) Statistically significant results mean performance is more likely to continue in the future.

      Gray arrows indicate the results are not statistically significant.

— Give your experiment time to render statistically significant results for either the control or the experimental item.

— Too little traffic can cause your results to appear insignificant.

e. At the end of the test, compare the results for the control ad and the experimental ad and end the AdWords experiment.

— Save a copy of your data at the end of your test period. AdWords deletes the performance data when you turn off the experiment.

— If your experimental ad results are statistically significant *and* better than the control group's, keep the ad.

f. Once you have decided whether your experimental ad is useful, you can launch it or delete it.

— Click on the *settings* for your campaign. Under *advanced settings*, click *experimental* and *apply: launch changes fully* if you want to add your experimental ad to the ad group. Click *delete: remove changes* if you do not want to keep your experimental ad.

— When you delete your experimental ad, AdWords purges the performance data and it no longer exists.

Experiments at the ad group or Keyword Levels operate the same as the previous example.

For more detailed instructions on executing experiments, search in AdWords Help for the topic "About campaign experiments."

Step 15: Use the Shared Library to Save Time

Shared library functions let you use certain options and restrictions with any of your campaigns, without re-entering your choices. This is a major convenience and time saver for a large account. The functions include:

- **Ads**: where you create a list with one or more ads and name it. You can then add the list to one or more ad groups. Google does not say why this feature is useful. (Perhaps, it is for experiments.)

- **Audiences**: where you can establish lists to use with different Remarketing Ads. (See Advanced Feature: Remarketing Ads for more information.)

- **Bid strategies**: where you create *flexible bid strategies* to use with one or more campaigns that you can apply to multiple campaigns. (See Flexible Bid Strategies (CPC) for more information.)

- **Budgets**: where you enter a budget(s) for specific campaigns to share.

- **Business data**: where you can upload a spreadsheet (called a feed) containing information about your chain of businesses, such as your business locations, phone numbers, customer reviews, sitelinks and app platform information (for example, Apple Store App #1233242). Click on the type of information you want to upload to see the column names you must use on your spreadsheet.

- **Campaign negative keywords**: where you create and name lists of negative keywords. You can then apply a named list to all campaigns (at the Shared Library level) or apply it to individual ad groups (when you setup keywords). See Level 5: Keywords, Targeting Methods, and Targeting Groups Targets for more information.

- **Campaign placement exclusions**: where you create a list (or lists) of placement that you prohibit from showing your ads. You can apply a list to all campaigns or to specific campaigns.

Step 16: Miscellaneous Time Savers

When you manage a large number of campaigns for your company, you need tools and tactics to help you monitor the status of each campaign. The following tips can help.

- **AdWords editor**: this AdWords tool resides on your desktop or laptop and lets you download account information to review off-line in a spreadsheet format. You can search and update data in your spreadsheet and upload your spreadsheet changes, in bulk, into AdWords.

- **Date selector**: the date selector lets you compare the performance of the current period with that of the previous period for a campaign, ad group, ad or keyword. It tells you if impressions, clicks or conversions have increased or decreased since the last period.
  — Select *all online campaigns* or *online video campaigns*, set the *date selector* to the desired period, click the *compare dates* to ON, check *previous period* and click *apply*.
  — Within the *statistics table*, a + *sign* (⊞) appears in the titles of the metrics. Click the + sign to see the performance for the two periods for that specific metric. You can quickly compare clicks, impressions and conversions for your campaigns without leaving the screen.

- **Copy and paste**: to setup similar campaigns, ad groups and ads quickly, use the *copy and paste* function under the *edit* button just above the *statistics table*.

177

- *Labels*: you can assign a label to a campaign, ad group, ad or keyword for reporting purposes. Labels let you:
  — Aggregate data across ads, ad groups and campaigns for reporting purposes. Use labels to group products, manufacturers or brands for reporting.
  — Mark things for quick reference. Use labels to designate a new bid so you can monitor it for the next few weeks. Add a date so you know how long it has been in effect. For example: Raised bid, 9/16/14.
  — Make a note. Use labels to remind you of your strategy. For example: Paused-Low CTR-Sept.

Setting Up, Monitoring, and Growing Your Search Network Campaigns

This chapter provides a "how-to" reference manual for Search Network ads, showing you how to setup and monitor the different Search Network ads. It dives into the details of evaluating Search Network ad results, and reviews a long list of options, at different account levels (campaign, ad group, ad, keyword, etc.), to use to improve performance. It provides best practices and repercussions for many of the options, and it outlines additional features and new ad types to add as your revenues grow.

More specifically, the chapter covers, in detail, how to setup and monitor the different Search Network ad types: Basic, Dynamic, Local, Mobile, Mobile App, Remarketing and Search-with-Display-Select ads. It also provides instructions for activating the advanced features of Conversion Tracking, Conversion Optimization and Remarketing.

A number of ad types exist that you can use to expand your AdWords campaigns. You can create most of the ads yourself, without involving graphic designers or programmers. Further, if you have a camera or phone with video capability, you can create a Video Ad to use in your marketing efforts.

- **Keep a "change log" as you setup and add new ad types and as you make significant changes to your campaigns.** It is frightfully easy to forget *why* you changed a campaign, ad group or ad. Even the most logical changes become a blur after a few weeks of looking at new data. When questions arise, clients and managers have little patience for "I don't remember" answers.

Chapter 5 discusses how to setup, grow and monitor each Search Network ad type, including:

- Basic Search Ads.
- Dynamic Search Ads.
- Local Ads using Google My Business, AdWords Express and AdWords.
- Mobile Ads for phones and tablets.
- Search ads targeted to previous visitors.
- Search ads with AdWords-selected Display Network options.

Chapter 6 covers Display Network ads.

SEARCH NETWORK ADS

All Search Network ads appear on Google.com search Engine results pages (SERP). These are the most common types of ad on AdWords. They work basically the same whether they are targeting the general public, local areas around your store, people who use mobile phones, people who use mobile apps, previous visitors to your website or people who use flip-phones.

Basic Search Ads

Full instructions for setting up your first ad are provided in Chapter 4, Getting Started. It is important you work through your first ad meticulously, so you learn the basics and understand how the many pieces of an AdWords campaign work together.

Setting Up Basic Search Ads

When you are ready to setup your next campaign, use these steps (Note that AdWords prompts and terms are in italics):

1. **Click on the *all online campaign* menu at left.**

2. **To setup a campaign, click on the *campaign* tab.**

3. **Click on the red +*campaign* button above the *statistics table*.**

4. **From the drop-down menu, click *Search Network only*.** Enter the appropriate information or options for your campaign for the following fields.

   - *Campaign name*: use a name that helps you remember what the goal is of this campaign.

180

- *Campaign type* should be *Search Network only*. Click the circle beside *All Features*.

- Ignore the follow prompts used with Google Shopping campaigns:
  — Merchant identifier.
  — Shopping settings.

- If you have a campaign you want to copy, click *load settings from existing campaign*. This can be a real time-saver.

- *Network*: unclick *include search partners*. Once you are converting visitors you can include Search Partners.

- *Devices*: leave it set to *all*. You can change it later if you want to restrict your ad to certain types of mobile devices.

- *Location*: click *edit* and on the next screen *advance search* to specify your desired locations. Enter your market in as granular detail as practical.

  For example, rather than use U.S., enter each state where you sell products. This lets you get performance information by state and, later, you can adjust bids by state as you learn more about your audience.

- *Location options (advanced)*: click *edit*. Select *people in your targeted areas* if you do not want to advertise internationally to people looking for products in the U.S. Otherwise, select *people in, or who show interest in my targeted location* to show ads to people everywhere—regardless of where they reside, or select *people who show interest in my targeted area* to show ads only to people outside your targeted location (as in the case of a hotel advertising to people who do not live near the hotel).

- *Language*: use *English*, the default, or select your own language.

- *Shopping channels*: ignore this prompt. It is used for Google Shopping campaigns.

- *Bidding and bids*: indicate whether you want AdWords to bid on your behalf or you want to manually set your bids.

  A prudent approach is to use *automatic bidding* to gather data about your costs-per-click before taking on the responsibility of *manual bidding*.

- Budget: enter the amount for your daily budget.

  Divide your monthly budget by 30.4 to determine the daily amount. AdWords multiplies your daily budget by 30.4 to get the maximum budget for your campaign per month. The costs for some days may go over the daily budget.

- *Delivery method*: indicate whether you want your ad to appear *evenly during* the day or if you want it to appear on an *accelerated basis*—as often as possible as early as possible.

Start with *evenly* to see how well your products sell at different times of the day. You can change it later.

Accelerated is used (1) for experiments when you want to see results quickly and (2) when you want to "get the word out" for a particular event or promotion.

5. **Advanced options are optional.**

Use any *advanced options* appropriate for your campaign.

- *Schedule:*
  — Enter a start and stop date.
  — Ad schedule: if you want to restrict your ad to certain hours of the day, click *edit* next to *ad scheduling* and then *+create custom schedule*. You can specify the exact hours of the day when you want your ad to show.

- *Ad delivery:*
  — Use the default, *optimize for clicks*, so your best ad shows most often.
  — Once you start use *Conversion Tracking*, the default becomes *optimize for conversions*, so the ad with the most conversions shows most often.
  — If you are running an experiment, the *rotation* options lets you rotate your ads evenly and for an extended period of time.

- *Experiment*: (See Step 13: Use AdWords Experiments to Improve Your Ads and Save Money, p. 170, for details on setting up an experiment.)

- *IP exclusions*: click *edit* to enter any IP addresses you want to exclude. Exclude your own company's network to prevent your staff from skewing results.

- *Tracking URL for dynamic links*: this is used with *Dynamic Search Ads* and *Google Shopping* campaigns if you use third-party tracking software.

- *Dynamic Search Ads*: this is used only with *Dynamic Search Ads*.

Click *save and continue*. Your Campaign Level options are now complete!

AdWords takes you immediately to the ad group setup screen. (If AdWords does not take you to the ad group setup screen, click on the *ad group tab*.)

6. **At the ad group** setup screen, enter the following:

- *Ad group*: enter a descriptive name. Including the type of product and the keyword theme is a good practice.
- *Create an ad*: click the circle beside *text*.

- Write your ad by entering:
  - A headline hawking your product.
  - Two description lines.
  - A display URL, which can be a simplified version of the real URL, using your domain, and a real destination URL using your domain name.

For example:

Mastering AdWords

www.multiplanetmarketing.com

AdWords Are Harder Than You Think!

Buy It Today to Make More Money.

- *Keyword*: put your best keyword in brackets (for an exact match) in the input box. You can broaden your match type later.
- *Ad group bid*: input your *default bid*.
- Click *save ad group*.

7. **Verify your ad.** Go to the *tools* tab and click *ad preview* (or use www.Google.com/AdPreview). If your ad appears, your ad is setup.

- If it does not appear, Google may not have given editorial approval yet. Go to the *ad tab* and check the ad for a message from AdWords, in red letters. You may need to wait 24 to 48 hours for Google to approve your ad.
- For details on gaining Google ad approval, search "Advertising principles" in AdWords Help. Correct any problems and repeat this task if necessary to gain Google approval.

8. **Add *ad extensions* to your campaign, ad group or ad.** For the desired campaign, ad group or ad tab, click the *ad extension* tab and then the *view:* button to the extension you want to add. (See Add Ad Extensions to Your Search Ads for details about *ad extensions*.)

- Repeat the previous steps for as many *ad extensions* as appropriate.

Monitoring Basic Search Network Ads

The following are tips for monitoring and improving your AdWords performance. Monitoring your account is important, not only to keep it performing at its lowest cost and peak revenues, but also to keep Google happy. Account monitoring is one of the items Google considers in determining your *quality score*. Google penalizes you if you are not interested in the success of your ads.

Use these tips to monitor your account and keep it at optimal performance. These tips are listed in priority order to guide you through a thorough review of your ad, from your conversion rate and ROI to your impressions.

A full review of your campaigns each month is prudent. You do not need to perform every step every time you look at your ads during the month. As you get more fluent, reviews will take less time. According to *Wordstream*, a major Boston AdWords agency with access to thousands of ads, only 1 percent of businesses review their ads monthly, so you can easily outrun most competitors.

Your ads must evolve to stay current. No market is stagnant. Over time, new products enter the market and other products wane in popularity; advertisers bid aggressively, throttle back or change focus, and searchers' tastes and needs change.

As a best practice, a professional AdWords marketer should experiment and freshen ads constantly, and a business owner should check ads weekly and review them monthly.

The following steps provide a well-rounded view of your campaign.

1. **Set a specific reporting period and include the comparison for the *previous period*.**
    *   Click the *date selector* menu on the top right corner of the page.
    *   Select the time period you want to analyze, either this week or this month. (Be aware that complete data for yesterday is not available until 3 p.m. PT today.)
    *   Click the *compare* button at the bottom of the date selector and click *previous period*.
    *   Click *apply*.

2. **Verify your ad is running.** While it is tempting to enter one of your keywords into Google.com to see if your new ad is running, do not yield to the temptation. Your search counts as an impression, and your ad may not show because of the competition.

    If you want to see your ad as it appears on a search page, use the *ad preview and diagnostic* feature under *tools* on the main menu. Enter a keyword and AdWords creates a page showing your ad without incrementing your impressions total.

    To determine definitively if your ad is appearing, go to the ad tab and check the *impression share (impr. share)* to see how many impressions your campaign received.

- If the column for *impression share* is not showing, click the *campaign* tab, then the *columns* button above the *statistics table*, choose *customize columns* from the drop-down menu, click *competitive metrics*, add *impr. share lost IS* (budget), *lost IS* (rank) and *exact match IS* and then click *save*.

- Further, click *attributes* and add *quality score*.

If your *impression share* is a positive number, your ad is showing. If your *impression share* is zero, your ad is not appearing and you need to fix it.

If your ad is not running, check these possibilities:

a. The bank declined your credit card or your credit card expired. Go to the *billing* tab and check the status. Update information as necessary.

b. Your ad is still *under review* or Google disapproved it. Go to the *ad* tab. The words "*under review*" or "*disapproved*" should appear next to the ad.

- Google emails you when your ad is disapproved (check your spam and junk folders, if you do not readily find it). Click the speech bubble in the *status* column of the *statistics table* to see why your ad was disapproved.

Under some circumstances, such as your website being down, a *re-submit my campaign for review* option appears. Use it, if appropriate.

If you believe Google should approve your ad, you can ask for a review by a Google employee. Disapprovals often happen with unusual product names, such as Campus SaVE Act (capitalization) and the *Ike Live!* show (italics and exclamation point). Google can override the rules.

Do not edit your ad until you are confident your change meets Google's requirements. Once you save your new ad it is immediately submitted to Google for approval. A history of disapproved ads can get your AdWords account suspended.

Click the pencil icon to edit your ad.

- To check ads *en masse*, add the *policy details* column to the *statistics table*. At the *All Online Campaign* Level click *column—customize columns*, then clicking *attributes* and add *policy details*.

- Contact Google if your ad is not reviewed after 24 hours. Google responds to user questions. (Call 1–866–2GOOGLE [1–866–246–6453] between 9 a.m. and 8 p.m. EST, Monday through Friday or enter "Contact Google" into AdWords Help to initiate a chat, email or video call.)

c. If you have a *prepayment billing account* (a legacy feature not available to new accounts), your budget may have run out. Other ads may have used your entire budget.

d. A single day where your ad did not appear may be the result of over-delivery on a prior day. AdWords works to stay within your monthly budget, but takes advantage of heavy traffic days. That means some days your ad is over-delivered and may show as not running in the ad preview.

e. You are using both AdWords Express and AdWords, and your AdWords Express ad is showing. AdWords shows only one ad from your account for any search.

3. **Verify your *ad extensions* are appearing.** Ad extensions affect your quality score, which affects the number of impressions you receive. It is very important that *ad extensions*, especially sitelinks and callouts, are up-to-date and showing.

To see the status of your *ad extensions*, go to the *keyword* tab and then click the *ad extensions* tab. All *ad extensions* appear, even if no clicks or impressions occurred. Recall that your *ad extensions* must be approved by Google before they appear.

To fix a missing ad extension, go to *ad extensions, view* <specific extension>.

- Add or re-add extensions to make sure you are using as many extensions as appropriate for your ad.

- Update sitelinks and callouts, if appropriate. Make sure they still fit with the ad. Do not let them get out of date; Google may stop running your ad.

When you edit an ad extension, AdWords removes the original ad extension (but keeps the performance data available) and adds the new one (starting the performance data at zero).

Check back in a day or two to make sure the ad extension is running.

4. **Verify that your ad is bringing buyers to your website.** You must determine if your ad is bringing buyers, not just visitors, to your website. You may need to ask people in Sales or Accounting how well the products are selling until you have enough clicks, consistently enough, to activate Conversion Tracking, which tracks online sales for you. Without sales information, you cannot maximize your AdWords performance.

If visitors are not buying, you are losing money. You do not need to increase your impressions or clicks if your visitors are not converting (e.g., buying, signing up, etc.).

To convert visitors to buyers, you must improve your landing page. If the number of buyers is lower than the number of clicks your ad

FIGURE 5.1 Ad extensions

received, you have room for improving your landing page. Review the quality score for your keywords. This shows you how AdWords rates your landing page.

With regard to landing pages, some AdWords professionals argue that small changes bring small improvements, while big changes bring big improvements. These pros often use experiments to compare landing pages.

Consider these ideas:

a. Change your landing page to sell only the product you are advertising. Remove all other products, so visitors do not need to make a choice.

b. Streamline your landing page. Remove any unnecessary information. The more information, the more indecisive visitors become.

c. Move the "buy" order form to the top of the page.

d. Improve your offer. Offer free shipping, a two-for-one sale, discounted price, free gift, free trial or a free audit.

e. Add testimonials and professional credentials, such as awards and memberships in professional organizations. For example, "BBB member," "rated #1 by PC World" or "in business since 1990."

f. Add statistics. For example, "over 1,000,000 sold."

Improving your landing page is a sure way to improve your overall AdWords performance. Improving your landing page should increase the number of buyers, and increasing the number of buyers will increase your *quality score*. In turn, increasing your quality score increases your ad rank, impressions and potential visitors. Your landing page is the heart of good AdWords performance.

187

Once you consistently have 15 conversions a month, turn on Conversion Tracking. Conversion Tracking takes your campaign to a higher level of capability.

5. **Verify your ad is receiving clicks (or maintaining its volume—if not increasing the number of clicks received since last month).**

   According to WordStream, 85 percent of the ads in the number one position have a click-through rate of only 7 percent. By contrast, the very best advertisers in the number one ad position have click-through rates of 24.01 percent. Such ads are so rare, however, some call them "unicorns." Unicorns require full-time, continuous experimentation with landing pages, ad copy, bids and market definitions.

   The chart that follows presents data about the CTR for ads in different ad positions (e.g., the top 15 percent, the top 5 percent and the top 1 percent). Median refers to the "middle" range of CTRs. Thus, for ads in position number one, 50 percent of all CTRs are above or below 6.69 percent.

   Data from the same agency indicates that norms differ widely by industry.

   If your ad is not enticing people to click, you can:

   a. **Buy traffic.** Raise your bids high enough that you get every available impression and, thus, get more visitors. This is an expensive way to get clicks, but it works. It does not necessarily increase the number of buyers or revenues.

Position	Best 15%	Best 5%	Best 1%
1.0 - 1.5	14.29%	18.88%	24.01%
1.5 - 2.0	8.82%	11.40%	14.48%
2.0 - 2.5	7.16%	9.20%	11.52%
2.5 - 3.0	6.18%	8.12%	10.33%
3.0 - 3.5	4.61%	5.91%	7.40%
3.5 - 4.0	3.93%	4.98%	6.18%
4.0 - 4.5	3.55%	4.67%	5.95%
4.5 - 5.0	3.21%	4.15%	5.22%
5.0 - 5.5	2.47%	3.11%	3.83%
5.5 - 6.0	2.44%	3.06%	3.77%

FIGURE 5.2 Click-through rate norms from a major agency

Conversion Rates by Industry					
	All Accounts	**Ecommerce**	**Legal**	**B2B**	**Finance**
Top 10%	11.45%	6.25%	6.46%	11.70%	24.28%
Top 25%	0.05%	3.71%	4.12%	4.31%	11.19%
Median Conversions Rate	2.35%	1.84%	2.07%	2.23%	5.01%

FIGURE 5.3 CTR norms by industry

b. **Improve your ad.** Use the experiment function to compare different ad copy.

To improve your ad, consider these suggestions and refer to Step 5: Write Attention-Grabbing Ad Copy, p. 142.

— **Change the flow of your page.** Move the order form to the top of the page.

— **Change the benefits you tout.** Look for benefits your competitors are not touting (if they are viable for your product). Re-describe your product.

— **Change the product feature you advertise.** Look for features your competitors are not advertising.

— **Change your adjectives.** Look for words your competitors are not using. Use the words your prospect uses (e.g., "stylish," "sophisticated," "cool," "rad" and "awesome" all mean the same thing, but speak to different prospects).

— **Focus on a sub-set of buyers.** Consider selling to novices, senior citizens, luxury seekers, mainstreamers, value seekers or some other subset of your market.

— **Sweeten your offering.** Add a freebie, such as "coupon with order" or "2-for-1" sale. Add money-savers, such as "free shipping" or "in-store returns." Add a stronger call to action ("Buy Today"). Express urgency, such as "limited time," "click now," etc.

— **Include product credentials.** Use facts. "Over 1 million sold." "The original. . ." "As seen on TV." Use cachet, such as an endorsement from a celebrity.

— **Differentiate your company.** Mention your success. "20 years experience," "Oldest Retailer in Pennsylvania," "Since 1925."

— **Update your language.** For example, replace "integrated marketing" with "cross-media marketing." Invent your own buzzwords. (Politicians do it all the time.)

— **Switch to lead generation tactics.** Offer something informational to get leads, rather than sales. White papers, e-books, videos, etc., work well for this. Then follow up via email where you have more space to advertise.

— **Change your tone.** Lighten up, with words that are more whimsical. "Bend it like Beckham Pretzels." Evoke desire: "Must-Have Summer Sandals," or "Fierce Halloween Masks." Evoke fear: "Do Not Be Caught Without Batteries."

— **Focus your efforts elsewhere.** Rather than work to improve a poorly-performing ad, you can decrease the maximum cost-per-click bid so you pay less for the keywords. This frees money for more productive keywords and makes this keyword less expensive to use (which in turn raises its return on investment).

To edit your ad, click the appropriate ad group under your campaign on the *all online campaign* menu. Click the *ad* tab and click the pencil icon next to your ad.

When you edit an ad, AdWords removes the original ad (but keeps the performance data available) and adds the new one (starting with performance at zero).

6. **Verify that your ad is improving or maintaining its level of impressions.** Click the small +sign (⊞) next to *Impressions Share* to see the number of impressions you received last period versus this period. (You should be comparing last period to this period.)

A sudden drop in impressions is not necessarily a problem but it can be the symptom of a problem. You need to determine if the drop is caused by seasonal activity, by the introduction of a new competitor or by more aggressive bidding by a competitor.

a. **Determine whether your ad is, in fact, receiving a lower *percentage* of impressions (rather than just fewer impressions).**

On the *ad* tab, check the *impression share (impr. share)* to see how many impressions your campaign received. Click the +sign (⊞) next to *impressions share* to see the number of impressions you received last period.

(If the column for *impression share* is not showing, click the *campaign* tab, the *customize columns* button, then *competitive metrics*, add *impr. share lost IS* (budget), *lost IS* (rank) and *exact match IS* and then click *save*.)

b. **If your ad has, in fact, dropped in impressions, determine why.**

— **Are fewer people searching for your product?**

(1) If your impression share percentage is close to the share you received last period but the number of impressions is lower, it means fewer people are searching for the product. This often happens with seasonal merchandise or services.

It also happens when (1) a new brand or a "disruptive-technology" product enters the market, as when the "iPhone" displaced the "cell phone" or (2) a new search term gains popularity, as when "Obamacare" became a term for "healthcare."

(2) Another way to find out if fewer people are searching for your product is to use the *auction insight report* to compare your percentage of impressions to other advertisers. Run the report for this period and last period and download them.

To create an *auction insight report*, click the *detail* button on the ad group tab and under *auction insights*, click *all*. Run the report for this period and for last period. Download them and compare the number. If your impression percentage is less, determine if it is because of new or more aggressive competition.

— **Are your competitors gaining market share?**

(1) On the *auction insight report*, note the names of any competitors that outrank you in number of impressions, especially those that did not appear in the previous period. These competitors may be bidding more competitively or may be using keywords you have overlooked.

Use the *keyword planner*, under the *tools* tab, to see suggested keywords for your competitors. Enter your competitor's URL into the *planner tool* and identify any keywords that you could apply to your product. (Be sure to use the URL that is for a webpage with a product similar to yours, not the homepage.) Download the report and compare their keywords to the ones you use.

Add any keyword that has significant impressions and applies to your product (and fits the theme of your ad group).

Once you are comfortable that you have the right set of keywords, move on to the next step.

c. **Improve your impression share.**

If you are losing impression share because of competitive pressure you can take one of two strategies:

• Strategy one: you can do research and (1) improve your keywords, (2) adjust your bids and/or (3) adjust your budget. This is a time-consuming, insightful and economical way to proceed. If this is your choice, proceed to the next step.

- Strategy two: if your budget permits, you can simply buy impressions. That is, you can raise your bids high enough that you receive a greater percentage of the *impression share*. This is the most expensive way to improve ad performance, but it is a great time saver.
  — If you use *automatic bidding*, you can raise the *CPC limit* for the campaign. This lets AdWords raise bids as needed to bring more impressions.
  — If you use *automatic bidding*, you can switch your campaign to manual bidding.
  — If you use *manual bidding* for Search ads, you can raise the *max CPC* for the ad group or the ad. More economically, you can raise the *max CPC* for your best converting keywords and offset those raises by lowering the bid for less productive keywords (or pausing those keywords).

7. **Evaluate your keywords.** If your *impression share* is falling, you may need to improve your keywords and/or your bids.

    a. Verify that all your keywords are running. Even though AdWords marks a keyword as *eligible*, it may not be in use. As a precaution, make sure your keywords are running.

    Go to the *keyword* tab, click the *details* button and click *keyword diagnosis*. Review the *status* column to see if any keywords need special attention.

    b. Determine if your keywords are matching appropriately with search terms.

    Go to the *keyword* tab, click the *details* button and select *search terms— all*. Review the search terms that brought visitors to your landing page. If a search term is not appropriate for your ad, add that term to the *negative keyword* list.
    — Be sure the keyword column shows on the report. Add it by clicking *column—customize columns, attributes* and *keyword*.
    — If your *negative keywords* applies to all the ad groups, use the *campaign—negative keywords* panel at the bottom of the screen to avoid setting the same keyword up for multiple ad groups or campaigns.
    — If you have large numbers of inappropriate matches for a keyword, switch your keyword to a narrower match (i.e., switch from broad-match to exact match).

c. Finally, review any messages in the *status* column related to bids. Common messages are:

— *Your keyword bid is below first page*. Being on the first page of Google search results is important because most clicks take place there. When this situation arises, consider these suggestions:

(1) Do not raise the bid on that keyword just yet. Focus on other, better performing keywords that bring in buyers before working to improve marginal keywords.

(2) If you are sure this keyword is worth the investment, raise your bid to the amount needed to appear on the first page. It is possible that you will not pay that full amount, so check the keyword in a couple of days. (Use a *label* such as "too expensive?" to remind you to check the keyword on your next visit to the page.)

(3) If you are sure you want to always be on the first page, consider using *automated rules* to raise your bids when your keyword falls below the first page.

(4) If it is imperative that your ads stay on the first page or at the top of the first page, consider switching to a *flexible bid strategy for page location*. (See Flexible Bid Strategies (CPC) under Key Concept 2: AdWords Supports Several Bidding Models to Maximize Your Budget, p. 88.)

(5) Improve the *quality score* for a good keyword.
On the *Keyword* tab, sort your keywords by *lost IS (rank)* percentage. The keywords with the lowest *lost percentage* are your best keywords and, if any have low quality scores, your landing page is not using the words your visitors expect to see. You should improve your landing page wording. Alternatively, you may want to make your keyword more descriptive and, thus, more relevant. This can raise your *quality score* and, in turn, your ad rank and ad position. For example, "black vintage leather jacket" may bring fewer impressions but more visitors (and at the same CPC) than does "leather jacket."

(6) Raise your bid 10 percent for your best keywords. If any of your best keywords have a high quality score, consider raising the bids for those keywords. You can use the *bid simulator tool* to determine how much to raise the bid on this keyword. Click the graph icon below the bid on the *statistics table* to invoke the bid simulator and see AdWords' recommendations. (See Bid Simulator/Traffic Estimator Tool under Tools and Reports for more information on the bid simulator.) Select

one of the recommendations AdWords provides. Alternatively you can raise your bid equal to the amount in the *est. first page bid* column or the *est. top of page bid* column.

Pause a keyword if it is not receiving clicks and its quality score is low. Such keywords drag down your overall quality score.

— *Your keyword(s) is not used by searchers often enough.* You can leave the keyword as is if you expect the term to gain in popularity, as happens with new brand names and new products. Alternatively, you can:

(1) Change the keyword from an exact-match type to a partial-match type to pick up searches for the same phrase but with the words in a different order.

(2) Change a partial-match type to a broad-match type to pick up searches using your keyword within other phrases. This can help you find long-tail keywords and new phrases, but watch the broad match keywords carefully. They can match to search terms you never considered and do not want. Add those unwanted phrases to your negative keyword list.

(3) Pause the keyword as not worth your time to nurture.

8. **If your ads cost too much. Consider these ways to reduce costs.**

   a. **Adjust your bids for mobile phones or tablets for the ad group or the ad.**

      — Compare the traffic for different devices to see which one most buyers (or visitors) use. Click the *ad group (or ads)* tab, click *segments* and select *device* from the drop-down menu. The *statistics table* shows data broken down by desktop, mobile and tablet.

      — Similarly, run an *auction insight report* to determine if your ads receive roughly the same percentage of traffic from different devices as your competitors. Click the *ad group (or ad)* tab, click the *details* button and *auction insights—all.* next, click *segment* and select *device* from the drop-down menu. The *statistics table* shows data for your competitors broken down by desktop, mobile and tablet.

      — Ensure your bids for mobile, desktop and tablet devices bear a relationship to their value. Google calls this process "equalizing your bids." To do this, divide the revenue generated by the mobile device by the revenue generated by desktop and tablet devices. For example:

$$\frac{\$10,900 \text{ in Mobile Ad revenue}}{\$12,100 \text{ in desktop and tablet revenue}} = 0.90$$

Next, subtract 1 from the result. This gives you the difference in value between mobile and desktop/tablet devices. In this example, the value of a Mobile Ad is *0.10 less* than a desktop ad.

$$0.90 - 1.0 = -0.10$$

Finally, multiply the difference by 100. Don't lose track of your minus sign if you have one!

$$-0.10 \times 100 = -10\%$$

Enter that percentage as a *bid adjustment* for mobile devices. (See Add Bid Adjustments for Devices, Locations, Ad Schedules and Targeting Methods for more information.)

b. **Adjust your bids for *location* for the ad group.**

Click on the *ad group* tab, click the *dimension* tab and select *geography* from the drop-down list.

Once you determine a need for a *bid adjustment*, see Add Bid Adjustments for Devices, Locations, Ad Schedules and Targeting Methods for more information.)

c. **Adjust your bids for *time periods* for the ad group.**

Click on the *ad group* tab, click the *segment* button and select *time* from the drop-down list along with the *day of the week*. Determine if certain days or time periods do not bring you buyers (or visitors). Lower your bid for those times to save money. This may also improve your *quality score* slightly.

Similarly, run an *auction insight report* to determine if your ads receive roughly the same percentage of traffic from different devices as your competitors.

Click the *ad group* tab, click the *details* button and the *auction insights— all*. Next, click *segment* and select *time* from the drop-down menu. The report shows data for your competitors broken down by *time of day*. Determine if your competitors are grabbing impressions when you are not, or vice versa.

(See Add Bid Adjustments for Devices, Locations, Ad Schedules and Targeting Methods, p. 276, for detailed instructions.)

d. **Consider narrowing your geographic market.**

Click on the *ad group* tab, click the *segment* button and select *geographic*. Determine if certain regions are not bringing you buyers. You may want to eliminate those areas and focus on areas where more buyers reside.

e. **Clean your keywords.** Ensure irrelevant search terms are not evoking your ads by adding irrelevant terms to *negative keywords*.

Go to the *keyword* tab, check the box next to your best keyword(s), click *details* and view the *search terms* that evoked your ad. If irrelevant keywords are evoking your ad, check the box next to them and click "*add to negative keywords.*"

f. **Cull your keywords.** On average, advertises sell only one in 500 clicks. Eliminate all keywords that cost more than 1/500th of the profit you make on a product.

g. **Switch bidding options.** Consider a *flexible bid strategy* such as *target ad spend* for lower performing ads, ad groups and campaigns. In short, let AdWords work on your behalf.

(See *Flexible Bid Strategies* under Key Concept 2: Bidding Strategies and Bidding Models, p. 81.)

h. **Focus your efforts.** Drop poor performing ads or ad groups in favor of others that are succeeding better.

9. **Evaluate your budget.** Now that you have improved your campaign from the bottom up, evaluate your budget.

a. If your daily budget is depleted early in the day, AdWords places a message next to your campaign. In response, you should evaluate your budget.

On the *campaigns* tab, check the lost impression share (*lost IS*) to see if you have missed opportunities to show ads. If you are missing substantial numbers of impressions, you can:

— Increase your budget. To compute the needed budget, multiply the *avg. CPC* by the number of impressions you lost during the period you selected. This determines approximately how much additional money you need to spend to obtain the maximum available number of clicks. Divide the amount by the number of days in the period you selected to obtain the amount to add to your *daily budget*.
If your ads are profitable (See Step 10: Evaluate Your Profitability, p. 159) and you want more clicks, raise your daily budget.
If your ads are not profitable, you do not need to pay more money for unproductive clicks—leave the budget alone.

— Use the budget simulation feature to see what AdWords recommends as your budget. Go to the *campaign* tab and click the graph icon in the *Budget* column.

— Again, if your ads are profitable (See Step 10: Evaluate Your Profitability, p. 159) and you want more clicks, raise your daily budget.

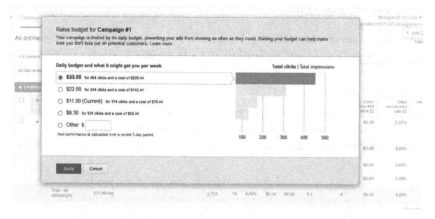

FIGURE 5.4 Campaign budget recommendations

— If your ads are not profitable, you do not need to lose more
money—leave the budget alone.

b. **You meet your daily budget almost every day.**

Review your *impression share* **to determine if you are missing
opportunities.** (Click the *campaigns* tab, click the *columns* button
above the *statistics table*, choose *customize columns* from the drop-down
menu, click *competitive metrics*, add *impr. share lost IS* (budget), *lost IS*
(rank) and *exact match IS* and then click *save*.)

If you are missing opportunities, use the *view recommended
budget tool* **to get AdWords' recommendations for your
budget.** Go to the *settings* tab and scroll down to the *bidding and budget*
section and click *view rec. budget*.

Based on the *recommended budget* **and the** *impression share*
data, you can:

— Increase your daily budget.
— Lower your bid on your better ads or keywords; your ad position
may drop, but you could pay less for your traffic and stretch your
budget to cover the day.
— Consider switching lower-performing ads, ad groups or campaigns
to the *flexible bid strategy*—*return on ad spend* or —*target ad spend*.
(See Flexible Bid Strategies [CPC] in Key Concept 2, p. 88, for
more details.) Carve out a small part of your budget for these ads,
leaving the bulk of your budget for your best performing ads, and
let AdWords manage them.

Dynamic Search Ads

Dynamic Search Ads (DSAs) **let you advertise hundreds of online products without writing individual ads for each product.** DSAs serve as a reminder to searchers that your store has the product they seek. Thus, DSAs build brand awareness, as well as bring traffic to your website.

DSAs **are a good choice for you if you offer many products, every product has its own page and you run frequently changing sales and seasonal promotions.** Many major retailers use *DSAs* for their e-commerce sites.

- *DSAs* are not a good fit for unique or customizable products, since many search terms may only partly describe your product and, consequently, leave searchers disappointed. Search Network ads where you describe the product in more detail are more effective.

- You can specify that all your webpages are eligible to support *DSAs* or you can specify a subset of webpages based on a product category, a URL, the HTML page title or a set of words that appear in the content.

- *DSAs* do not compete with other search ads you are running within the same Ad Group with one exception: when price and match-type are equal between a *DSA* and a regular *Search Ad*, the ad with the higher quality score is used. (Note that AdWords treats DSA keywords as broad or partial match-types.)

With DSA ads, you must continually build your negative keyword list, so only the most relevant search terms trigger your ad. In contrast, DSAs can help you find keywords you may never have considered.
In a nutshell, here's how DSAs work.

- When a searcher enters a query, AdWords determines whether you have a webpage using the query term or a similar term in the URL. If so, AdWords treats the words in your URL like keywords and enters your ad in the auction.

- If you win the auction, AdWords constructs a headline using the searcher's query term and adds the generic description you provided along with your URL.

- You use *keyword insertions* to make the searcher's own query term appear in your ad and, presumably, make the searcher more receptive to your ad.

- If you enter a coding parameter into your designation URL, AdWords collects information about the parameter. You can use multiple parameters, including search term, landing page or match type (among many other parameters) that trigger your ad and webpage. (See Step 6, p. 201)

Using Keyword Insertions

DSA ads let you format a word or phrase in your ad text as if it were HTML code. The formatting lets AdWords know you want to replace the formatted word with the keyword triggering your ad. You can insert the HTML code any place in your ad—headline, description lines or URL.

The HTML code must follow this format:

{keyword:default-text},
where the "default-text" is a generic keyword.

For example: if your keywords are dark coffee, rich coffee, Kona coffee and Columbian coffee, set your ad to look like this:

Your	Big {keyword:coffee} Sale
setup:	*www.coffeekatcher.com/coffee*
	Now through May 1
	Free Shipping. Try it today!

When your ad shows, the {keyword:coffee} is replaced with the keyword that triggered your ad:

Searcher's query:	robust coffee
Ad shows query word:	**Big robust coffee sale**
	www.coffeekatcher.com/darkcoffee
	Now through May 1
	Free Shipping. Try it today!

If the searcher's term is too long, AdWords uses your default-text:

Searcher's query:	Rich, dark, almond-flavored Kona Coffee
Ad shows query word:	**Big coffee sale**
	www.coffeekatcher.com/darkcoffee
	Now through May 1
	Free Shipping. Try it today!

AdWords determines how to capitalize the keyword based on your capitalization of the word "keyword." In essence, AdWords shows your default-text just as you capitalized "keyword." For example, where the searcher enters rich, dark coffee, your ad uses the rich, dark coffee query, capitalized according to these rules:

Format	How to Treat the Keyword Phrase	You Enter:	Ad looks like:
keyword	no caps	{keyword:coffee}	Big rich, dark coffee Sale
Keyword	cap the first letter of the first word	{Keyword:coffee}	Big Rich dark coffee Sale
KeyWord or KEYWORD	cap the first letter of each word	[KeyWord:coffee] Or {KEYWORD:coffee}	Big Rich Dark Coffee Sale
KEYword	cap the whole first word	{KEYword:coffee}	Big RICH dark coffee Sale
KEYWord	cap the whole first word and the first letter of all others	{KEYWord:coffee}	Big RICH Dark Coffee Sale

Once your *DSA* runs, you can use performance data in the *statistics table* to refine your DSAs. For example, you can (1) change your target from "all webpages" to just the product categories that searchers seem to like, (2) add certain words in the title or content of your webpage to resonate better with viewers or (3) include certain words in your display URLs (or actually change your destination URLs) to reflect searcher queries as well as create more targeted ad copy.

Setting Up Dynamic Search Ads

Note: You may need a programmer's help to create *DSA*s.
   To create a *DSA*, do the following:

1.   Create a separate *Search Network* campaign just for DSAs.

2.   As your campaign type, select *Search Network* and *Dynamic Search Ads*.

3.   With regard to bidding, try *automatic bidding* first. Google claims *DSA*s can improve click-throughs by 10 percent with less cost. See if it works for you.

4.   Enter your domain under the advanced option prompt: *Dynamic Search Ads*.

You can create one ad group for your entire website or one ad group and ad for each set of products. At the combined Ad group/Ad Level screen, do the following:

5. Enter your generic description (two lines). Your copy should relate to all your products, so be very generic. For example, "See our wide selection. Free shipping and delivery."

6. If you want to have each webpage tracked separately, enter the following *ValueTrack* parameter (i.e., a word the HTML code is programmed to understand) with your domain:

   - Add a slash, a question mark, the variable and the variable's programming name enclosed in brackets. Note the brackets around the HTML word.

     For example:

       www.multiplanetmarketing.com/?url={lpurl}

       Asks AdWords to capture the landing page URL and include it in performance data in Google Analytics.

   - ValueTrack results are viewed in Google Analytics, not AdWords.

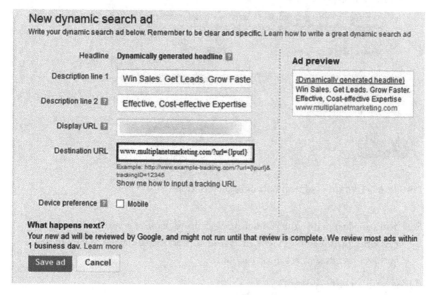

FIGURE 5.5 Dynamic Search Ad with ValueTrack destination URL

   - A number of HTML code words (called parameters) are available. Search in AdWords Help for "Track clicks with ValueTrack."

7. Set *add all webpages* as your dynamic ad target unless you want to designate a certain subset of pages. You can identify the pages you want to breakout using up to three of these parameters:

a. One of the *categories* defined by AdWords after running your ad.

b. A *URL* (usually a URL that covers a set of services or products)

c. The *page_title* embedded in your webpage code (it appears at the upper-left top line of your webpage).

d. The *page_content*, meaning a word or string of words that appear somewhere on your webpage(s).

You can use up to three of these criteria within an ad group, but be aware that a website must match all your criteria to be eligible for the *Dynamic Search Ad*.

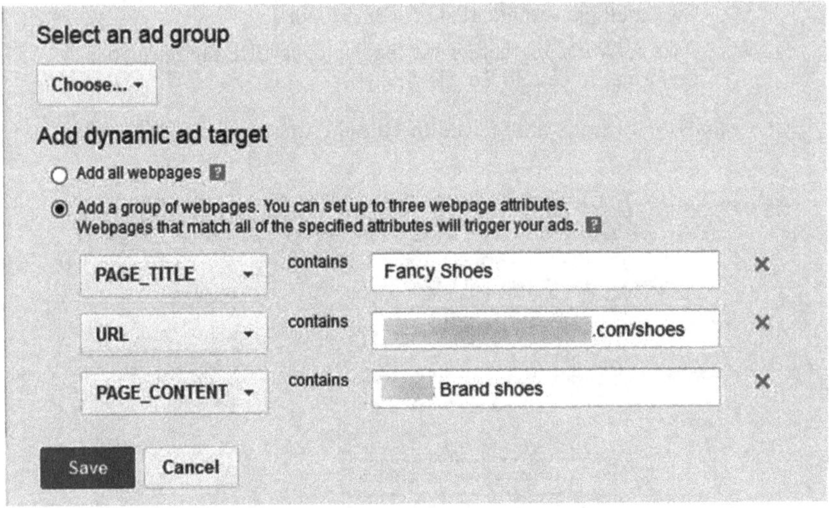

FIGURE 5.6 Dynamic search sub-category options

8. You can designate your Dynamic Search Ad as *mobile preferred*, to have it run only on mobile devices. It is a best practice to have a *mobile preferred* and *non-preferred* version of each ad.

After you create your DSA,

9. You can (and should) add any appropriate *ad extensions* such as address, phone number, sitelinks, Google +1, etc., by going to the Ad Extension tab.

10. You can apply *bid adjustments* to increase or decrease your max CPC for different devices and/or different locations. (See Add Bid Adjustments for Devices, Locations, Ad Schedules and Targeting Methods for more about *bid adjustments*.)

Monitoring Dynamic Search Ads

Dynamic Search Ads are essentially Search Ads using a headline that includes the searcher's query terms. Their campaign, ad group and ad options are the same as for other Search Network ads.

Refer to Growing Basic Search Network Ads and Monitoring Basic Search Network Ads for suggestions for improving your ad.

Local Ads—Google My Business

Google My Business is an organic search listing. However, because it figures into your AdWords results, it is a best practice to set it up for your business.

Setting Up a Google My Business Listing

To setup your local business on Google My Business, do the following:

1. Make sure you meet Google quality guidelines. (Search in Support.Google.com for "Local business information quality guidelines.")

2. Create a Google Account and a Gmail address (at accounts.google.com/signup), if you do not have one.

3. Go to Google My Business (www.google.com/business).

4. Indicate whether you are a storefront or a service business.

5. Select your business' name and address from the drop-down list. If it is not there, enter the information when prompted.

6. Click submit.

7. Verify your business. Opt to:

   a. Receive a postcard from Google containing a verification code you enter into your dashboard on Google My Business.

   b. If you have a pre-existing Google account, receive a phone call with a verification code you enter into your dashboard on Google My Business.

   If your programmer has verified your website using Webmaster Tools, your account is instantly verified.

   c. Make any final changes to your information.

8. Click *Done editing.*

Monitoring Google My Business Listing

Google My Business does not require frequent monitoring. However, to get the most out of the listing, you can use it as your social media conduit to your following by posting a daily status.

Local Ads—AdWords Express

AdWords Express is the no-expertise-needed version of AdWords, so setup and monitoring is simple—and limited.

Setting Up AdWords Express Local Ads

AdWords Express ad setup has only six prompts:

1. Select your city, state, or country.

2. Select the product or service you want to advertise. (Select the specific category from the ones AdWords offers.)

3. Enter your headline (25 characters) and two description lines (35 characters each).

4. AdWords fills in your website URL.

5. Enter your daily budget.

6. Preview and approve your ad.

Monitoring AdWords Express Local Ads

AdWords Express ads are basically Search Network ads, but with limited capabilities. To make the best use of them, monitor them in AdWords. The *AdWords Express* screen provides a link to AdWords so you can view your campaign in AdWords.

Refer to Growing Basic Search Network Ads and Monitoring Basic Search Network Ads for suggestions for improving your ad, especially the suggestions concerning Geography.

Local Ads—AdWords Search Network

Local Ads let you compete aggressively with national companies when a person in your area searches for your product or when a searcher specifies your geographic area in his or her search query.

Essentially, *Local Ads* are simply Search Network ads targeted to people in your business' geographic area. They show on Google.com results pages after someone enters a search query for your product.

Setting Up Local AdWords Ads

To create a Local Ad, do the following.

1. **Create a campaign for the *Search Network Only* or use an existing campaign.**

   Under *location*, select *let me choose* and click *advance search*. Define your local area by entering either your city or the zip code(s) around your business location.

   Optionally, under the *location options (advanced)*, you can restrict your ad to only people in your geographic area. To do so, select *edit* next to *target (people in, searching for, or viewing pages about my targeted location)*. Click *people in my targeted area. Save* your ad.

2. **Setup an ad group and ad as you normally would for a Basic Search Ad.** (See Basic Search Network ads for instructions.)

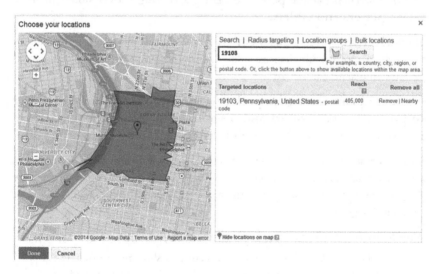

Figure 5.7. Location selection screen

Enter your zip code and your campaign is now targeted to your local area.

- As with all Search Network Campaigns, you specify the geographic area, language and device requirements the searcher must meet before you allow your ad to show.

- For each individual *Local Ad* you create, you specify a list of keywords describing your product. A searcher must use one of your keywords for your ad to appear.

Monitoring Local Ads On The Search Network

Ads need a few weeks to begin showing trends. *Local Ads* may take longer if the level of traffic is low. You may want to review your ad for a few weeks before you make any change to its composition.

1. **Refer to Monitoring Basic Search Network Ads for suggestions for monitoring Local Ads.**

2. **Refer to Growing Basic Search Network Ads for suggestions about growing your campaign.** Again, pay special attention to items related to geography, search terms and auction insights. (You may need to have a few months of data before trends show.)

Mobile Device Search Ads

Mobile Search Ads **reach people on the go, through their smartphones, music players and tablets.**

By default, AdWords runs on all devices. Consequently, it is not necessary to create ads for mobile devices as long as you have text or text-and-image ads in your campaign.

However, many marketers prefer to run ads only on mobile devices to promote special offers and discounts and/or to direct searchers to a website optimized for mobile viewing.

To restrict an ad to mobile devices you must (1) designate your Mobile Ad as *mobile-preferred* and (2) create a regular ad (a non-mobile-preferred ad) in the same ad group using the same ad type as the mobile-preferred ad (i.e., either a text or text-and-image ad).

Mobile Search Ads **have special requirements:**

- *Mobile Search Ads* look like desktop ads and show most often as 320 x 50 pixel banners (about 3"x 1/2"). If you create an image ad, your image must be 320 x 50 pixels.

- You should select your keywords with care. Do not assume the keywords you use with desktop/laptop ads are as productive with smartphone ads. People often use different keywords on mobile phones.

- To create *Mobile Search Ads* you must designate the ad group as *mobile preferred.*
    - As a best practice, you should create at least one *Mobile Search Ad* in each of your *Search Network Ad* groups. Similarly, an ad group for *Mobile Search Ads* must contain at least one regular ad.
    - If the searcher is on a mobile device, a *Mobile Search Ad* takes precedence over a regular ad—as is logical.
- Your ad should not include Adobe Flash because Flash does not show correctly on some devices, and iPhones do not support Flash at this time.

Mobile Search Ads **use the following** *ad extensions,* **all of which bring prospects to your business**. Use them!

- *Call extension*: lets you include a clickable phone number in your ad. (Do not put your phone number in your ad copy; use this ad extension.)

- *Location extension*: lets you add information about the store closest to the viewer with a "get directions" link.

- *Promotional offers*: lets you add a promotional ad or in-store promotion that viewers can email or text to themselves for later use.

- *Sitelinks*: lets you add a hyperlink to a landing page other than your destination URL. You need at least one *sitelink* used only by your mobile device ad.
    - **Be aware that AdWords sometimes shows your most clicked** *ad extensions* **instead of the second description line (unless your extensions prove to lower your click-throughs).**

A *Mobile Search Ad* **can contain a** *click-to-download* **link to your app on iTunes or Google's Android market.** (However, the *Mobile App Install Ads* give you more targeting options, so use them instead.)

- AdWords automatically presents iTunes download ads to iPhone users and Android download ads to Android phone users.

- iTunes and Android *click-to-download* ads must be in different ad groups.

- If you are selling mobile apps such as ringtones, wallpapers, quizzes, etc., you must clearly state the price, billing interval and the fact it is a subscription on your website.

The *cost-per-click* **for a** *Mobile Search Ad* **on a smartphone or a tablet often differs from that of a desktop/laptop ad.** Consequently, AdWords lets you adjust the bid (1) for mobile devices (smartphones) with full browsers and (2) for tablets with full browsers.

- *Bid adjustments* for mobile devices are available at the Campaign, Ad group or Ad Level. They are an increased or decreased percentage of the max CPC.

If you use a mobile website with your *Mobile Search Ad* (and you should), it should:

- Load quickly.
- Be easy to navigate with your thumbs.
- Make it easy to buy, sign-up, whatever.
- Provide local information.
- Let users switch between mobile and desktop sites, depending on their device.
- Review AdWords' policies for mobile device ads to make sure your ad meets its requirements. Learn more at the "Mobile Ads—what's the policy?" topic on AdWords Help.

For *Mobile Search Ads* you also can use Google Analytics to monitor the performance of your website.

Search in AdWords Help for "Types of Mobile Ads" to learn specific technical requirements for mobile device ads.

Setting Up Mobile Device Ads on the Search Network

To deploy a mobile device ad for full browsers:

1. **Setup your campaign.**
   - Set up a radius *location* for your stores of one, two and three miles (or whatever mileage you think appropriate for different CPC bids).

2. **Create an ad group for the campaign and enter a regular *Search Network Ad* aimed at desktop and tablet users.** Use the same type of ad you plan to use for your *Mobile Search Ad*.

3. **Create your *Mobile Search Ad*.** Within that same ad group, create your *Mobile Search Ad*, using the same type as your desktop ad, but this time check the box next to *mobile preferred* to designate the ad for use only on smartphones and tablets.

   Provide a URL for a mobile-optimized website or landing page, if you have one.

4. **Add all the appropriate *Ad Extensions*.** Click the *ad extension* tab and then the *view <option>* button for the extension you want to add. At a minimum, add a *call extension*.

- If you have a physical store, add a *location extension*. (You must have a *Google My Business* account to add location extensions.)
- Consider using different *sitelinks* for desktop/tablet and Mobile Ads. *Sitelinks* for *Mobile Ads* are invaluable for moving viewers quickly to a specific webpage.

5. **Make any *bid adjustments* you want for your mobile and desktop ads.** If you have no experience with *Mobile Ads,* wait until you see definite CPC cost differences between devices before making *bid adjustments.*

   Click the *settings tab* and the *device* button. Enter a percentage increase or decrease for smartphones and/or tablets.

For more information, search in AdWords Help for "Create a high-end Mobile Ad."

Monitoring Mobile Device Ads on the Search Network

To monitor *Mobile Device Ads,* do the following:

1. **Check that you are not paying too much (or too little) for your *Mobile Search Ads.***

   Review the data for mobile devices and desktops/tablets to see which is bringing you the most conversions. Click on the *ad group* tab for your Mobile Ad and the *device* button.

   You should "equalize" your bids across devices, so the bids bear a relationship to their value. To do this, divide the revenue generated by your Mobile Ads by the revenue generated by your desktop/tablet ads.

   $$\frac{\$10,900 \text{ in Mobile Ad revenue}}{\$12,100 \text{ in desktop and tablet revenue}} = 0.90$$

   Next, subtract 1 from the result. This gives you the difference in value between mobile and desktop/tablet devices. Here, the value of a Mobile Ad is 0.10 less than a desktop ad.

   $$0.90 - 1.0 = -0.10$$

   Finally, multiply the difference by 100. Don't lose track of your minus sign if you have one! Enter that percentage as a *bid adjustment.*

   $$-0.10 \times 100 = -10\%$$

2. **Check your Mobile Ad position.** Raise your bid if you are falling below the third position.

3. **Review the keywords that drive traffic to advertisers.** Click the box beside a keyword and then click *details* and *search terms* to see the search terms people are using on their mobile phones. Add new terms to your list of keywords, and determine if the match type of any keyword should change. (See Change Keyword Match-Types, p. 223, for information about changing keyword match type.)

4. **Make your ad text very specific to the viewer.** For example, tell customers to "Call now."

5. **Upgrade your landing page to work like a mobile website or a touch-screen, so it is easier to use on a mobile device.** Talk with your website programmer.

6. **Refer to Growing Basic Search Network Ads and Monitoring Basic Search Network Ads for general suggestions for Search Network ads.**

Mobile Search Ads for Flip Phones

AdWords offers a special ad type for flip phones (also called feature phones). AdWords calls these phones by their technical name, WAP-based phones.

- **To accommodate the feature phone's small screen, you must use a WAP-based landing page.** The landing page must be built in a WAP version that AdWords supports. Further, it must fit one of the many sizes AdWords supports.

- **WAP-based ads require their own WAP-only ad group(s).** Do not combine WAP and non-WAP ads in the same ad group.

- **WAP-based ads are shorter than normal ads: 18 characters for each line.** AdWords supports both text-only and text-and-image ads. URLs can be 20 characters.

- **Select your keywords with care.** Do not assume the keywords you use with desktop/laptop ads are good for mobile device ads. People often use different keywords on mobile phones.

- **You can add a *call extension* that a customer can click to call you without tapping in numbers.**

- **Ads must meet AdWords' policies and be approved, and WAP-based ad requirements differ by country.** (Search in AdWords Help for "WAP Mobile Ads".)

Setting Up WAP-Based Flip Phones

Note: You must have a WAP landing page to support a WAP ad.

To setup a WAP-based ad:

1. **Create a separate campaign.** Determine your campaign options as you would for a search on Display Network ad, except for the following items:

   - Campaign type: select either the *Search Network only* or *Display Network only* and *all features.*

2. **Create your WAP-based ad.** Create one of the following ad types:

   a. A text ad, which shows on the *Search Network* or the *Display Network.*

   b. An image ad, with a 320 x 50 image-with-text, which shows on the Display Network.

3. **Specify your mark-up language.** You also have the option of selecting operating systems, devices and WiFi carriers for feature phones.

4. **Add all the appropriate *ad extensions.*** Click the *ad extension* tab and then the *view <option>* button for the extension you want to add.

   - At a minimum, add a *call extension.*

   - If you have a physical store, add a *location extension.* (You must have a *Google My Business* account to add location extensions.)

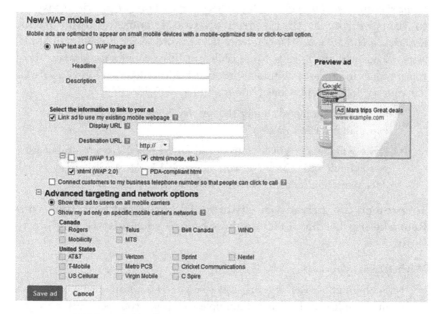

FIGURE 5.8 WAP mobile ad setup screen

- Consider using different *sitelinks* for desktop/tablet and Mobile Ads. Sitelinks for Mobile Ads are invaluable for moving viewers quickly to a specific webpage.

For more information, search in AdWords Help for "Create a WAP Mobile Ad."

Monitoring WAP-Based Flip-Phone Ads

1. If your WAP-based Mobile Ad is on the Search Network, monitor it as you would a smartphone Mobile Ad on the Search Network.
   - Refer to Monitoring Basic Search Network Ads for review suggestions.
   - Refer to Growing Basic Search Network Ads for suggestions for expanding your campaign.

2. If your WAP-based Mobile Ad is on the Display Network, monitor it as you would a smartphone Mobile Ad on the Display Network. Refer to Mobile Ads on the Display Network for mobile device monitoring
   - Refer to Monitoring Basic Display Network Ads for the review process.
   - Refer to Growing Basic Display Network Ads for suggestions for expanding your campaign.

Remarketing Lists for Search Ads (RLSA)

Remarketing Lists for Search Ads **(RLSA) lets you target previous visitors to your website as they search on Google.com for other items.** *Remarketing Lists for Search Ads* combines the keyword search capability of Search Network ads with the *Remarketing* capability that uses cookies to show ads about your product to previous visitors as they surf the Internet. In effect, *Remarketing* lets your ad "follow" a previous visitor.

- (See Remarketing Ads under the Display Network for a fuller explanation of *Remarketing*.)
- *Remarketing* was originally introduced for Display Network ads but use was extended to Search Network ads in 2013. (Most AdWords documentation focuses on Display Network uses.)

To protect the privacy of visitors, AdWords requires that your Remarketing list has 1,000 cookies before your ads are eligible to show.

With *RLSA*s, you can:

- Setup multiple Remarketing lists (the same visitor appearing on multiple lists if they visited multiple web pages you specified).

- Have multiple ads using the same list, as when you advertise a product and a website-wide sale at the same time.

- Have multiple ads qualifying to show to a visitor, in which case AdWords uses the ad with the highest *ad rank*.

- Bid at the Ad Group Level for all underlying ads or bid at the *Remarketing List Level* for all ads using a particular *Remarketing list*.

RLSAs use the *cost-per-click* bidding model.

- **You can set *bid adjustments* for individual *Remarketing lists*.**

You must have 1,000 previous visitors on your Remarketing list (i.e., 1,000 cookies) before AdWords shows your ad.

- **However, you can use the *bid only* option to bid higher for previous visitors in regular Search Network and Display Network ads, while your *Remarketing list* is building to the 1,000 level.** (Essentially, you are enabling *bid adjustments* for the *Remarketing lists*.) This lets you make use of AdWords' knowledge of previous visitors before your *Remarketing* campaign is eligible to run.

  Once your *Remarketing list* hits 1,000 visitors, you can remove your *bid only targets* from your regular Search Network or Display Network campaign and use your Remarketing campaign, which lets you show ads aimed at returning visitors. (If you do not remove your *bid only targets* from your basic Search or Display campaign, those ads will compete against your *remarketing Ads,* possibly raising your costs.)

  Recall that the *bid only* options permit you to enter a percentage increase or decrease to the *max CPC* at the Ad Group Level.

RLSA ads to not compete against a Search Network or Display Network campaign even if they use the same keywords. If the searcher is a previous visitor, your RLSA ad appears. If the searcher is not a previous visitor, your regular Search Network ad appears.

- You can run a *RLSA* campaign that is exactly like your Search Network campaign—including the keywords.

- To quickly create a RLSA campaign, create a new *search only* campaign and *load settings from an existing campaign.* Be sure to include *Remarketing* or *RLSA* in the campaign's name.

Some AdWords users have reported strong click-though rates with RLSAs. Consequently, Google recommends you use *RLSAs* with your *all site visitors* list at first. Further, you may find that running *Remarketing Ads* for all products on a website is more time-consuming than the results merit.

AdWords provides performance data for each ad and for each *Remarketing List*.

Setting Up Remarketing Lists for Search Ads

1. You must be using the *Remarketing* feature. (See Setting Up Remarketing Ads for setup instructions.)

2. Create your *Remarketing lists* for the Search Network. You can create lists in the *shared library* and use the lists for any campaign. Alternatively, you can create lists as needed when you setup an ad group.

   For *Remarketing lists for the Search Network*, you can:

   • Use existing *Remarketing lists* with Search Network ads.

   • Use the *all site visitors Remarketing list,* which is created automatically when you activate *Remarketing*.

   While you can use any of the *Remarketing lists* you created previously when you setup *Remarketing for the Display Network*, it is not recommended that you use the same Remarketing list in Search Network and Display Network ads.

3. Setup your RLSA campaign. Use one of these methods:

   • Create a new *Search Network only* campaign, ad group and ad. (To quickly create a RLSA campaign, create a new *Search Network only* campaign and *load settings from an existing campaign*. Be sure to include Remarketing in the campaign's name.)

   • Use an existing *Search Network only* campaign.

   • Assign your *Remarketing list(s)* to your ad group.

4. Setup your *Remarketing lists*.

   a. Click the *audience tab*.

   (If the *audience tab* does not appear to the right of the *keyword tab*, click the down arrow at the end of the row and select *audience* from the drop-down menu.)

   b. Click the red *+Remarketing* button.

   c. Select your ad group.

   d. Click *add targeting* and select *interest and Remarketing* from the drop-down menu.

   e. Click *select category* and click *Remarketing lists*.

   f. Next to the desired list, click *add*.

— As a best practice, attach only one *Remarketing list* to an ad. Otherwise, you cannot discern which *Remarketing list* is coaxing visitors back.

g. Select *Target and Bid or Bid only.*

— Click *Target and Bid* to use the *Remarketing list(s)* as a *targeting method* (with or without a *bid adjustment*). With this option, your *Remarketing lists* controls who sees your ad. Once your *Remarketing list* hits 1,000 cookies, your ad will show.

— Click *bid only* to use a *bid adjustment* when a searcher on the list is using one of your keywords. Your ad will not show, but you can increase your bid when a previous visitor searches. You may want to use this option until your *Remarketing list(s)* hits 1,000 cookies.

h. *Save* your input.

Monitoring Remarketing Lists for Search Ads

Monitoring *RLSAs* is like monitoring basic Search Network ads except that you also must monitor the success of your Remarketing lists.

1. If you used *bid only* for a Remarketing list while your list built to 1,000, be sure to change it to *target and bid* so your Remarketing Ads appear.

   (Click the *audience tab*, click the red *+Remarketing* button. Select the ad group. A panel with *interest and Remarketing* appears. Click the pencil in the right corner and, at the bottom of the screen, change *bid only* to *target and bid*.)

2. To conserve your budget, use *bid adjustments* for the *Remarketing lists* that bring back visitors (rather than increasing the max CPC at the Ad group or Keyword Level).

3. Refer to Monitoring Search Network Ads for suggestions for monitoring the ad.

Search Ads with Select Display

Search-Ads-with-Display-Select lets you advertise on the Search Network as well as highly-relevant Display Network websites. For new advertisers, these ads let you ease into the Display Network, using your existing budget.

Setting Up Search-Ads-with-Display-Select

The easiest way to setup a *Search-Ads-with-Display-Select* is:

215

1. Convert a *Search Network only* campaign to a *Search-Ads-with-Display-Select* campaign and let your text ad run on both networks. (Go to *settings* and change the ad type.)

2. Later, add an ad group with a *Display Network* ad or a *Dynamic Search Ad*. (See Setting Up Basic Display Network Ads and Setting Up Dynamic Search Ads, respectively for instructions.)

Alternatively, you can create a new *Search-Ads-with-Display-Select* campaign.

1. Create a *Search-Ads-with-Display-Select* campaign. The options are the same as for *Basic Search Network Ads*. (See Setting Up Basic Search Network Ads for instructions.)

2. Create an ad group with a text ad for the Search Network.

3. If you want to have a different ad run on the Display Network, you can create an ad group for an image ad, *ad gallery* template ad or digital ad. (See Setting Up Basic Display Network Ads for instructions.)

Monitoring Search-Ads-with-Display-Select

A Search-Ads-with-Display-Select campaign is a search ad and a display ad running in the same campaign. You must monitor each individually.

1. For *Search Network ad*s:
   - Refer to Monitoring Basic Search Network Ads for review suggestions.
   - Refer to Growing Basic Search Network Ads for suggestions for expanding this aspect of your campaign.

2. For *Display Network ad*s:
   - Refer to Monitoring Basic Display Network Ads for the review process.
   - Refer to Growing Display Network Ads for suggestions for expanding your campaign.

GROWING BASIC SEARCH NETWORK ADS

The following presents numerous ways to easily and quickly expand your Search Network ad campaigns.

Remember, do not expand a campaign until it is converting visitors to buyers! You do not need to pay Google for more visitors if your landing page is not converting them to buyers.

Once your first search ad is converting visitors, you can begin to expand using the following techniques.

Activate Conversion Tracking and Conversion Optimization

Activating *Conversion Tracking* is the first thing you should do to grow a Search Network campaign. This is the fastest way to maximize your budget and AdWords success.

1. **If your campaign is successfully converting visitors to buyers and you have at least 15 conversions within the last 30 days, turn on Conversion Tracking.**

    Conversion Tracking captures information about visitors when they see your ad, click your ad, view your landing page, navigate your site and make a purchase. It also switches your campaign to the enhanced CPC (eCPC) bidding option and, thus, adjusts your bid so you win more auctions and appear before more people who exhibit the same online behaviors as your customers.

2. **Activate the Conversion Optimizer feature after you install Conversion Tracking and have at least 15 conversions a month.** This puts more of the power of AdWords behind your campaign.

If your campaign has not reached 15 conversions a month, make that a goal!
(See Conversion Tracking (Data Collection) for activation details.)

Increase Your Daily Budget

If your campaign is successfully converting visitors to buyers and you are not getting 100 percent of the available impressions, try increasing your daily budget. This can help you gain more ad impressions, click-throughs and, ultimately, more conversions without increasing the cost of each click.

1. To change your daily budget, go to *all online campaigns* and click on your campaign. Click the *settings tab* and scroll down to the daily budget prompt. Enter a new amount. The change is effective immediately.

2. If you share your budget across campaigns, consider moving this campaign out of the shared budget if it is performing better than the other campaigns.

Change to Search Network with Display Select Campaign Type

If your campaign is successfully converting visitors to buyers and most of your keywords are capable of converting visitors, you may

want to convert your campaign from Search Network to Search Network with Display Select.

Changing to Search Network with Display Select makes your ad eligible to compete for ad positions on Display Network Partner websites with content highly relevant to your keywords. Ad costs on the Display Network are often cheaper than on the Search Network, which makes your budget go further.

1. To change your campaign type, go to *all online campaigns* and click on your campaign. Click the *settings tab* and change the campaign type from *Search Network* to *Search Network with Display Select*.

2. Review your campaign to ensure none of the keywords for your *Search Network with Display Select* ad are duplicates of keywords you have for Display Network ads. If the same keyword appears in two ads, they will compete against each other and the one with the highest bids shows.

Add Google Search Partners

If you excluded Google Search Partners when you setup your campaign, add them back now that your keywords and landing page are working well.

To evaluate Google Search Partners in your campaign:

1. At the Campaign Level, click the *segment* button and select *network* from the drop-down menu to see which network is performing the best.

2. After you add Google Search Partners, monitor Google Search Partners periodically to ensure they are bringing buyers, not just click-throughs.

Change Your Geographic Market to Reflect Local Markets

If your campaign is successfully converting visitors to buyers, consider adjusting your geographic area to reflect your best market(s).

*   If your visitors are coming from specific areas, you may want to narrow your geographic market from "U.S." to specific zip codes, cities or radius areas. Alternatively, you might create separate campaigns with different bids for each specific area.

*   Local advertisers often outrank national advertisers (depending on the product). By narrowing your market, you could gain a higher ad placement than advertisers with broader markets, including advertisers with national markets.

*   Conversely, if your visitors are scattered across your local region, consider creating one or more new campaigns for different regions.

By using additional campaigns for different regions (rather than simply increasing the geographic area of your original campaign), your original ad keeps its "Local Ad" advantage.

Recall that changing your geographic area affects all ads within the campaign. Thus, you may need multiple campaigns if you want to target multiple "local" areas.

To change your geographic market:

1. View your current performance data by geography to see where your visitors reside. Click the *dimensions* tab, click the *view: <option>* tab and select *geographic* or *user location* from the drop-down menu.

2. View the geographic performance data to see where your users reside. Click on *All Online Campaigns* and then the appropriate campaign. Next, click the *Settings Tab.*

3. Scroll to the *locations* prompt. Click *edit* and, after the input screen opens, click *advanced search* and narrow or enlarge your geographic market.

Change the Max CPC for Keywords

If your landing page is converting visitors to buyers, you may want to consider changing your maximum *cost-per-click* (max CPC) for some keywords. (Note, you must use *manual bidding* to do this.)

Depending on your ad position, you may be able to lower your max CPC and gain more traffic. Some ads attract visitors even if they are in a lower position on a page.

- If you are willing to accept a lower ad position, you can lower your CPC on good keywords and increase your traffic. After you make such a change, keep an eye on your keywords to make sure your traffic increases, rather than decreases.

- This approach is not recommended if your ad appears in a *top of page* position, above the Google.com search results. Over time, a *top of page* ad position can gain you a discounted cost, as Google rewards you for your high quality score.

To determine whether to increase your max CPC, do the following:

1. Identify the keywords that bring you visitors. Click the *click* column on the *statistics table* to sort the table by number of clicks.

2. For the keywords with the most clicks, review the *search impr. share* column to see what percentage you received of all the possible

impressions. If the percentage is low, you may want to raise your bid to capture more impressions for your top keywords. (Further, you may want to lower your bid, or pause, poor performing keywords.)

3. Use the *bid simulator* to determine what to bid. Click the bid simulator icon next to a keyword to quickly move to the *bid simulator / traffic estimator* tool (discussed in the *Tools and Reports* section, p. 327). The icon is not always available, in which case you must go to the *keyword planner* tool under the *tools* tab and click *get traffic estimates for a list of keywords.*

FIGURE 5.9 Bid simulator icon

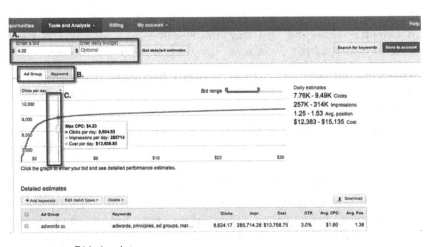

FIGURE 5.10 Bid simulator

Alternatively, you can add the bid recommendation columns on the *statistics table*. Move to the *keyword* tab, click the *columns–customize* button, then bid simulator and add the available columns.

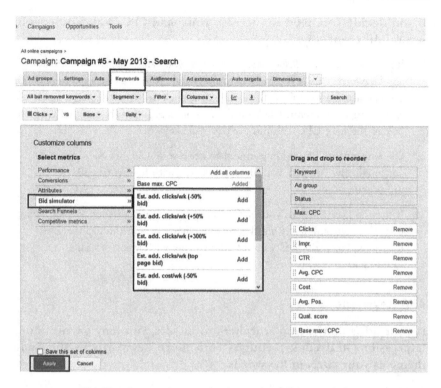

FIGURE 5.11 Bid Simulator column selections

Bid Simulator columns are available only on the *Keyword* tab.

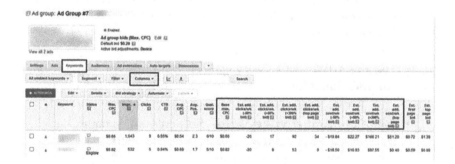

FIGURE 5.12 Bid Simulator columns

With the Bid Simulator columns showing you quickly see the impact on clicks and costs of cutting your bid by 50% or increasing it by 50% or 300%.

If you decide you need to increase your max CPC, you can do so in several different ways:

1. If you use *Focus on Clicks—manual bidding*, you can enter a new CPC for any keyword. This is the most common method for increasing a max CPC. To increase the max CPC for a keyword, click on your campaign in the *all online campaigns* menu. Click on the *keyword tab*. Enter the new CPC in the box in the max CPC column next to your keyword.

2. Use enhanced CPC bidding model to raise your CPC up to 15 percent automatically. This lets you bid aggressively with less work and monitoring.

3. If the top positions are your sweet spot use automated rules to raise your max CPC automatically and keep your keyword(s) in the top three positions. This, too, lets you bid aggressively with less work and monitoring.

Add Keywords

If your ad is converting searchers to buyers, you may garner more impressions and click-throughs with more keywords in the same theme as your current keywords.

To evaluate your keywords:

- **Review the search terms that triggered your ad and add new, similar terms to your list of keywords.** (To see the search terms that bring you visitors, check the box next to a keyword, click the *details* tab at the top of the table and select *search terms*.) If irrelevant terms trigger your ad, add them to your *negative keyword list*.

- **Use the AdWords' *keyword planner* tool to obtain suggestions for additional keywords.** Enter your best keyword phrases into the *keyword planner tool* and see the additional keywords recommended.

- **Pause unproductive keywords.** Keywords that do not produce clicks or sales drag down your *quality score*. Pause them and see if the remaining keywords perform better.

- **Review your competitors' keywords using the AdWords** *display planner tool*. Put the URL of a competing advertiser into the website box to see the search terms that appear. Know that other third-party tools exist online to find the keywords of your competitors.

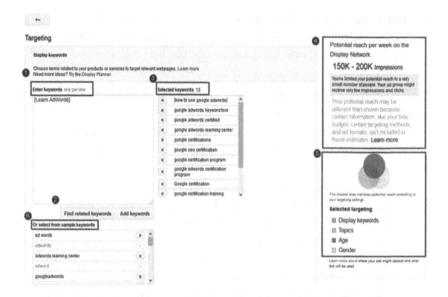

FIGURE 5.13 Add keywords to Display Network ad

The Display Network screen for adding keywords lets you (1) enter keywords, (2) find related keywords (3)select from a list of keywords, (4) see the potential weekly reach for a keyword, (5) see how your targeting methods narrow your audience and (6) select sample keywords. Do not forget to specify the desired match-type for each keyword; otherwise, the keyword is designated a broad-match keyword.

To add keywords:

- On the *all online campaigns* menu, click the ad group for your campaign. Click the *keyword* tab for your ad and then the *+add keywords* button. Remember to include the appropriate keyword-match type for each new keyword. Save your entries.

Change Keyword Match-Types

To improve your results, you may want to change your keyword-match strategy.

When it comes to keywords, basically two strategies exist:

1. **The broad-match strategy**: you start with broad-matching keywords to see which phrases people use most often. You continually cull out the unproductive keywords. This is the strategy Google recommends. While it garners you a lot of traffic, it can be expensive because the visitors are not well qualified (if you have enough budget, you may not care) and it is time consuming because you must constantly cull bad keywords.

223

2. **The exact-match strategy**: you start with exact match keywords—words you believe are most descriptive of your product or service. Then, you move to broad-match keywords once you have a level of success and revenues.

Either way, changing your strategy may increase your traffic. To fine-tune your keywords, consider these actions:

- Use the *search term report* to see which user search terms match your keywords and bring shoppers versus buyers. You may have some surprises.

  To produce a *search term report*, go to the *keyword tab* for your ad, click the checkbox beside *keyword*, click the *details* tab, choose *search terms* and then *selected*. You can make corrections on this report.

  Make sure the keyword that matched the search term appears to add it, then go to the *keyword tab*, click *columns* in the submenu and select *customize columns*. Click *attributes* and select *add* next to *keyword*. Click *apply*. The options to *add as keyword* and *add as negative keyword* now appear above the *statistics table*.

  (Alternatively, you can produce a *search term report* for a campaign, ad group or ad by clicking *dimensions*, clicking *view* and selecting *search terms*. You cannot use this version to make corrections.)

- The search terms shown are those used most frequently during the last 30 days (exclusive of today, since data are current as of 24 hours ago). To see search terms used in the past, change your date range (in the upper-right corner of the screen) to the historical date range you want.

- Consider changing the designation on your keywords from an exact match to a broader match type, such as exact, partial, modified broad or embedded broad so your keywords match against more searches.

- Or, consider changing your keyword matching from broad-match to a tighter match, such as exact, partial, etc. to get more qualified visitors.

- When you change the keyword-match type, the new version replaces the old version; however, data for the old match type remains visible.

To change the keyword-matching for your keywords:

1. Click the ad group under the campaign on the *all online campaigns* menu.

2. Click the *Display Network tab* and then the *display keyword* button.

3. Edit the keywords based on the number of clicks. Change broader match types to tighter match types and vice versa.

Switching to a Flexible Bid Strategy

Flexible bid strategies are very useful for managing low priority or low performing campaigns while you focus on more productive campaigns. You must use automatic bidding to use flexible bid strategies. Further, you can apply a single flexible bid strategy to more than one campaign or ad group and/or you can setup multiple strategies. (See Flexible Bid Strategies (CPC) under Key Concept 5 to refresh your memory about flexible bid strategies.)

- Recall that applying a flexible bid strategy to a campaign automatically applies it to the underlying ad groups and ads. Similarly, applying the strategy to an ad group automatically applies it to the underlying ads.

- Use the *maximize clicks* strategy to save time and to control low priority or long-tail keyword campaigns and ad groups.

- Use the *enhanced CPC* strategy if your landing page is converting well and you want to make an aggressive effort to bring traffic to your site and use your entire budget.

- If you use Conversion Tracking, you can use the *return on ad spend (ROAS)* to tell AdWords to try to meet your ROI (the value of your sales divided by the cost of your AdWords.) (You must provide an average conversion value.) Be sure to set a realistic ROI, just slightly above your current ROI. Google recommends not setting a maximum or minimum bid limit.

- Use the *target search page location* strategy, with its many additional options, if you want to control a campaign or ad groups for a particular ad position.

Add Ad Extensions to Your Search Ads

The more information in your ad, the easier searchers can decide whether your product or website is appropriate for them *before clicking your ad*. Then, if they click, they usually are more predisposed toward your product.

AdWords lets you expand the "pre-click" information you provide a searcher through *ad extensions* for: address, sitelinks, phone number and the Google +1 social extensions.

AdWords considers *ad extensions* when computing your *quality score*, so it is essential for you to include as many *ad extensions* as appropriate in your ads.

(Refer to the discussion of ad extension under Key Concept 3, Level 2: The Campaign.)

Your Search Network campaign must use the *all features* option to use *ad extensions*.

Ad extensions include:

- *Call extension*: where you add a clickable phone number or, alternatively, a call forwarding phone number provided to you by Google. One phone number per ad group is allowed.

  For more information about call forwarding phone numbers, search in AdWords Help for "Add phone numbers to your ads."

- *Location extension*: where you show a location based on the searcher's physical location (or location of interest if he or she enters one).

  You must have a Google My Business account to use location extensions. AdWords inserts the city, phone number, postal code and phone number of your nearest store. (See Local Ads—Google My Business for setup instructions for a Google My Business account.)

- *Offer extension*: where you can add a coupon or special deal.

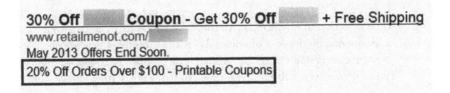

FIGURE 5.14 Offer extensions

- *Social extensions*: where the number of followers of your Google+ page shows. If you are posting on your Google+ page and have a "significant number of followers" (about 100 people), AdWords includes the +1 icon and comment box in your Search ads if space permits. Viewers can share a comment about your ad on their Google +1 social networking page.

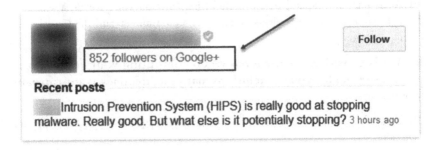

FIGURE 5.15 Social extensions

You can opt out of social extension ads by submitting a form to Google. To obtain the form go to services.google.com/fb/forms/ socialannotations.

To activate an ad extension,

1. Determine where you want to apply the ad extension. Bear in mind the following:

   • Ad extensions can be added (1) to your campaign to apply to all ad groups and ads, (2) to an ad group to be applied to the underlying ads or (3) to a specific ad.

   • The *ad extension* at the Ad Level has top priority to show in your ad, followed by any ad extension at the Ad Group Level and, finally, at the Campaign Level.

2. To add an *ad extension*, click on the *ad extension* tab and the *view <extensions>* button for the extension you want to add.

3. Enter the information required by the specific *ad extension*.

Conduct Experiments

Unless you keep learning about your keywords, other advertisers can overtake your ad position. Search terms used to describe your product can change over time, and you can overpay for ad impressions.

By experimenting you can keep your ad fresh, and your understanding of the market current. Experiments let you:

   • Test different keywords and learn more about your customers.

   • Find more effective messages to attract more visitors.

   • Improve your landing page using more effective keywords and messages.

   • Determine the best promotional offers or the best content to generate sign-ups.

Ultimately, experiments help you generate more revenue for Search Ads and reduce your costs for Display Network ads.

(See Step 13: Use AdWords Experiments to Improve Your Ads and Save Money, p. 170, for an overview of AdWords experiment capabilities.)

ADVANCED SEARCH NETWORK FEATURES

Two features, unique to the Search Network, put the trend analysis logic of AdWords to work for you: *Conversion Tracking* and *Conversion Optimization*. Use these features to take your campaign to the next level of success.

Conversion Tracking (Data Collection)

Conversion Tracking captures information about the searches and viewing behaviors of your ad viewers, website visitors and buyers. AdWords then uses that data to help you compete more aggressively.

Conversion Tracking does the following:

1. **Reveals a customer's path through your website prior to a purchase.**
   - This helps you understand the customer's thought process, priorities and interests (i.e., the steps in their search funnel).
   - It reveals the keywords your customers use early in their search as they explore your site versus the keywords your customers use later in their searches as they make the decision to buy.
   - It helps you identify repeat buyers.

   You may want to use this information to fine-tune your landing page or create different landing pages for different phases of the decision-making process.

2. **Maintains data for up to 90 days about customers who view your ad, who visit your site and who buy.**
   - This helps you determine which Search Network ads, Display Network ads, videos or interactive ads, keywords, etc., are building awareness for future sales. You may want to increase your bid for ads or keywords that introduce new buyers to your site (even though it may be days, weeks or months before they buy).

3. **Attempts to estimate the number of conversions resulting from searchers who use "multiple screens" (i.e., multiple devices, browsers and visits) before making a purchase.** Today many searchers switch between smartphones, tablets and desktops to research products and make multiple visits to a landing page before converting. In response to this, AdWords is attempting to capture, or extrapolate, more insights about the behavior of searchers to help you refine your campaigns and bids.

4. **Comes with a set of reports called search funnels.** As with the sales funnel reports that marketers use to distinguish the different steps prospects go through before buying, the Conversion Tracking search funnel reports help you understand how people search for your product. It also helps you understand where your funnel may be "leaking" (i.e., losing) prospects.

5. **Varies data depending on your *view-through* option.** A *click-through* occurs when a searcher sees your ad, clicks it and buys. By contrast, a *view-through* occurs when a searcher sees your ad, does not click on it, but returns to your website within the number of days you specify (up to 90) and buys.

    - If you want AdWords to count this scenario as one conversion only, you *enable the view-through* option.

    - If you want AdWords to count this scenario as one view-through and one conversion, you *disable the view-through* option.

    - Disabling the view-through option (i.e., counting view-throughs) helps you determine which Display Network ads are bringing future buyers to your site.

    Before reviewing Conversion Tracking data, bear in mind that:

    - Data at the Campaign Level provides insight into the patterns of buyers across the demographic, geographic, language, etc. characteristics you selected for the campaign.

    - Data at the Ad Group Level provides insight into the most appealing product attributes (i.e., keywords used to describe the product).

    - Data at the Ad Level provides insight into the message that resonates best with buyers.

    Note that Google Analytics, Google's robust website tracking software, also reports search behaviors. It also provides information about non-buying visitors to your site and buyers coming from sources other than AdWords ads.

6. **Lets you import offline sales to provide a full picture of your AdWords success.** When a visitor prospect fills out a form on your website to request a call from your sales representative, AdWords records the ad and keyword that brought the visitor to your site, along with a Google click ID (GCLID) number to represent that visitor.

    Once your sales rep calls the prospect and makes the sale, you load the visitor's GCLIDs into AdWords and AdWords records the sale for the ad, keyword and GCLID involved. Thus, you then know which ad and keyword initiated the offline sales.

You can upload your offline sales through the tools tab—*conversion* function using an Excel or .csv file. You also can use AdWords' application programmer interface (API). For information on this feature, search in AdWords Help for "Tracking offline conversions" and "How to import offline conversions."

In a nutshell, Conversion Tracking works like this:

1. You place a snippet of code on pages of your website.

   - To recognize and track a sale, put the code on the webpage that appears *after* a visitor takes the action you want (i.e., the "thank you for your order" page).

   - If you want the code snipped you can capture the value (dollar amount) of the merchandise sold. Alternatively, you can set a flat amount to represent the value of a customer (as you might do if you have an average-value-per-customer statistic).

2. When someone comes from Google.com to your site, AdWords places a temporary cookie on that visitor's computer (or smartphone or tablet) and records the cookie ID on AdWords along with (1) the path your customer took through your website before buying/downloading/signing up or leaving the site, (2) the keyword(s) that brought the customer to your site, (3) other searches the customer executed for the product before coming to your site and (4) the keywords used by customers in those searches.

3. A notification on your webpage tells your customer you are using Google Conversion Tracking and lets them opt out. The cookie expires before 90 days, depending on the duration you select.

   Note: Google states that AdWords does not relate a customer's behavior to any identifying customer information such as email, username, IP address, etc.

Setting Up Conversion Tracking

You must have at least 15 conversions in the last 30 days to use Conversion Tracking. If you have reached that milestone, you should deploy Conversion Tracking immediately. Also, you can import historical conversion data from Google Analytics.

The following describes the major steps to implement Conversion Tracking.

1. **Make a copy of your CPC and CTR data before you implement Conversion Tracking.** This data is your baseline and is invaluable in measuring your success after you implement Conversion Tracking.

2. **Add Conversion Tracking data elements to your statistics table.** Go to the *campaign* tab, click the *column* button and then *customize columns* in the drop-down menu. Click *conversions* in the *select metrics* column and select *add* to add all the conversions data columns to the *statistics table*.

3. **On the *tools* tab, click *conversions* in the drop-down menu and then click the +*conversion* button.**

4. **AdWords creates a snippet of code for each type of conversion and each webpage your want to track. Each snippet requires you answer short set of questions, such as the following:**

    a. *Conversion name*: a name you devise to let you quickly recall the campaign or ad group name.

    b. *Source*: the landing page where the conversion took place: (1) your website, (2) a smart phone (i.e., a call) or (3) the download of an app from a mobile app. (Downloads initiated from Search Network ads or Display Network ads cannot be tracked.)

    On the next page, indicate your conversion category and tracking choices:

    c. Conversion category:

    *Purchase/*sale: if a purchase is selected, you must also add one of the following:
    — *The price of the product*: if you want to track the value of each sale for a single product, you need to insert the item's price into the snippet.
    — *Total of all items*: if you sell multiple items, you must put the name of the transaction field for the total purchase amount into the snippet so AdWords captures the amount. The amount subsequently appears in the *value* column on Conversion Tracking reports.

    Lead: tracks calls or an inquiry form.

    Sign-up: tracks a form or email.

    View of a key page: tracks specific pages you designate, such as the Contact page.

    Other: not specified.

    d. *Conversion window*: the length of the normal buying period (one, two, three or four weeks; 30, 45, 60, 90 days). If in doubt, choose 90 days.

e. *Page security level*: either HTTP or HTTPS, depending on your webpage.

f. *Markup language*: either HTML, CHTML, XHTML or WML.

g. *Conversion value*: enter the monetary value you believe a new customer is worth (consult your company's Chief Financial Officer to determine this number). Alternatively, if you want AdWords to record the amount of a sale, leave this blank for now.

h. *Notification*: this adds a notification on your website's order confirmation page that you are using Google Site Stats (i.e., Conversion Tracking). You have a choice of one-line or two-line notification, the color of the font and the language. You are not required to add this notification, but Google recommends it.

i. Under *advanced options*, enter your *view-through conversion window*: the period of time after viewing your ad that AdWords' cookie remains active on the visitor's device. (The *view-through* option tracks visitors who *see* your ad and do not click on it, but return to buy within the period you specify. This is where you specify the time period.)

j. Tell AdWords who runs your campaigns. AdWords needs to know the webmaster who should receive an email with the code.

4. **Paste the snippet AdWords creates into your order confirmation page and on any page you want tracked.**

5. **Know that you cannot use Conversion Tracking with certain other AdWords features, namely:**

   - *Ad scheduling*: Conversion Tracking ignores ad schedules.

   - *Bid adjustments*: Conversion Tracking ignores *bid adjustments* except for mobile devices' *bid adjustments* of –100 percent. A *bid adjustment* of –100 percent sets the bid to zero, and the Conversion Tracking then excludes your ad from auction for mobile devices.

6. **Be aware of the following limitations:**

   - Not all Display Networks Partners can provide the data needed by AdWords for Conversion Tracking.

   - If you use *managed placements*, you may want to remove websites that do not support Conversion Tracking.

   - Some customers do not permit cookies, and some knowingly disable cookies. This can skew your results.

   - A visitor may return to your site using another search engine, which also skews results.

7. **To view the Conversion Tracking Reports, go to the** *tools* **tab and click** *conversions* **in the drop-down menu.** In the lower left-hand menu, click *search funnels*.

Remember, the longer Conversion Tracking runs, the more data AdWords has to work with and the better your results.

Detailed instructions for implementing Conversions Tracking are available under "Understanding Conversion Tracking" in AdWords Help.

The following provides an overview of the Conversion Tracking data elements in AdWords. (If you do not see these elements on the *statistics table*, click the *column* button, click *customize columns*, select *conversions* and add the desired element.)

- **Conv. (1-per-click)**: the total number of unique buyers. AdWords counts each buyer only once during the period, regardless of how many times he/she bought something. This number also includes clicks on phone numbers in Mobile Ads, regardless of whether that number is your business number or an 800-number from Google that forwards to your business number.

- **Cost/conv. (1-per-click)**: the total cost of your clicks divided by number of unique buyers.

- **Conv. rate (1-per-click)**: total number of unique buyers divided by number of impressions shown.

- **View-through conv.**: the number of ads your buyer saw before buying.

- **Conv. (many-per-click)**: the number of purchase transactions. This number counts the same person more than once if he/she bought more than once.

- **Cost/conv. (many-per-click)**: the total cost of all clicks divided by number of purchase transactions. This number counts the same person more than once if he/she bought more than once.

- **Conv. rate (many-per-click)**: the total number of purchase transactions divided by number of impressions.

- **Total conv. value**: the value of all conversions (based on either the per-item value that you plugged in the code snippet or the total amount at checkout if you designated in the code snippet the transaction field where the amount is stored).

- **Conv. value/cost**: the total value of conversions divided by the total costs of ads.

- **Conv. value/click**: the total value of conversions divided by the total clicks on ads.

233

- **Value/conv. (1-per-click)**: total value of all conversions divided by the total number of unique visitors (1-per-click, meaning a visitor is counted only once, regardless of the number of times that individual returns to purchase during the period).

- **Phone call conversions**: the number of calls to your Google-provided phone number, if you use Google's call forwarding option.

AdWords provides the following fields to help you determine the impact and value of conversions resulting from searchers who use multiple devices before purchasing.

- **Estimated total conversions**: at the Campaign Level for campaigns with 50 or more conversions a day, the number of conversions on your website plus the number AdWords estimates from:
  - Calls of a set duration from a landline phone to your Google-provided 800 number, if you elected to have that data reported.
  - A count of every conversion a visitor made during one visit (i.e., formerly called the many-per-click total); Google does not say how this is determined but, logically, it could be determined by multiple appearances of your Thank You page while the visitor is on your site).
  - A count of calls from a mobile phone to the phone number in your ad by a person who visited your website (i.e., cross-device conversions); Google does not say how this is determined but, logically, Google could match the phone number called against cookies on the phone.

  Since AdWords has no way to determine whether these actions resulted in a sale, it calls them estimates.

  Estimated total conversions indicate how many additional conversions you could attribute to AdWords usage. Based on this information, your ROI for AdWords changes, and you may want to increase your usage of AdWords.

  Further, since estimated total conversions give some indication of how big a role Mobile Ads play in bringing you customers, you may want to run more Mobile Ads and/or increase your bid (or *bid adjustment*) for Mobile Ads.

- **Estimated cross-device conversions**: at the Campaign Level for campaigns with 50 or more conversions a day, AdWords estimates the number of searchers who used more than one device to visit your landing page before buying. This information indicates whether Mobile Ads assist your desktop/tablet conversions.

234

AdWords estimates the number based on data from users who signed into Google from multiple devices. (It attributes a conversion to the last ad the searcher clicked before converting.)

For the purposes of estimated conversions, AdWords considers *cross-device conversions* to involve a device (smartphone, tablet or desktop) and a browser (Safari, Chrome, Windows, etc.).

- **Cost/estimated total conversion**: the estimated average amount you paid for each conversion, as determined by dividing your total costs by the estimated number of conversions.

- **Estimated total conversion rate**: the estimated total conversions divided by the total number of clicks. Remember that many-per-click conversions are included, so your rate may be over 100 percent.

- **Estimated total conversion value**: the estimated number of conversions times the amount you set as the value of a conversion.

- **Estimated total conversion value/cost**: your estimated return on investment (ROI), as determined by dividing the estimated value of your conversions by the cost of your ads.

- **Value/estimated total conversions**: the average value of an estimated conversion, as determined by dividing the value of your conversions by the estimated number of conversions.

- **Estimated total conversion value/click**: the average value of an estimated click, as determined by dividing the value of your conversions by the estimated number of clicks.

Search funnel—data for Conversion Tracking and Conversion Optimization features that help you determine what visitors do when they are (1) researching vendors (at the top of the sales funnel), (2) learning about products (in the middle of the sales funnel) and (3) ready to buy (at the bottom of the sales funnel).

- *Top conversions*: shows which types of conversions (i.e., sales) bring the greatest revenue.
  - *Assist clicks, assist impressions*: show how many times an ad was viewed, clicked or viewed-and-clicked before a purchase *excluding the last one immediately before a purchase*. Thus, as the names imply, this shows you which ads are assisting your sales by bringing people to your site, even though the ad may not be the one to bring them when they buy.
  - *Assist Clicks*: shows all ads clicked before a buy except the last click.
  - *Assist impressions*: shows data for Search Ads shown-but-not-clicked before a conversion.

— *Assisted conversions*: shows the keywords that drive the most conversions. For the keyword bringing you the most buyers, consider moving it and the ad with the highest relative CTR into their own AdWords Group and increasing the max CPC.

- *First click analysis*: shows the frequency with which each campaign, ad and keyword is the first one clicked by a buyer. This highlights the campaigns, ad groups and keywords that contribute the most to conversions.

- *Last click analysis*: shows the frequency with which each campaign, ad or keyword is the last one clicked by a buyer. This highlights the campaigns, ad groups and keywords that contribute the most to bring sales-ready buyers to your website.

- *Top paths data*: shows the most common paths your customers take to complete purchases and the value of the purchases they make.
  — *Top paths (clicks)*: shows the many different sequences of *ads buyers clicked* on before buying and how frequently each sequence happened among your buyers. The report is available at the Campaign, Ad group and Ad Levels.
  — *Top paths (impressions)*: shows the different ad impressions *a buyer saw* before a conversion, whether the searcher(s) clicked on them or not.
  — *Top paths (query paths)*: shows *ads customers clicked before buying* (as opposed to the top paths—impressions, which shows the ads matching the searcher's query [whether or not the people bought]).
  — *Top paths (transitions)*: shows the sequence of keywords, ads, ad groups and campaigns a buyer viewed before buying.

- *Transition ratios*: provide insight into the relationship between two elements. You select two elements to compare.

- *Time lag*: shows how much time passed (1) between the first impression and the conversion, (2) between the first click and the conversion and (3) between the last click and the conversion.

- **Path length**: shows the number of clicks-before-conversions or, alternatively, the number of impressions-before-conversions.

Monitoring Conversion Tracking

The more data AdWords has to work with (i.e., the longer Conversion Tracking runs), the better your results.

Recall the following key concepts:

- **Whether you selected the click-through option or view-through option matters.** A click-through occurs when a searcher sees your ad, clicks it and buys. By contrast, a view-through occurs when a searcher sees your ad, does not click on it, but returns to your website within the number of days you specify (up to 30) and buys. If you enabled view-throughs, these two visits count as one conversion.

- **Data at the different AdWords levels provide different insights for decision-making.**
  - Data at the Campaign Level provide insight into the patterns of buyers across the demographic, geographic, language, etc. characteristics you selected for the campaign.
  - Data at the Ad Group Level provide insight into the most appealing product attributes (keyword theme).
  - Data at the Ad Level provide insight into the message that resonates best with buyers.

- **Before monitoring your ads, make sure the Conversion Tracking data columns appear on the** *statistics table.* If they do not appear, go to the *campaign* tab, click the *column* button and click *customize columns* on the drop-down menu. Click *conversions* in the *select metrics* column and add *all* the conversion data columns.

To monitor ads under Conversion Tracking, do the following:

1. **At the Campaign Level, determine if you are making more sales using Conversion Tracking.** Compare your previous period's conversions with your current period's conversions. (Use the comparison capability on the date selector in the upper right corner.)

2. **At the Campaign Level, determine if you are maintaining your** *cost-per-acquisition.* Compare your cost-per-acquisition (CPA) and click-through rate (CTR) after deploying Conversion Tracking to your CPAs and CTRs before you deployed Conversion Tracking. Alternatively, compare your current CPA and CTR with your CPA and CTR for the prior 30 days.

   a. If your CPA is the same or lower *and* your CTR is the same or higher, Conversion Tracking is working for you.

   b. If your CPA is higher *and* your CTR is lower, Conversion Tracking is not bringing you more business.
      - Consider whether this is a normal or seasonal fluctuation (i.e., a fluctuation you have seen before in your sales activity). Have you seen the same trend in other campaigns? Has a new competitor entered the market?

— You may want to increase your max CPA during times of change.

— Consider whether the initial maximum CPA or target CPA was too low. If you guessed your target CPA (as often done when little history exists), your target CPA may be too low, and fewer impressions and fewer click-throughs are the result. Consider raising your target CPA.

— Be aware that it takes Conversion Tracking a while to respond to build buying patterns.

— If you disable Conversion Tracking, you cannot re-enable it until you again reach 15 conversions in 30 days.

To improve Conversion Tracking results, consider the following:

3. **Ads that assist in conversions.** These ads may not have many impressions, clicks or conversions but they are contributing to your sales. *Label* these ads as assisters to discourage you from pausing or deleting the ad because of poor performance.

4. **Keywords that assist in conversions.** These keywords may not have many impressions, clicks or conversions but they are contributing to your sales. Label these keywords as Assisters to discourage you from pausing or deleting them because of poor performance.

5. **If your campaigns are bringing in buyers, consider increasing your CPC and/or CPA.** This gives AdWords more leeway in auctions, which can bring more impressions and, ultimately, sales.

Conversion Optimization [Bidding]

One of the major benefits of using Conversion Tracking is the opportunity to add the *Conversion Optimizer* feature to Search Network ads.

• The *Conversion Optimizer* is available only after you have a history of at least 15 conversions a month and have installed Conversion Tracking.

The *Conversion Optimizer* calculates an estimated *cost-per-acquisition* (CPA) when you select *Optimize for Conversions* as your campaign bidding option. The CPA represents the amount you pay, on average over a 30-day period, for a buyer. Thus, CPA is the total cost of all the ad impressions for 30 days divided by the total number of unique buyers during the same 30 days. AdWords knows the total number of buyers because the *Conversion Tracking* maintains a running total.

• Note that cost-per-acquisition and cost-per-customer are the same metric. They both count a person only once. Thus the cost-per-acquisition is your total costs for AdWords for 30 days divided by the total number of unique visitors.

- The cost-per-conversion or the cost-per-lead is the total costs of AdWords for 30 days divided by the total number of purchase transactions.

- A *conversion* refers to a visitor who takes whatever action you promote on your site. Thus, a conversion refers to a buy, a lead sign-up, a newsletter sign-up, etc.

- A *lead* is someone who comes to your site and leaves enough information that you can contact him/her later by email, mail, phone or social media.

- A *buyer* is a visitor that makes a purchase on your site (i.e., executes a transaction). Generally, this number does not count a visitor more than once, even if he or she returns several times.

- In marketing and sales parlance, customers are "acquired" (not "converted" as AdWords' terminology implies) and cost-per-customer is a more commonly used term than cost-per-acquisition.

The *Conversion Optimizer* attempts to bring you more buyers at the same (or better!) *cost-per-acquisition* (CPA). When a searcher follows the same search and click behavior your buyers exhibited in the past, the Conversion Optimizer increases your max CPC bid as much as 30 percent to obtain an ad impression before that searcher. This helps you win more impressions at the lowest price possible before your best prospects.

- To identify searchers with high purchase potential, AdWords compares the conversions history of your buyers to the current searcher's location, sites visited, search query and other factors.

- To bring more potential buyers to your site while staying at or below your current CPA, AdWords may bid very high for one searcher and later offset that high bid by bidding very low for another searcher.

The *Conversion Optimize* sets an initial Max CPA bid to help you get started. You can use it or enter a maximum *cost-per-acquisition* of your own determination.

- Because the Conversion Optimizer is optimizing your bid based on your *cost-per-acquisition*, it ignores any max CPC or *bid adjustments* you set.

According to Google, the Conversion Tracking and the Conversion Optimizer together give you a better chance of capturing profitable clicks. Google cites examples of double-digit increase in conversions and double-digit decrease in CPA for some Conversion Tracking/automatic bidding users.

Setting Up Conversion Optimization

To implement the Conversion Optimizer:

1. **You must be using Conversion Tracking.**

2. **Go to your campaign, click the *settings* tab and change your *bidding option* to *Focus-on-Conversion*.**

Detailed instructions for implementing the Conversion Optimizer are available under "About Conversion Optimizer" in AdWords Help.

Monitoring Conversion Optimization

1. Ensure that Conversion Optimization is garnering more clicks and buyers than your campaign (ad group or ad) received previously. Use the comparison feature in the date selector to review date before and after the activation of Conversion Optimization.

2. The only control you have over Conversion Optimization is the target CPA, which you set at the Campaign Level.

   • Raise it if you are successfully converting visitors to buyers but are still missing impression opportunities. (i.e., your lost impression share is greater than 10 percent or so).

   • Lower it if your impression share is high (approaching 100 percent) and you need to lower costs or believe a drop in ad position will not affect your results.

3. Review the steps for monitoring Search Network ads to improve keywords and landing pages.

Chapter 6

Setting Up, Monitoring, and Growing Your Display Network Campaigns

This chapter provides a "how-to" reference manual for Display Network ads, showing you how to setup and monitor the different Display Network ads. It dives into the details of evaluating Display Network ad results, and reviews a long list of options, at different account levels (campaign, ad group, ad, keyword, etc.), to use to improve performance. It provides best practices and repercussions for many of the options, and it outlines additional features and new ad types to add as your revenues grow.

More specifically, the chapter covers, in detail, how to setup and monitor basic display, engagement, impression, local (and on YouTube), mobile (and on YouTube), video (and on YouTube), Google Shopping, and Google Ad/Mob app ad types.

If you are comfortable with your understanding of your buyer, you can add Display Network ads to your campaign.

BASIC DISPLAY NETWORK ADS

Display Network ads, including Engagement Ad, impression ads and image ads, need careful monitoring to ensure:

- Your max CPC is not too high for you to make money.
- Your ads are appearing on appropriate sites for your desired prospects and, conversely, are not appearing on sites damaging to your brand.
- Your ads are bringing not just visitors, but buyers.

Display Network ads run on the websites of thousands of publishers who opted into Google's AdSense program, as well as on YouTube, Google Blogger, Gmail and Google Finance.

Display Network uses images, animation, color, shape, size and more to entice viewers to click your ad. AdWords provides a number of ways to Display Network ads, including:

1. Text ads: like those you create for Search Network ads.

2. Unique template ads: created by AdWords by scanning your website. You can modify the copy and button text.

3. Image ads: created using an image that you upload. Your image represents the entire message; AdWords does not add a headline or description lines. You will need different sizes to fit different ad spaces. Ad sizes include:

   Rectangle:

200 × 200	Small square
240 × 400	Vertical rectangle
250 × 250	Square
250 × 360	Triple widescreen
300 × 250	Inline rectangle
336 × 280	Large rectangle
580 × 400	Netboard

   Skyscraper:

120 × 600	Skyscraper
160 × 600	Wide skyscraper
300 × 600	Half-page ad
300 × 1050	Portrait

   Leaderboard:

468 × 60	Banner
728 × 90	Leaderboard
930 × 180	Top banner
970 × 90	Large leaderboard
970 × 250	Billboard
980 × 120	Panorama

   Mobile:

320 × 50	Mobile banner
320 × 100	Large mobile banner

4. *Ad gallery ads*: created using one of the more than 200 templates available. Templates are easy to use, and the end result is a professional looking ad. Many of the templates contain animation, and you can modify the template to use your brand colors and typeface. The major template styles are:

   — Dynamic ad templates: ads for schools, travel, hotels and rental businesses, along with a custom image template that lets you

242

provide a spreadsheet of items to sell (similar to a Google Shopping feed).

— Social ads templates: ads that show your Google+ post.

— Lightbox ads (Engagement Ads) templates: ads that expand, use animation, etc.

— Video Ads (CPC-based) templates: ads that support video clips.

— General purpose ads templates: ads that use animation to attract attention.

5. *WAP Mobile Ad*: an ad format for the Google/AdMob Network and cell phones that do not have full web browsers (i.e., are not smart phones). Read Display Network Ads for Mobile Devices, later in this section, if you want to use this option.

As you work with Display Network ads, keep these important characteristics in mind.

- **Generally, Display Network ads have lower click-through rates.** It is harder to get people's attention while they are reading.

- **You set the *max CPC* at the Ad Group Level for Display Network ads.** However, you can override the max CPC at the Keyword Level using *custom bids*. Further, you can add *bid adjustments* to your other targeting methods.

  (See Key Concept 2: AdWords Supports Several Bidding Models to Maximize Your Budget, p. 88, for more details about custom bidding and *bid adjustments*.)

- **You can assign a different destination URL (landing page) to each *managed placement*.** This lets you align the message on your landing page with the look, feel and approach of the website sending you the prospect.

- **Some Display Network Partner websites support text ads along with image ads, while others support only text ads.** For these reasons, it is wise to include a text ad in each of your Display Network ad groups.

In a nutshell, Display Network ads work like this:

1. **You can add Display Network ads to an existing campaign for Display Network ads, or you create a separate ad group for Display Network ads.**

   - You can use *Automatic Placements* and let AdWords place your ads. This lets AdWords find your most productive sites for you. However, you should watch your budget closely. It may take a while to find your ideal buyer.

243

- Alternatively, you can target your audience using the Display Network targeting methods—keywords, managed placements (websites and webpages you specify), topics (items you select from AdWords predefined list), interests (items you select from AdWords predefined list), ages, genders and site categories.

- You can show an ad exclusively on YouTube by entering YouTube.com as your only *placement*.

- You can set different *destination URLs* for managed placements.

- You can exclude specific keywords, managed placements and certain types of sites (using *site categories*) to keep your ad off sites you find unproductive.

- You can exclude ads from appearing on apps by adding AdSenseForMobileApps.com as an excluded placement.

- As with all Display Network ads, you must win the auction for your ad to appear.

2. **You develop ads with images and animation without the services of a graphic artist.** The Display Network +Ad function can create image and animation ads for you. (This capability was once called the *display ad builder*.)

3. **Based on your targeting methods, AdWords includes your ad in the auction for a webpage.**

For detailed instructions on implementing Display Network ads, refer to "Display Network getting started guide" in AdWords Help.

Setting Up Basic Display Network Ads

The major tasks to implement Display Network ads are:

1. **Setup your campaign options.** Select *Display Network only* and the *all features* option.

2. **Setup an ad group.** At the Ad Group Level, enter these options:

   - *Ad group name*: enter a name that describes the theme of this group of ads and keywords.

   - *Default bid*: Enter your *maximum CPC* bid.

   - *Targeting method(s)*: select either:

   a. *Display keyword: show ads on sites related to your keywords.* Use this option if you want to target your audience based on your keywords. You can also add additional targeting methods after you add your keywords.

b. *Interest and Remarketing*: *show ads to people based on their interests.* Use this option if you want to target your audience based on affinity, in market for x, or interests. If you use Remarketing, you can select your Remarketing Lists here or target people similar to those on your Remarketing lists.

c. *Use a different targeting method* (note that it does not offer keywords as an option): use this option if you want to target your audience by topics, placements, age, gender or parental status. Use this option if you want to run ads on YouTube.

The following *targeting methods* are available after you setup either option a or b above. All the targeting methods except *keywords* are available after you setup option c.

Remember, targeting methods are cumulative—a website must meet all your targeting methods.

— *Keywords*: enter 10–20 tightly themed keywords related to your ad. Note that all keywords are broad match and cannot be designated as exact match or partial match.

— *Topics*: specify areas of interest from AdWords' predefined list. AdWords then targets web surfers whose interests match the ones you listed, based on their previous sites visited and social media data.

— *Managed placements*: specify websites, sections of websites or specific webpages to include or, alternatively, to exclude.

(1) Use the *display planner* tool to find sites for your ad.

(2) If you have multiple landing pages for the ad, determine which landing page (destination URL) to associate with each managed placement.

(3) If you want your ad to only appear on YouTube videos, enter YouTube.com as your only placement.

(4) If you want to prevent your ad from appearing on apps, enter AdSenseForMobileaApps.com as an excluded placement.

— *Interests*: select as many categories and/or sub-categories as you want from the following:

(1) *Affinity*: to target people with certain interests, such as theatre aficionados, auto buffs, beauty mavens, foodies, DIY, etc.

(2) *In market*: to target people who are researching your product and looking to buy (based on their search history).

(3) *Interest*: to target people based on their interests, such as art, business, computers, hobbies, education, jobs, etc.

— *Remarketing lists*: specify the Remarketing list you want to view this ad. This option is available only if you use the Remarketing feature.

— *Gender*: specify male or female and whether you want to include people whose gender is unknown.

— *Age*: specify the age ranges you want.

If you want to *exclude* certain types of sites, you must: (1) first save your ad group, (2) go to the Display Network tab and (3) under the *statistics table*, select *site category options*. There you can exclude websites based on subject, type, video type and ad location, indicate where you do not want to show your ad.

d. Select your choice for *targeting optimization*: *let AdWords automatically find new customers for you*. Leave this item checked if you do not want to specify placements for the ads in the ad group.

If you opted to let AdWords *find new customers for you*, select your level of pursuit. (Using the option, called the *display campaign optimizer*, is recommended.)

— *Conservative targeting: find additional customer at your current costs-per-customer*. Use this option if you need to keep close control on your cost-per-customer.

— *Aggressive targeting: discover even more customers around your current cost per customer (display campaign optimizer)*. Using this option authorizes AdWords to increase your current cost-per-acquisition in order to bring in more likely buyers. Google does not say how much of an increase is permitted.

Google documentation says your campaign must have 15 conversions before aggressive targeting can be used; however, the question appears when your setup your first ad group (when presumably you have no conversions). Logically, *aggressive targeting* waits until you have 15 conversions, but that is not stated.

3. **Setup your ad.** At the Ad Level, select a *type of ad* and enter your ad information. Each requires a headline, two description lines, a display URL and a destination URL, along with any additional elements mentioned here:

- *Text ad*: an ad like the ones you created for the Search Ad network. You can use this ad type for YouTube *overlay banner ads*.

- *Image ad*: two variations exist:
  — An ad designed by you or a graphic artist and uploaded to AdWords. You will need different sizes.
  — An ad created by AdWords from a scan of your website.

  You can use this ad type for YouTube *overlay banner ads*. You need a 320 × 50px ad.

- *Ad gallery*: a text-and-image ad generated automatically from free templates. Modify the ad to use your brand colors and typeface. This tool offers over 200 templates, some with animation. Using it is easy, and the end result is professional looking.

  You can use the *in-video static image* template for YouTube *overlay banner ads*.

- *WAP Mobile Ad*: an ad format for the Google/AdMob Network and cell phones that do not have full web browsers (i.e., are not smart phones). Read Display Network Ads for Mobile Devices, later in this section, if you want to use this option.

4. **For Video Ads, go to *all video campaigns* in the left-hand menu column and use that function to create ads.** The latest video formats are available there. Refer to Video Ads later in this section.

Monitoring Basic Display Network Ads

Display Network ads need careful monitoring to ensure:

- Your *max CPC* is not too high for you to make money.
- Your ads are appearing on appropriate sites for your desired prospects and, conversely, are not appearing on sites damaging to your brand.
- Your ads are bringing not just visitors, but buyers, to your website.

To monitor your Display Network ads, do the following:

1. **Set a specific reporting period.**

   - Click the date range menu on the top right corner of the page and select the time period you'd like to analyze.
   - Be aware that complete data for yesterday is not available until 3 p.m. PT today.

2. **Verify your ad is running.**

   - On the *tools* tab, click *ad preview and diagnosis* and enter one of your keywords. This tool lets you view your ad without affecting your click-through rate.

3. **Click on the *Display Network* tab and select each *targeting method*, in turn, to determine if each underlying item is active and generating clicks (and conversions if you use Conversion Tracking).**

   On the *statistics table*, under the *status* column, click the *speech bubble icon* (🖵) to see if the item is active.

Check the impressions and clicks (and conversions) to identify items that are not productive.

To raise your *quality score*:

- Pause or delete items with no impressions or clicks. Also, add the unproductive placements to the *excluded placement* list.

- Unproductive items drag down your *quality score*, which depends heavily on your overall click-through rate (CTR).

- Add unproductive keywords to the *negative keywords* list to remove your ad from unproductive sites. Review the keyword terms that brought people to your site using the search term report (*keyword* tab— *details—search terms—all*). Add the irrelevant terms to your negative keywords list.

4. **Use the *segment* button to see your ad performance by time of day, device, network, top positions, click type and Google+1 annotation.**

   - Delete or lower bids on unproductive device types, networks or click types.

   - To lower costs, consider *ad scheduling* with different bids for peak and off-peak time for *managed placements*.

5. **Review your ad performance by geographic area and user location to determine where your buyers reside.** (Click the *dimensions* tab, click the *view* tab and from the drop-down menu, select *geographic* to see data for the users' physical locations or their locations of interest. Select *user location* to see data based only on the users' physical locations.)

   - Reduce your geographic area to attract prospects close to your location. Conversely expand your geographic area to increase impressions.

   - Compare the geographic report to the user location report to see if you have a significant number of visits searching from outside your area. You may want to allocate more budgets to an outlying area. (Use the *location bid* feature to do that.)

6. **Review the *mouseover time* for your ads, to see if customers show any interest in your ad even though they did not click it.** (Click on the *dimensions* tab and click *free click* on the drop-down menu.)

   - Experiment with different call-to-action lines to see if your ad improves.

7. **For Engagement Ads,, review the number of people who clicked through to your landing page.** Go to the *dimensions* tab and click *free click* on the drop-down menu. Be aware that the clicks column in the *statistics table* shows the number of people who clicked your ad to view it, not to go to the landing page.

8. **Review the performance of your *destination URLs* to determine which ones need text, imagery or layout changes to entice more visitors to purchase.** (Click the *dimensions* tab, click the *View* tab and select *destination URL* from the drop-down menu.)

   • Review Step 4: Create a Compelling Landing Page.

9. **Review the *relative click-through rate* (CTR) for your Display Network ads.** Relative CTR is a measure of how well your ad is performing in comparison to other advertisers' ads appearing on the same websites.

   More specifically, relative CTR is the result of dividing your CTR by the average CTR of all advertisers on the placements where your ads appear. AdWords computes this number for you.

   Relative CTR is available at the Campaign and Ad Group Level. If it does not appear on the *statistics table*, click the *columns* button, select *competitive metrics* and *add* relative CTR.

   Relative CTR changes based on the websites where your ad appears and what other ads are running against yours. Thus, it changes as the competition changes.

   • The average relative CTR is always 1.00. If your relative CTR is above 1.00, your ad is doing better than average.

   • If your relative CTR is below 1.00, the ad is not competing well against other advertisers. Move poorly performing placements and categories to the excluded sites and categories. Improving your ad text and/or your keywords can improve your results. Run experiments to see which changes work best.

   • Relative CTR shows which ad is the most competitive against other advertisers, and your most competitive ad may or may not be the ad that gets the most clicks. An ad may be very relevant but receive few impressions because of a low bid. Lower the bids on the less competitive ads (or pause them), so the most competitive ad competes in more auctions.

   • Consider raising your bid on the most productive targeting method items if it does not erode your profits too drastically.

10. **Use the auction insights report to see who your competitors are.** The report tells you who is getting the most impressions and best ad positions, whose ads appear above yours and whose ad you compete with head-to-head.

    If you segment the report by device or time, it tells you where and when your competitors are getting clicks.

11. **Use the *tools—display planner* to see which keywords and placements AdWords recommends for your competitors.** Put a competitor's URLs into the display planner to see the recommendations. Determine if any of the recommendations are appropriate for your ad.

12. **Review Step 3: Identify Lucrative Keywords, p. 138, and Step 5: Write Attention-Grabbing Ad Copy, p. 142, for suggestions for improving your ads and keywords.**

To further improve your Display Network ads:

13. **Consider using the *display targeting optimizer*.**

    With the *display targeting optimizer* in use, AdWords automatically selects placements and, if you permit, raises your bid to win auctions—an especially helpful action if the reader visits some of the same sites your buyers visit. AdWords works to keep your overall cost-per-acquisition (CPA) below the dollar amount calculated by the Conversion Tracker or set by you. You can stop the *display tracking optimizer* at any time.

ENGAGEMENT ADS

Engagement Ads attract attention and engage the viewer. They are especially useful for building brand awareness, though you can also use them to sell products and, even, present catalogues of items.

Engagement Ads run on the Display Network and you can use any or all of the Display Network targeting methods.

Not all Display Network Partner websites can run Engagement Ads.

In a nutshell, Engagement Ads work like this:

1. You create a separate campaign for the Display Network, and you select the cost-per-engagement bidding option (which works just like the CPC bidding option).

2. You develop the type of ad you want to show, either a lightbox ad or a hover-over ad that uses an image, video, animation, etc. You can use the *ad gallery* to create your Engagement Ads.

3. You select your targeting methods and enter your choices.

Setting Up Engagement Ads

To Implement Display Network—Engagement Ads, do the following:

1. Determine your campaign options as you would for a Display Network ad, except for the following, which have changes:

   - *Campaign type*: select the Display Network and the sub-campaign feature, Engagement Ad.

   - *Bidding options*: select *Focus-on-Engagements, manual maximum CPC bidding.*

2. Setup an ad group for your Engagement Ads.

   - As usual, enter a default bid and any targeting methods you want to use.

   - On the next panel, select either the lightbox or the hover-over template.

   - Upload the required resources (your logo, beginning and ending images, etc.).

   - Enter your headline, *display URL* and *destination URL*.

   - Review your ad and save it or add additional ads before saving the group.

   For more on Display Network ads—Engagement Ad, refer to the topic, "Create an Engagement Ads campaign" in AdWords Help.

Monitoring Engagement Ads

Refer to Basic Display Network Ads for suggestions for monitoring and improving ads.

IMPRESSION ADS

For Impressions Ads, or cost-per-thousand (CPM) impression ads, you bid a specific amount for 1,000 impressions, called a max CPM. You are charged each time your ad appears, regardless of whether the viewer clicks your ad.

Impression ads work best for high-intensity, short-run campaigns, where you want as many people as possible to see your ad (rather than visit your website). CPM ads are best when you want to attract attention, build brand recognition or announce a new product or upcoming event.

Your ad should contain your entire message. When your ad contains your entire message, it does not need to link to a landing page. This makes these ads quick and easy to deploy.

- Impression ads run only on the Display Network.
- When you select the CPM bidding option for your campaign, specify that your ad be "viewable" (i.e., that 50 percent of the ad must be on-screen for one second or longer in order to be billable).

Consider the following when determining your bid:

- Many publishing (e-zines) websites outside of AdWords offer CPM advertising. Check their CPM prices before you advertise on AdWords so you do not bid too high. It may be more affordable and more productive to use a publisher's website that is tightly focused on your market rather than AdWords.
- Your ad still must win its position, which means a reasonable max CPM is important.
- The higher your bid, the higher the ad position your ad is likely to achieve and the more often it is likely to appear.
- You can specify a max CPM for the ad group or for each *managed placement* (i.e., each Display Network partners' websites you specify).
- Use CPM ads in conjunction with *managed placements* as an inexpensive and highly-targeted "get-the-word-out" campaign.

In a nutshell, Impression Ads work like this:

1. You create a campaign for the Display Network, select the CPM bidding option and select your targeting methods (usually, keywords and/or placements).

2. You develop the type of ad you want to show, either a text-only ad or an ad that uses an image and text. You can use the *ad gallery* to create your image ads or have your graphic designer create them.

3. Your ad appears before your desired audience.

4. Add the performance metrics (active view) data to your *statistics table*. Go to *columns*, click *customize columns*, then *performance* and *add the active view metrics*.

Refer to the topic, "Cost-per-thousand-impressions bidding" in AdWords Help for more information about impression ads.

Setting Up Impression Ads

To implement an Impression Ad:

1. **Determine your campaign options as you would for a Display Network ad, except for the following, which have changes:**

   * *Campaign type*: select *Display Network only*.

   * *All features*: select this option to gain access to additional options, such as Ad Extensions.

   * *Bidding options*: select *advanced options* and *Focus-on-Impressions*. Check *enable viewable CPM (with active view reporting)* to ensure that your ad appears in an ad slot where your viewer is most likely to see it and that AdWords charges you only if 50 percent of the ad is visible for one second or longer.

   * *Default bid*: enter your max CPM.

     Do not bid more than you would if you advertised directly with a website owner. Many websites offer advertising impression-based advertising (e.g., "X impressions per Y dollars," or, for example, 100,000 impressions for $5,000, which is 20¢ per impression). Use the going rates on websites that your prospects visit to determine your bid for impressions on AdWords.

     A reasonable CPM bid is somewhat higher than the CPC bid for the same target audience.

   * *Frequency capping*: if you use the *Focus-on-Impressions (CPM)* bidding model, you can set a maximum number of times a Display Ad can appear on a website per viewer per day.

2. **Setup an ad group for your impression ads.**

   * *Ad group name*: enter a name for your ad group.

   * *Default bid* (for this ad group): enter a CPM bid to override the one at the Campaign Level, if you want.

   * Select your targeting method(s). Remember that targeting methods are cumulative. A searcher or website must meet all your criteria for your ad to show.

     If you want your ad to appear on certain websites, enter those websites or webpages as *managed placements*. Set a CPM bid for each, if you like. You may want to bid more for the best placements for your ad.

     Make sure your ad format is compatible with the placements you select.

Monitoring Impressions Ads

1. Refer to Basic Display Network Ads for suggestions for monitoring and improving ads.

LOCAL ADS—ADWORDS DISPLAY NETWORK

Local Ads on the Display Network are basic text ads targeting the immediate area around your business.

Setting Up Local Ads on the Display Network

To create a Local Ad, do the following.

1. **Create a campaign for the Display Network only or using an existing campaign.** Under *location*, select *let me choose* and click *advance search*. Enter your local area by entering either your city or the zip code(s) around your business location. Save your ad.

2. **Setup an ad group and ad as you normally would for a Basic Display Ad.** See Basic Display Network Ads for instructions.

3. **Local Ads, like all Display Network ads, show on all devices—desktops and such mobile devices as smartphones, phablets**

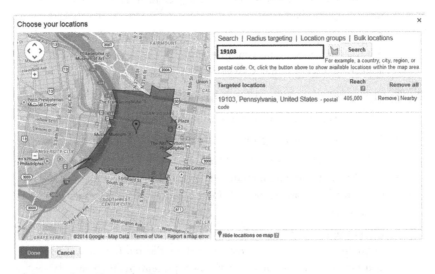

FIGURE 6.1 Location selection screen

Your campaign is now targeted to the area you specified. You can create ad groups for different products. Within each ad group, you may want to create a Local Ad for desktops and one for mobile devices.

254

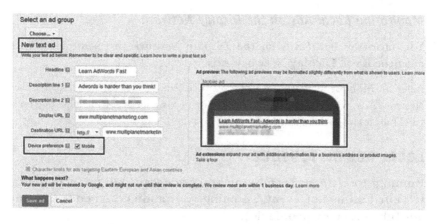

FIGURE 6.2 Local Ad for Mobile Devices

To designate a Local Ad to run on mobile devices check the box next to mobile when you setup the ad.

and tablets. However, you may want to create Local Ads especially for mobile devices.

To designate a Local Ad for use only on a mobile device, create a text ad and check the box for *device preference: mobile*.

4. You may want to exclude some devices from showing your campaign—especially if you are running image or Engagements Ads, which may not show well on small screens.

   To do this, you can set a *bid adjustment* of –100 percent for the device(s) you do not want to show your ad:

   a. Click on the *setting* tab and, then, the *devices* tab.

   b. Click the box next to the ad(s) you want to exclude from mobile devices.

   c. In the *bid adjustment* column, enter –100 percent to deactivate the desired device(s).

5. Depending on the size and type of your ad, you can include certain smartphones and tablets based on operating system, device model and/or carrier. This may come into play more often as the screen sizes of mobile devices continue to change.

   To include certain smartphone and tablets:

   a. Click on the *setting* tab, scroll to the bottom of the screen to *device: target selected mobile devices and tablets* and click *edit*.

   b. From the drop-down menus, select the devices you want to target.

Monitoring Local Ads on the Display Network

You monitor *Local Ads on the Display Network* the same way you monitor **Basic Display Network Ads.**

Refer to Monitoring Basic Display Network Ads and Growing Basic Display Network Ads, where the section on changing geographic areas and adjusting max CPC bids are especially relevant.

LOCAL ADS ON YOUTUBE

Running *Local Ads on YouTube* **can be a great way to draw an audience to your business or event, assuming your audience spends time on YouTube (as many people do).**

- For example, you might use *local overlay banner ads on YouTube* videos to advertise the grand opening of your ice cream store, to sell tickets to a local community theater production, to remind people of the school fund-raiser, etc.

- Alternatively, you might use *local Video Ads on YouTube* to talk about the service you offer or to demonstrate your work.

Setting Up Local Ads on YouTube

You can setup *Local Ads on YouTube* for overlay banner ads or Video Ads in two ways:

1. On the *all online campaign* screen, as a *Display Network only* campaign, using the *cost-per-click* bidding method, as a text ad or image ad. Refer to Setting Up Basic Display Network Ads for instructions.

   - This is the easiest way to setup YouTube ads. If you are not going to use videos, this is by far the preferred method.

2. On the *all video campaign* screen using the *cost-per-view* bidding method, as a banner ad and/or as a Video Ad. Refer to Setting up All Video Campaign Video Ads (CPV) for instructions.

   - This format provides the ability to bid by audience and to view performance data for different segments (such as format, network, device, etc.).

Monitoring Local Ads on YouTube

You monitor *Local Ads on YouTube* on the screen where they were created, either the *all online campaign* screen or the *all video campaign* screen. (AdWords shows the campaign only on the screen where it was created.)

1. If you created your *Local Ads on YouTube* campaign on the *all online campaign* screen, refer to Monitoring Basic Display Ads for instructions for monitoring your ad.

2. If you created your *Local Ads on YouTube* campaign on the *all online campaign* screen, refer to the section "To Monitor YouTube Ads" under Monitoring All *Video Campaign* Video Ads for instructions for monitoring your ad.

MOBILE ADS ON THE DISPLAY NETWORK

By default, all Display Network ads appear on mobile devices. However, you may want to create ads especially for mobile device. This lets you:

- Target people near your store with a more specific message or, better yet, with a special promotion to pull them in for a visit
- Streamline your ad to fit the small screen
- Send your visitor to a mobile landing page so they can easily peruse your site.

To run an ad only on mobile devices, you merely set the *device preference* **as** *mobile* **for the ad.** You can add a Mobile Ad to an existing group, which forces *non-Mobile Ads* (i.e., *device preference* is not set to *mobile*) to appear only on tablets and desktops.

In fact, it is a best practice to create a Mobile Ad and a non–Mobile Ad in every ad group.

AdWords automatically sends ads marked *mobile* **to your** *mobile-optimized landing page*, **if you have a** *mobile-optimized* **and a desktop-optimized landing page**. (But you should enter your mobile-optimized landing page in your ad anyway.)

- A mobile-optimized landing page or website is designed for the small screens of smartphones. Webpages are very narrow with larger type and long, scrolling pages.

Mobile Ads **have special requirements and advantages:**

- *Mobile Ads* show most often as 320 × 50 pixel (about 3″ × 1/2″) banners or image ads.
- Your ad should not include Adobe Flash because it does not show correctly on some devices, and iPhones do not support Flash at this time.
- You should select your keywords with care, if you use keywords as a targeting method. Do not assume the keywords you use with desktop/laptop ads are as productive with smartphone ads. People often use different keywords on mobile phones.

- *Mobile Ads* can use the following *ad extensions*, all of which bring prospects to your business. Use them!
  — *Call extension*: lets you include a clickable phone number in your ad. (Do not put your phone number in your ad copy; use this ad extension.)
  — *Location extensions*: lets you add information about the store closest to the viewer with a "get directions" link.
  — *Offer extension*: lets you add a promotional ad or in-store promotion that viewers can email or text to themselves for later use.
  — *Sitelinks*: lets you add a hyperlink to a landing page other than your destination URL. You need at least one sitelink used only by your mobile device. Location extensions take precedence over sitelinks.
  — *Callout*: lets you add one line touting a company benefit. The message is not clickable.
- The *cost-per-click* for a *Mobile Device Ad* on a smartphone or a tablet often differs from that of a desktop/laptop ad. Consequently, AdWords lets you adjust the bid (1) for mobile devices (smartphones) with full browsers and (2) for tablets with full browsers.
- *Bid adjustments* for mobile devices are available at the Campaign, Ad Group, or Ad Level. They are an increased or decreased percentage of the max CPC.

  (See Key Concept 2: Bidding Strategies and Bidding Models, p. 88, for an overview of *bid adjustments*. See Adding Bid Adjustments for Devices, Locations, Ad Schedules and Targeting Methods for implementation details.)
- To advertise a mobile app in a Mobile Ad, use the Mobile App Install or Mobile App Engage ad types. They offer more capabilities.
- You should link your *Mobile Ad* to a *mobile-optimized website*, and it should:
  — Load quickly.
  — Be easy to navigate with you thumbs!
  — Make buying, signing-up, etc., easy.
  — Provide local information.
  — Let users switch between mobile and desktop versions of your website, depending on their device.
- Know that Google Analytics also shows performance data by mobile device.

Review AdWords' policies for *Mobile Ads* to make sure your ad meets its requirements. Learn more at the "Mobile Ads—what's the policy" topic on AdWords Help.

Setting up Mobile Display Ads

If you create a second ad within an ad group and mark its preferred device as *mobile*, AdWords shows only that ad on mobile devices. Thus, you should create two ads in every ad group—one for desktops and one for smartphones and tablets.

Further, AdWords automatically sends ads marked *mobile* to your mobile-optimized landing page, if you have one. (But you should enter your mobile-optimized landing page in your ad anyway.)

Mobile Device Ads on the Display Network must be text or image ads. You cannot use ad templates from the *ad gallery* on mobile devices.

To create a *Mobile Device Ad* on the Display Network, do the following:

1. In an existing Display Network ad group that already has an ad for the product you want to advertise, create a text or image ad being sure to:
   - Use less ad copy. Keep your headline at 25 characters, but shorten your description lines.
   - Use the URL for a mobile-optimized landing page.
   - If you want your ad to appear only on YouTube, set *placement* as a *targeting method* and enter YouTube.com.
   - Next to *device preference* box, check the box for *mobile*.
   - *Save* your ad.

You may want to give your Mobile Ad a different bid than your desktop ad. You do this by entering a *bid adjustment* for mobile devices and/or tablets.

To apply a different bid to your *Mobile Ads*, do the following:

1. Click on the desired campaign, ad group or ad on the *all online campaign* screen.

2. Click the *settings* tab. Click the prompt: *change campaign settings*, if it appears.

3. On the submenu that appears, click *devices*.

4. Enter your *bid adjustment* in the *bid adj.* column in the *mobile devices with full browsers* row. Enter it as either a percentage increase or a percentage decrease from the max bid. If you change your mind and do not want to enter a percentage, clear the field and leave it blank.

   If you put a zero in the field, your campaign is marked as having a *bid adjustment* (even though the amount is 0.) Clearing the field prevents this issue.

   The amount is saved as soon as you exit the field.

Monitoring Mobile Display Ads

Monitor your Mobile Display Ads by device to determine which device brings you buyers and, thus, should have the highest bid.

Further, monitor your ads by device to see which device seldom brings you buyers and should have a low bid or be turned off.

You can monitor Mobile Ads at the Campaign or Ad Group, Ad Level or at the Targeting Method level.

1. To monitor Mobile Display Ads, go to the desired campaign, ad group, ad or targeting method.

2. Click the *segment* button and select *devices*.

    Review the column for *conv.* (if you use Conversion Tracking) to see which device brings more buyers to your site. If you do not use Conversion Tracking, review the *clicks* column.

    Review the column for *display impr. share* to see what percentage of impressions it receives.

    Decide whether to raise your *bid adjustment* in an effort to receive more impressions for a device performing well or to lower your *bid adjustment* for a device performing poorly.

3. To change your bid, click in the *bid adj.* column and enter your new bid. Set the bid to minus 100 (−100) to completely stop a device from showing impressions.

VIDEO ADS

AdWords offers two ways of creating Video Ads. The two methods differ by:

1. The screen you use to setup the Video Ad.

2. The bidding method choice you have.

3. The level of performance data you receive.

The steps to write you ads are very similar regardless of which method you use.

More specifically, AdWords offers:

1. Video Ad formats that are created on the *all online campaign* screen, use the *cost-per-click* or *the cost-per-thousand* bidding method and provide no special performance information.

2. Video formats that are created on the *all video campaign* screen use the *cost-per-view* bidding method with the ability to bid by audience and provide performance information for different segments (such as format, network, device, etc.). Note that Google calls these "AdWords for Videos" ads in some of their Help documentation and makes mention of the fact that these Video Ads use TrueView video technology, which lets videos appear on many different browsers.

All Online Campaign Video Ads (cost-per-click):

Video Ad Name	Description	Setup Steps
In-Stream Video Ads	Short-clip video ad, 20-seconds or less, using CPC or CPM bidding	1. *All Online Campaign* screen 2. Select *Display Network Only* campaign. 3. Select *Ad Gallery* 4. Select In-Stream video template
YouTube Overlay Banners	Using Cost-per-Click or Cost-per-1000 bidding	1. *All Online Campaign* screen 2. Select *Display Network Only* campaign. 3. Select *Ad Gallery* Ad 4. Select the *YouTube Promotion* video template.
YouTube Promotions	Using Cost-per-Click or Cost-per-1000 bidding	1. *All Online Campaign* screen 2. Select Display Network Only campaign 3. Select *Ad Gallery* 4. Select the TrueView In-Display Promotion template
Engagement Video Ad	Hover-To-Play Video Ads Cost-per-Engagement	1. *All Online Campaign* screen 2. Select Display Network Only campaign and the Engagement ad sub-type. 3. Select Hoover-to-play template.
Engagement Video Ad	1-Video or 3-Video Ad using Cost-per-Engagement	1. *All Online Campaign* screen 2. Display Network Only campaign and the Engagement ad sub-type. 3. Select either the 1-video or the 3-video template, whichever fits your needs

Setting Up All Online Campaigns Video Ads (CPC)

1. **If you expect to specify placements (i.e., specific websites) for your ads on the Display Network, use the** *display planner* **tool to find appropriate videos and websites before starting your ad.**

   - To capture a consistent audience choose a specific *theme* (e.g., topics such as outdoor sports) or interests exhibited by your prospects (such as hunting and fishing). Keep a list of the videos and websites you want as placements.

2. **Setup a new campaign or use an existing** *Display Network only* **campaign with the** *All features* **sub-type for all CPC-based Video Ads except** *Engagement Video Ads.* **For** *Engagement Video Ads* **select the** *engagement* **sub-type.**

   - *Ad group name*: enter a name that describes the theme of this group of ads and keywords.

   - *Default bid*: enter your *maximum CPC* bid.

   - *Targeting method(s)*: select your *targeting method(s)*.
     - If you want to use keywords, select *display keyword—show ads on sites related to your keywords*. Enter any keywords you want to use.
       - (1) To garner lots of viewers for a YouTube overlay banner, use keywords associated with the most popular, viral or trending videos. Take your keywords from the video's description, tags, theme and comments.
       - (2) If you set your campaign's geographic area to your local zip code, a YouTube overlay banner can reach hundreds of people in your local business area as they partake of the latest YouTube sensation. This is a great way to announce a grand opening, new product, sales promotion or upcoming event.
     - If you want your ad to appear only on YouTube, select *use a different targeting method*. Select *placements*. Enter *YouTube.com* as your only placement.
     - If you want to setup more *targeting methods*, click *narrow your targeting further* under the placement panel, but remember: *targeting methods* are cumulative. The more *targeting methods* you use, the smaller your market.

   - Select your choice for *targeting optimization*:
     - Leave this item checked, so AdWords puts its logic to work for you: *let AdWords automatically find new customers for you.*

   - Select the level of effort you want AdWords to use. Aggressive targeting (i.e., using the *display campaign optimizer*) is recommended.

— *Conservative targeting: find additional customer at your current costs-per-customer.* Use this option if you need to keep close control on your cost-per-customer.

— *Aggressive targeting: discover even more customers around your current cost per customer (Display Campaign Optimizer).* Using this option authorizes AdWords to increase your current cost-per-acquisition in order to bring in more likely buyers. Google does not say how much of an increase is permitted.

Google documentation says your campaign must have 15 conversions before aggressive targeting can be used; however, the question appears when you setup your first ad group. Whether aggressive targeting begins immediately or waits until you have 15 conversions is not stated.

3. **Setup your ad.** On the *Ad tab,*

   a. Click the red *+Ad* button.

   b. Select *ad gallery.* (This option does not appear if you are doing an Engagement Video Ad.)

   c. Select *Video Ads.* (This option does not appear if you are doing an Engagement Video Ad.)

4. **Select your desired template:**

   a. **For a YouTube overlay banner, select** *in-video static image.*
      — Enter your headline, description lines, *display URL* and *destination URL.*

   b. **For a YouTube promotion to promote your video to people watching YouTube, select the** *TrueView in-display YouTube promotion* **template.**
      — Your video must reside on YouTube.
      — Use "YouTube.com" as your only placement under *targeting methods.*
      — You can specify whether you want the viewer to go to your channel or to a watch page.

   c. **For an** *In-Stream ad* **(15–20 seconds non-skip-able video), select** *in-stream video Ad* **template.**
      — You are charged when the viewer completes the video. If you want to use a video over 30-seconds, you must contact Google.
      — The viewer goes to your YouTube video page (or channel) when they click your ad.
      — Some Display Network Partner websites require a static image. Use this to entice the viewer to watch your video.

263

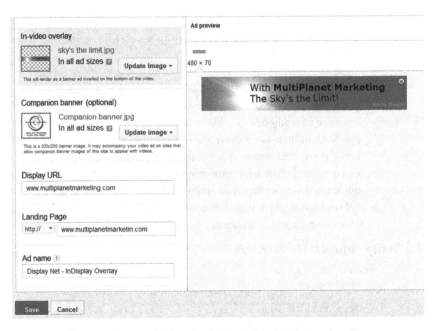

FIGURE 6.3 Overlay banner setup screen (in-video static image ad)

FIGURE 6.4 YouTube promotion setup screen (TrueView in-display Video Ad)

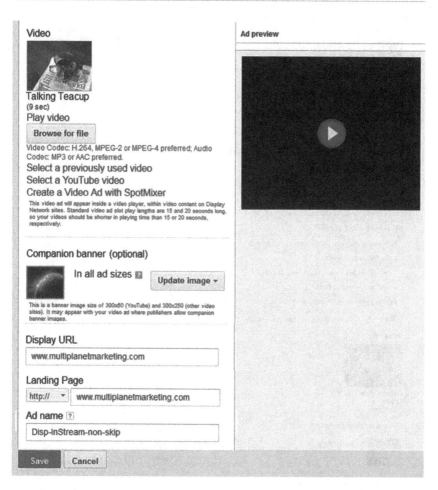

FIGURE 6.5 In-stream Video Ad

 d. **For an Engagement Video Ads, select one of the following choices:** *hover-to-play, one video lightbox, and lightbox with multiple videos.*

  — Setup is very similar for these ads. The *lightbox with multiple videos and image gallery* is the most complicated, so we use that as an example here.

  (1) Upload your logo.

  (2) The URL where your viewer goes upon clicking your logo.

  (3) Select your theme (dark or light), your accent color, your background color and the opacity of the background fade.

  (4) Enter the message for the first message, second message and third message, along with your call to action button.

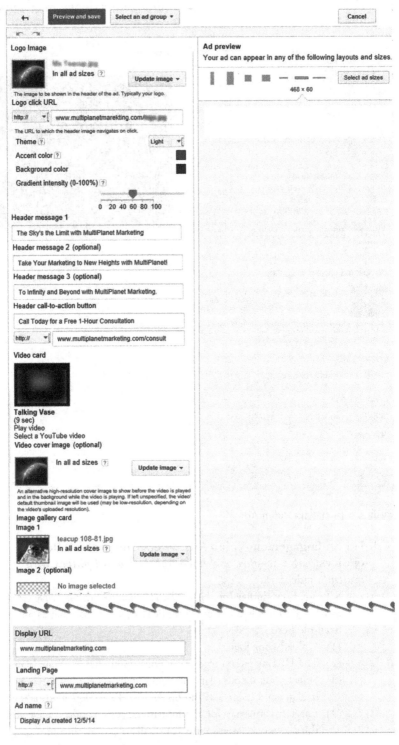

FIGURE 6.6. Lightbox with video and image gallery

(5) Enter the links to your videos.

(6) Upload your images from your computer (or select images you have previously uploaded).

(7) Enter your *display URL* and *landing page*.

(8) Name your ad.

(9) At the top of the page, select your ad group.

(10) Preview your ad. If your ad does not fit a particular ad size, uncheck it so it does not appear in that size space.

(11) Save your ad.

5. At the top of the page, select your ad group.

6. Preview your ad. If your ad does not fit a particular ad size, uncheck it so it does not appear in that size space.

7. Save your ad.

Monitoring All Online Campaign Video Ads (CPC)

Refer to Basic Display Network Ads for suggestions for monitoring and improving *all online campaign Video Ads*.

Setting up All Video Campaign Video Ads (CPV)

The *all video campaign* screen lets you setup your video to run on YouTube as well as the Display Network in one process. This is a quick and easy way to make sure your ads appear everywhere possible.

Video Ads created through the *all video campaigns* screen use the *cost-per-view* bidding model. You set the cost-per-view for each targeting group (audience) you create, rather than for each Video Ad.

- This lets you bid higher for one audience rather than another audience for the same video. AdWords charges you only when a viewer watches all or at least 30 second of your video, whichever comes first.

To deploy Video Ads via the *all video campaigns* screen:

1. **You must have a YouTube account and you must link your AdWords and YouTube accounts.** To link your accounts,

   - Go to the *all video campaigns* screen and click *linked YouTube accounts* in the left hand navigation menu.

   - Select either *I own the YouTube channel I want to link to AdWords for Videos* or *someone else owns the YouTube channel I want to link to AdWords for Video*.

- If you selected *someone else*, AdWords provides a link that you email to the owner of the site.

  When the owner of the site clicks the link, a YouTube screen opens asking the owner to grant permission to link the two accounts and to permit AdWords to (1) access video statistics, (2) add overlay banners to your videos, (3) remarket to previous visitors and (4) track visitor behaviors on the channel.

2. **Upload your video to YouTube before you build your Video Ad.**

3. **Create a new video campaign or add a video to an existing campaign.**

   - To create a new campaign, click *all video campaigns* on the left-hand menu, click the *campaign tab* and the red *+new campaign* button.

   - To add to a campaign, click *all video campaigns,* click the video campaign you want to expand and click the red *+new video* button.

   - Enter with other Display Network campaigns, enter a descriptive campaign name along with your daily budget, delivery, location and language and *advanced settings options you want to use.* See Setting Up Basic Display Network Ads for information on these options.

   - Finally, enter the URL of the video you want to advertise.

4. **Define your *target audience*.** Click on your campaign, then click the *target* tab and finally click the red *+new target* tab to define your audience.

   a. Give the target audience a descriptive name.

   b. Enter your *max cost-per-view*. AdWords provides an estimate of the number of views you will receive and the estimate cost-per-view based on your max CPV and budget.

   c. By default, your Video Ad is shown to anyone viewing YouTube videos. However, you can narrow that audience using (1) demographics (age, gender and parental status) and/or (2) interests (affinity, in-market or other interests).

5. **Create your Video Ad.**

   a. Click the *ad tab* and the red *+new Video Ad.*

   b. Enter the URL of your YouTube video. (Your YouTube video must be on YouTube and designated as *public*.)

   The screen refreshes and shows a cover picture for your video.

   c. Check the box next to *in-stream* if you want to show your video as a commercial before, during or after the YouTube video the viewer selected. Do not check the box if you want to show your ad only as an *In-Display* Ad (i.e., an overlay banner ad, aka a static image ad).

— You can supply a static image, called a *companion banner*, to use to advertise your video in YouTube search results. It links to your YouTube video. According to Google, the less your cover image looks like a professionally produced ad, the better it does.

— The companion banner must be a 640 × 90px rectangle or 300 × 70px small rectangles, depending on the ad's position in search results.

d. Enter the *display URL* you want to appear in your ad.

e. Enter the *destination URL* of the webpage you want the ad to take your visitor to; either your website, your YouTube channel or your YouTube video.

f. Before your video plays, a cover image shows. Select either:

— Use auto-generated cover image from the video (which is quick and easy since AdWords does this for you), or

— Upload my own image (which lets you create an enticing or eye-catching cover).

AdWords provides a sketch of your *In-Stream* Video Ad format.

g. Check the box next to *in-display*, if you want to show your ad as an overlay banner on YouTube videos (on yours and on those of other people who permit such ads) and/or as a promotional ad on YouTube.

h. Select a thumbnail image for your video. All thumbnails are generated by AdWords.

i. Enter the headline and description lines for your ad.

j. Select the landing page where you want the visitor to watch your video, either:

— My channel page on YouTube, or

— The video watch page on YouTube.

AdWords provides a sketch of your In-Display Video Ad format.

k. Enter an ad name. Enter a descriptive name for your ad.

l. Select your target audience from the *targets* you created.

m. *Save* your ad group.

Monitoring All Video Campaign Video Ads (CPV)

The *all video campaign* screen presents a *statistics table* to help you track the performance of your Video Ad campaigns.

269

- The *statistics table* shows who viewed your video, how long they watched it for and what other actions they took, so you can improve your videos over time.

- The *statistics table* also permits you to look at your ads and your video by segment. Segments include networks, formats, campaigns, times, devices and percentage of the video watched.

- **Video data on AdWords may not match view counts on your YouTube account.** You should use only the All Video Campaigns statistics table to monitor your ad performance.

  AdWords data does not include views of your video by people who find your video in ways other than clicking on your ad (e.g., a search on Google, an email link from a friend, etc.), and AdWords does not bill you for such views. Thus, your YouTube view-counts are often higher than AdWords' website clicks.

- Know that YouTube Analytics also provides more information about your video. It lets you drill down to learn how people find your video, the demographics of your audience, which parts of your video keep your viewers most engaged, where in the world most people watch your video, how your videos are trending, etc.

To monitor YouTube ads:

1. **Set your reporting period.**

2. **Select your campaign.** Select the campaign you want to view from the navigation menu on the left.

3. **For a general understanding of your video performance, cycle through the *segmentation* data and check the view rates.**

   Be aware that you need to give your ad some time (a few weeks) to generate views. You are competing against other videos, but over time they stop running or saturate their audience, which gives your Video Ad a chance to be seen.

   The *view rate* is the number of times someone viewed your ad/video divided by the number of times it appeared. This tells you the percentage of times people played your ad once you are the thumbnail.

   Make sure your *column* setting is on *views* and cycle through the following *segmentation* screens to learn where your video is most effective.

   a. On the *no segmentation* screen, determine how well your ad performs.

   b. On the *segmentation by video screen* determine how much of your video usually played (25, 50, 75 or 100 percent). If people consistently leave your video early, your content is not holding their attention. You need a shorter video or stronger content.

c. On the *segmentation by format on network* screen, determine where your video finds the biggest audience. (You are unlikely to have your ad showing on Google Display Network, given the previous setup scenario.) Over time, one format and network may outshine the others.

d. Click the other *segmentations* button and go to *segments by device* to see:
   — If your audience prefers computers, mobile phones or tablets. Knowing which device your audience prefers helps you create ads using the best length and format.
   — If your video is earning views (i.e., if people are watching other videos on your channel after clicking your ad).
   — If your audience views your video longer than average on a particular device (25, 50, 75 or 100 percent). If people consistently leave your video early on a mobile device, but watch it to the end on a tablet or computer, you may need a shorter, more to-the-point video for mobile phones.

4. **To determine if you are meeting your marketing goal, do the following:**

   a. **If your goal is to build subscriptions, you need to check your *earned actions*.** Go to the *column* button, click on *audience* and then click the *no segmentation* link.

   Check the number of earned views, earned subscribers, earned shares and earned likes to see how well your Video Ad is triggering additional actions by your viewers.

   Check the *segmentations by format by network* and *by device* to see which format/network combination and which device garner the most earned actions.

   b. **If you goal is to build brand awareness, you need to check *unique viewers, average view frequency, impressions* and *average impression frequency*.** Go to the *column* button, click on *brand* and then click the *no segmentation* link.

   Check the number of *unique viewers, average view frequency, impressions* and *average impression frequency* to see how engaged your audience is. Clever and entertaining videos are often viewed over and over.

   Check the *segmentations by format by network* and *by device* to see the format/network combination and the devices that engage the viewer the most.

c. If your goal is conversion (whether a sell or a signup) and you use Conversion Tracking, you need to check your conversion data. Go to the *column* button, click on *conversion* and then click the *other segmentation* button and click *conversions by name*.

Check the number of conversions, view-through conversion along with the conversion rate and cost-per-conversion to see if your ad is bringing in buyers.

Check the *segmentations by format by network* and *by device* to see the format/network combination and the devices that bring in the most buyers.

The following provides suggestions for correcting various performance problems and for improving your ads:

1. **Your video is not showing.** Check that your YouTube video is *public*.

2. **Few people watch your ad.** To improve your *view rate*, consider:
   - Changing your description lines to add a more enticing call-to-action.
   - Changing your cover images to be more attractive or eye-catching.
   - Changing your ad format; clicks often vary by type of format, and an Engagement Ad or a click-to-play ad may work better with your particular audience and subject matter.
   - For *in-stream* ads, consider shortening your video to 15 seconds.

3. **The number of impressions are low.** Consider raising your bid. As with all ads, your Video Ad must win auctions to get impressions. Raising your bid is the easiest way to increase your auction wins and, thus, your impressions.

4. **The costs are too high.** Consider using the *ad scheduling* feature with higher bids during the times that viewers are online and watching.

5. **Refer to Monitoring Basic Search Network Ads for additional suggestions for improving ads**.

GROWING DISPLAY NETWORK ADS

The following presents numerous ways to easily and quickly expand the Display Network ad campaigns you created previously.

Remember, do not expand a campaign until it is converting visitors to buyers. You do not need to pay for more visitors if your landing page is not converting them to buyers. Once your first Display Network ad is converting visitors, you can begin to expand using the following techniques.

Change Your Geographic Market

If your campaign is successfully converting visitors to buyers, consider adjusting your geographic area to reflect your best market(s).

Recall that changing your geographic area affects all ads within the campaign.

- **Before making any changes to your geographic market, view your current performance data by geography to see where your visitors reside.**

   Click the *dimensions* tab, click the *view: <option>* tab and select *geographic* or *user location* from the drop-down menu.

   — If your visitors are coming from specific areas, you may want to narrow your geographic market from "U.S." to specific zip codes, cities or radius areas and create separate campaigns for each specific area.

   — Local advertisers often outrank national advertisers (depending on the product). By narrowing your market, you may gain a higher ad placement than advertisers with broader markets, including advertisers with national markets.

   — Similarly, if your visitors are scattered across your local region, consider creating one or more new campaigns for adjacent regions. By using additional campaigns for the adjacent areas (rather than simply increasing the geographic area of your original campaign), your original ad keeps its "Local Ad" advantage.

To change your geographic market:

- Click on *all online campaigns* and then the appropriate campaign. Next, click the *settings tab*. Scroll to the *locations* prompt. Click *edit* and, after the input screen opens, click *advanced search*.

- Use the links at the top of the panel to choose the criteria for narrowing or enlarging your geographic market.

Add or Remove Keywords

The more generic your keywords, the more impressions you receive and the less qualified the visitors to your site. The more specific your keywords, the more qualified your visitors.

To increase the number of well-qualified visitors, review your keyword performance data (click on the *keyword* tab) and do the following:

- **Ensure keywords with zero clicks are active.** A keyword marked as *eligible* may not participate in the auctions for a variety of reasons,

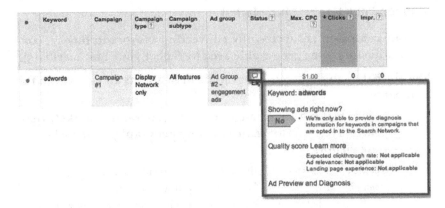

FIGURE 6.7 Checking keywords

Be aware that an *Eligible* keyword may not be active.

including nullification by a negative keyword or duplication of a keyword in another ad group or low ad rank.

To evaluate keywords click the speech bubble icon next to each keyword.

- **Add more specific keywords.** Review the search terms that triggered your ad and add new, similar, longer or more specific terms to your list of keywords.

(To see the search terms that bring you visitors, check the box to the left of a keyword, click the *details* tab and select *search term*.) If irrelevant terms trigger your ad, add them to your negative keyword list.

- **Pause unproductive keywords.** Pause keywords that produce clicks but not sales.

Change Your Bids

AdWords offers several ways to increase your bid for an ad:

1. Increase the max CPC for the ad group.

   By increasing the max CPC for an ad group that is performing well, you may win more auctions and garner more impressions. Adjusting your max CPC affects all the keywords and targeting methods for the ad group.

2. Set *custom bids* for any or all criteria within one targeting method.

   Using *custom bids* or *bid adjustments* lets you set different max CPCs for each criterion within a targeting method. They let you set higher bids for productive criteria or lower for less productive criteria. Recall that a *custom bid* is a dollar amount.

You cannot set a custom bid and *bid adjustment* for the same targeting method.

3. Set a *bid adjustment* for devices, locations, ad schedules and any or all criteria within your targeting methods

    Using *custom bids* or *bid adjustments* lets you set different max CPCs for each criterion within a targeting method. They let you set higher bids for productive criteria or lower for less productive criteria. Recall that a *bid adjustment* is a percentage increase.

    You cannot set a custom bid and *bid adjustment* for the same targeting method.

4. Create or designate a *bid only* target method.

Change the Max CPC

-   Go to all online campaigns and click the appropriate ad group.
-   Click the edit link in the ad group description next to the ad mock-up and enter your new max CPC.

FIGURE 6.8 Max CPC edit screen for an ad group

Add Custom Bids

Custom bids let you override your max CPC at the Targeting Methods Level for Display Network ads (in the same way you can override your max CPC at the Keyword Level).

Custom bids are used most often for keywords in Display Network campaigns.

275

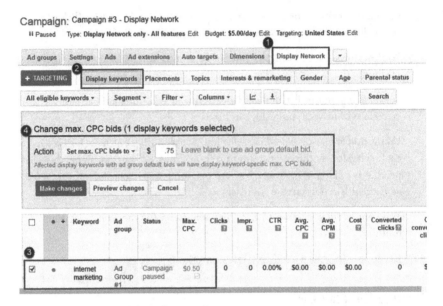

FIGURE 6.9 Custom bid for a keyword

To add a custom bid:

1. From the *all online campaigns* menu, select the campaign, ad group or ad you want to have custom bids.

2. Click *Display Network tab* and click the tab for the appropriate *targeting method*: *display keywords, placements, topics, interest and Remarketing, gender* or *age*. Your targeting method items appear in the statistics table.

3. Just above the statistics table, click the *edit* button and select *change bid adjustment* from the drop-down menu. In the box that appears, enter your increase for the line item. Click save.

Add Bid Adjustments for Devices, Locations, Ad Schedules and Targeting Methods

You can set *bid adjustments* for *devices, locations, ad scheduling* (days and hours) and any of the *targeting methods* used by your Display Network ad groups or ads.

- *Bid adjustments* are percentage increases or decreases applied to your default bid (max CPC). Bids must be between –90 percent to +900 percent. (Note that you cannot completely eliminate a max CPC, since –90 percent is the lowest offset you can apply.)

- To eliminate mobile devices (i.e., smartphone or tablet) from your campaign, enter a –100 percent. A –100 percent bid brings your max CPC bid to zero and, thus, AdWords omits that item from all auctions. Do this for computers and tablets when you want an ad to run only on mobile devices (i.e., smartphones).

- To remove a *bid adjustment* for a device, clear the field. Note that leaving a zero in the bid adj. field causes the "active *bid adjustment*: device" notation at the campaign description to remain.

- *Bid adjustments* apply on top of your default bid, and multiple bids apply on top of each other. For example, the 20 percent *bid adjustment* for a tablet *device* increases your $2 max CPC from $2 to $2.40. Next, the 10 percent *bid adjustment* for a New York City *location* increases your max CPC from $2.40 to $2.64. Your adjusted CPC is $2.62, for a total increase of 32 percent.

- The *bid adjustment* screen also shows performance metrics (clicks, impressions, CTR, etc.). Once your ad starts running, you return to this screen to check its performance. Thus, this screen is both a data input screen and a report screen.

- The maximum amount you can increase your default bid is 900 percent.

- AdWords provides a calculator to show you the percentage increase/decrease for your *bid adjustments*. (See Figure 6.11.)

FIGURE 6.10 Bid calculator icon

To find the bid calculator, click the small icon at the end of the campaign description line.

You can apply *bid adjustments* to:

1. **Devices.** Click on *all online campaigns*, then click the appropriate campaign. Note that your campaign appears at the top of the screen. Click the *settings* tab and then the *device* tab on the submenu. The different

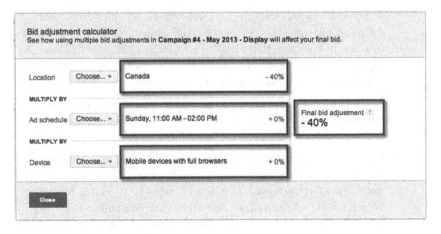

FIGURE 6.11 The bid calculator

The bid calculator applies all the adjustments you have made to the campaign and renders a final bid adjustment.

FIGURE 6.12 Device bid adjustments

Note that the campaign description alerts you to the presence of active bid adjustments and that the breakout of the bid adjustment by device shows on the Statistics Table. Thus, this screen is both a data input screen and a report screen.

devices appear in the statistics table. Enter the appropriate percentage *bid adjustment* next to one or more devices. (See Figure 6.12.)

2. **Locations.** Click on *all online campaigns*, then click the desired campaign. Click the *settings* tab and then the *location* tab on the submenu. The geographic areas you have set for the campaign appear in the statistics table. Enter your percentage *bid adjustment* next to one or more locations.

   Note that the more granular you make your locations, the more performance data you receive and the more opportunities you have to make specific bids. For example, entering all 50 states in your location option at the Campaign Level lets you see more data and easily set bids by state.

3. *Ad scheduling.* Click on *all online campaigns,* then click the desired campaign. Click the *settings tab* and then the *ad schedule* tab on the submenu. The ad schedule appears in the statistics table. Enter the appropriate percentage *bid adjustment* next to one or more time periods.

4. **Targeting methods.** Click on *all online campaigns*, then click the desired campaign. Click the *settings* tab and then the desired *targeting method* tab on the submenu. The targeting method appears in the statistics table. Enter the appropriate percentage *bid adjustment* next to one or more items.

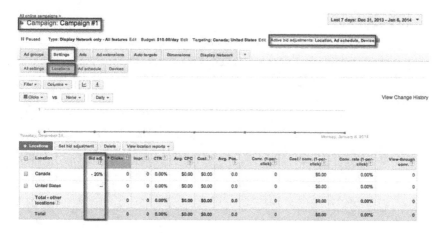

FIGURE 6.13 Location bid adjustments

Note that the campaign description alerts you to the presence of active bid adjustments and that the breakout of the bid adjustment by location shows on the *Statistics Table*. Thus, this screen is both a data input screen and a report screen.

FIGURE 6.14 Ad schedule bid adjustments

Note that the campaign description alerts you to the presence of active bid adjustments and that the breakout of the bid adjustment by day shows on the *Statistics Table*. Thus, this screen is both a data input screen and a report screen.

FIGURE 6.15 Bid adjustment on the statistics table

The above table shows a bid adjustment of 20 percent for the topic Business & Industry, Advertising and Marketing.

Add a Bid Only Target

In some instances, you may want to bid higher or lower for certain topics, placements, interests, Remarketing lists, ages or gender criteria, even though you do not necessarily want to target them. You can do that using the *bid only target* features.

- For example, say you find your ad gets clicks every time your keyword "HR evaluation software" appears in the Wall Street Journal. While you do not want to add managed placements as a targeting method, you want to bid higher than your max CPC when an auction involves the Wall Street Journal. The *bid only target* lets you enter the Wall Street Journal as a placement as a *bid only target* and specify a *bid adjustment*.

- Recall that a website must meet one criterion in *each* of your targeting methods to show your ad. If you were to add managed placements with only the Wall Street Journal as a placement, your ad would appear only on the Wall Street Journal website! This is not the outcome you want in this situation.

To create a bid-only targeting method, you mark an unused targeting method as "bid only" and enter your criterion (i.e., the placement, topic, whatever). Next, go to the *Display Network tab* and select the targeting methods on the *view:<choice>* drop-down menu. Enter a default bid for the item on the *statistics table*.

Add Ad Groups with Different Targeting Methods

Having the same ad with different *targeting methods* can help you determine the attributes that most closely represent your buyers.

- For example, if you are converting visitors interested in certain *topics*, you might want to create another ad group that targets *interests*. Similarly, you may want to create another ad group that targets certain *age ranges*.

- Note that stacking multiple *targeting methods* in one ad group will not give you the same results as the previous example. *Targeting methods* are cumulative. That is, a website must meet one criterion in every targeting method for the ad group if your ad is to show.

To create Display Network ads with different targeting groups, follow the instructions for creating an ad group (item 2) under Setting Up Basic Display Ads.

ADVANCED FEATURES FOR DISPLAY NETWORK

AdWords offers two important "power features" that help you gain more customers. Use these options if at all possible.

Display Targeting Optimization

Once your ad has 15 conversions a month, you can use *display target optimization* to seek customers more aggressively. With targeting optimization, AdWords shows your ad in place and before people not within your targeting methods because AdWords' algorithm indicates they could be advantageous to you.

Under *conservative targeting*, the targets selected by AdWords do not increase your *target cost-per-acquisition*; however, under *aggressive targeting*, the targets can increase your *target cost-per-acquisition (CPA)*.

Using the *display campaign optimizer* is recommended unless you *must* stay within your *targeted CPA*.

Setting Up Display Targeting Optimization

You can turn on display targeting optimization when you setup a Display Network campaign, or activate, change your choice or deactivate it at any time.

1. Click the *Display Network* tab.

2. Click the + *targeting* button.

3. Select your ad group.

4. In the *targeting optimization* section, click *Let AdWords automatically find new customers.*

5. Select either *conservative* or *aggressive targeting.*

6. Click *save.*

Remarketing Ads

Remarketing enables you to reach people who previously visited your site, your YouTube channel or your YouTube video. It helps you coax them back for a second look or a second purchase, using different ads and/or offers.

- **You must use Conversion Tracking and you should use the *Conversion Optimizer* with Remarketing.** This ensures ads show to the best prospects at the most competitive bid.

- ***Remarketing* works with the Search Network.** You can advertise to people who visited your website previously, bidding more aggressively this time and showing either the product they viewed previously or other products they might find interesting.

- **_Remarketing_ works with the Display Network.** You can advertise to people who visited your website previously. In addition, you can fine-tune your _Remarketing lists_ using these _targeting methods: keywords, topics, managed placements_ and _interest categories_.

  For example, you can advertise your new athletic shoe to people who previously visited your site who are male and aged between 18 and 24.

- **_Remarketing_ works with YouTube.** You must associate your YouTube account with your AdWords account and Remarketing to people who visited your YouTube video or channel.

- **_Remarketing_ works with Interest-Based ads.** Once you have 100 people on your Remarketing list, AdWords can identify people who have search and viewing patterns similar to the visitors to your site and show them your ads. Thus, AdWords helps you expand your market.

- **_Remarketing_ works with Mobile Apps Ads.** You can remarket to people who have downloaded your app.

Remarketing let you show ads to a specific group of previous visitors to your website.

- For example, you can show an ad for wedding veils to people who looked at wedding dresses on your website, or you can show an ad for hiking boots to people who looked at hiking boots on your website but abandoned their shopping carts.

To define the previous visitors you want to see your ad, you create a _Remarketing list_ and specify the webpages the visitor must have visited.

- For example, you can create a _Remarketing list_ called "Brides-to-be" for people who visited your webpage www.departmentstore.com/wedding_dresses; or, you create a _Remarketing list_ called "Serious Hikers" for people who visited webpage www.departmentstore.com/hiking_boots and www.departmentstore.com/shopping_cart.

Remarketing lists are extremely flexible. To define the previous visitors you want to see your ad, you create a _Remarketing list_, give it a name and use one of the following three methods to specify the webpages the people visited:

1. **A URL.** A URL consists of "www" designating the World Wide Web, the domain name and an extension (.com, .net, or .biz). For example, www.departmentstore.com.

Be aware that a *Remarketing list* defined by a URL includes all pages of your website that bear that level of domain name.

- For example, a *Remarketing list* with the URL www.departmentstore. com includes people who visited any page of the website, since all pages have www.departmentstore.com in their names.

- In contrast, a *Remarketing list* with the URL for a lower-level webpage, such as www.departmentstore.com/shoes/athletic, includes people who visited pages that have /shoe/athletic in their names.

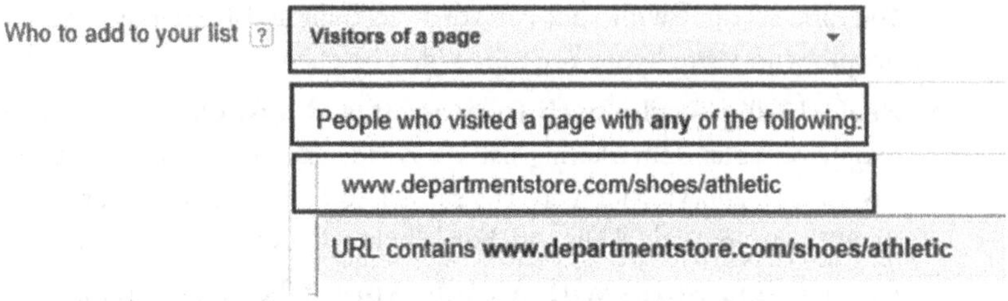

FIGURE 6.16 Remarketing list for visitors to a section of the website

2. **A rule.** A rule consists of a domain name (www.departmentstore.com), an *operator* (a word that AdWords recognizes) and a value.

   Rule *operators* include: *containing, equal to, starting with, ending with, not containing, not equal to, not starting with,* or *not ending with.*

   For example, a rule for all webpages for athletic shoes might be:

   > *URL:* www.departmentstore.com
   > *Operator:* URL CONTAINS
   > *Value:* /shoes/athletic

   As a result, the Remarketing lists includes the following sections of the website:

   > www.departmentstore.com/shoes/athletic/mens/sneakers
   > www.departmentstore.com/shoes/athletic/mens/cleats
   > www.departmentstore.com/shoes/athletic/mens/golf

   Further, you can use URLs and rules together to create sophisticated Remarketing lists for:

   - People who visited a page/section during a *specific period* (before or after a date, or between two dates)

   - People who visited a page(s) with a *dynamic Remarketing tag*

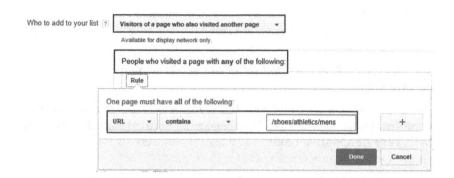

FIGURE 6.17 Remarketing list rule defining a section of a website

- For *Display Network Remarketing Ads* only, people who visited *two or more* pages/sections
- For *Display Network Remarketing Ads* only, people who visited one page/section but *not* another page/section.

3. **Custom combinations.** You can *include* or *exclude* people on more than one list. *Custom combinations* use the operators *and* and *or*.

Thus, you can create *Remarketing lists* that:

- *Include* only people who appear on *all the lists* you specify (using the *and* operator). Note that the more lists you include the fewer people you include.

- *Include* people on *at least one* of lists you specify (using the *or* operator). Note that the more lists you include the more people you include.

- *Exclude* people who appear *on all the lists* you specify (using the *and* operator). Presumably, few people appear on all your lists, so the more lists, the more people eligible to see your ad—however, be sure you understand the consequences of your rule.

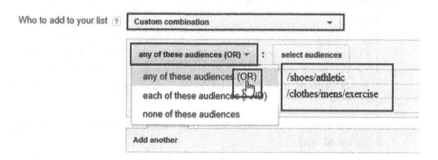

FIGURE 6.18 Custom combination remarketing list

- *Exclude* people on *at least one* of the lists you specify (using the *or* operator). Note that the more lists, the fewer people eligible to see the ad. *Exclude* all your lists and you defeat the purpose of Remarketing.

You can create *Remarketing lists* as you need them, over time, for your ad campaigns.

As a best practice, use one *Remarketing list* per campaign (use a custom combination to create a list if necessary), and give each *Remarketing list* a very descriptive name. You do not want to unknowingly pepper your previous visitors with too many ads.

In a nutshell, this is how *Remarketing* works on Display Networks:

1. **First, you add the *Remarketing* "*tag*" (i.e., a snippet of code) to your homepage to track every webpage or to the webpages you want to track.**
   - For example, you place a tag on the page www.website.com/Shoes, where you show shoes, and on www.website.com/thank-you, the Thank You webpage that visitors see after they buy something.

2. **Next, on AdWords you create your *Remarketing lists*.** An *all site visitors* list is created for you automatically, but you can create *Remarketing lists* for people visiting a particular page; a set of pages; two or more particular pages; one page but not another; etc., as well as for people not having visited a page; a set of pages; etc.
   - For example, you create a *Remarketing list* called "Shoe Shoppers" for people who looked at shoes on www.website.com/shoes and another list for "Buyers" for people who saw the Thank You webpage (www.website.com/thank-you) after a purchase.

3. **When someone visits your webpage (or buys something), AdWords adds a cookie (i.e., a file) with a unique ID number to the visitor's device.** AdWords also adds the cookie ID to the *Remarketing lists* for the www.website.com/Shoes and (www.website.com/thank-you).
   - For example, a visitor looks at shoes on your website and buys a pair. AdWords places a cookie with ID#-123 on the visitors PC and adds ID#-123 to all your "Shoe Shoppers" *Remarketing list* and to your "buyers" *Remarketing list*. (Note that the visitor's name, email, etc. is not stored.)

4. **Next, you create a Display Network campaign with an ad group for "Shoe Shoppers."**
   - For example, you create an ad for your "Really Big Shoe Sale" and associate the "Shoe Shoppers" *Remarketing list* with it.

286

5. **When the visitor surfs the Internet and visits a Display Network partner site, AdWords checks to see if the visitor has a cookie ID on his/her computer that matches the *Remarketing list* for your ad.** If the visitor does, AdWords includes your ad in the auction (even though the visitor is not searching for, or reading about, shoes).

   - If you use *conversion optimization*, AdWords raises your bid, if necessary, to win an ad position. (Otherwise, you win or lose the auction based on your *max CPC bid*.)

6. **Your ad appears and the visitor sees it.** He or she may or may not click on it. Regardless, when the visitor moves to another Display Network site, AdWords repeats step 5–7 again. In this way, your ad "follows" the visitor for up to 30 days.

   - More specifically, when the visitor with ID#-123 lands on a Google Partner website, AdWords recognizes that ID#-123 is on your Shoe Shoppers *Remarketing list*. It includes your ad in the auction, helps get your ad bid high enough to win an ad position if you use *conversion optimization* and shows your Really Big Shoe Sale ad to your previous visitor.

Setting Up Remarketing Ads

The major steps for implementing Remarketing Ads are:

1. **Review AdWords' "Remarketing Program Policies" before you start.** Search in AdWords Help for "Interest-Based advertising policy" and read the section on "Policies."

2. **Obtain the *Remarketing code* created by AdWords.**
   - Go to *shared library* in the left-hand menu and click *Audience*.
   - In the upper right-hand corner, click *Remarketing tag*. On the next screen, click setup and select your business type. AdWords walks you through a set of questions and creates the code snippet.
   - Enter the membership duration (how long your ad will follow a previous visitor), a name for the list (using the same name as on the webpage is a good idea) and, optionally, a description, such as "site visitors." Click *save*.
   - The tag code appears on the upper-right corner of the *audiences* page of the *shared library*. Click the *view tag details, then details, view AdWords tag for websites*, to see the code and re-send it to your programmer. Notify your programmer via email that the code is coming from Google.

287

3. **Paste the Remarketing tag immediately before the closing tag </body> at the bottom of each webpage or, alternatively, place it inside the footer area of your homepage.**

   - Putting a tag on every page is a straightforward setup method for a small website. When you create your *Remarketing lists*, you use the exact URL for each page.

   - Alternatively, you can put a tag in the footer of the website. When you create your *Remarketing lists*, you use *Remarketing rules* to define the pages you want to include in the list. This is explained in greater detail as follows.

4. **Determine which products you want to remarket. Note their webpage URLs.**

5. **Create your *Remarketing list*(s).** To setup a *Remarketing list* for a specific campaign, click the campaign in the navigation menu at left. Click the *audience tab*. (If the *audience tab* does not appear to the right of the *keyword tab*, click the down arrow at the end of the row and select *audience* from the drop-down menu.)

   You need to enter the following:

   a. *Remarketing list*, where you give your *Remarketing list* a very descriptive name.

   b. Create your *Remarketing list* using (1) URLs and/or (2) rules or (3) custom combinations.

   c. *Include past users who match these rules*, where you help your list achieve 1,000 visitors faster by checking the option to *include people who have visited this page(s) in the past*.

   d. *Membership duration*, where you indicate how long you want a visitor to remain on the *Remarketing lists*.

   e. *Description*, where you enter notes on the marketing opportunity this *Remarketing list* addresses.

6. **Setup your campaign options.** Select *Display Network only* as your ad type and *Remarketing* as your sub-type. You cannot mix *Remarketing Ads* with other types of ad in a campaign.

   - Use the same bidding and budget options that you used in the original campaign that brought the visitor to your site.

   - If you already use *Conversion Tracking*, you use *Focus-on-Conversions* and *optimize for clicks* bidding choices.

Using *Conversion Tracking* with **Remarketing is a powerful accelerator for your ads. Implement it as soon as you can.**

- Do not use location, language or device restrictions in your campaign. The settings for the ad that drove the visitor to your site already filtered your audience. Narrowing the group further at this point defeats the purpose of Remarketing.

- Keep the two defaults set by AdWords:
  - — *Ad rotation—optimize for conversions*: show ads expected to provide more conversions.
  - — *Frequency capping*: no cap on impressions.

9. **Set up your ad group.**

- Keep your *Remarketing Ads* as simple as possible. It is easy to end up with ads competing against each other for the same visitor.

- Use one *Remarketing list* per ad group. (Create a *custom combination* if you need to combine, differentiate or exclude visitors.)

- Use only *keywords* as your *targeting method*. Adding more *targeting methods* decreases the number of sites where you can advertise to previous visitors and buyers.

Remember a visitor must meet *all* your targeting methods.

10. **Set up your ads for your Remarketing audience.** To make the most of Remarketing capabilities,

- Create ads for people who visited 30, 60, 90 and 120 days ago.

- Use text-and-image ads in various sizes and give ads the same look and feel as your site.

- Create highly relevant ad copy for your Remarketing list and include a call-to-action.

Detailed instructions for implementing Remarketing Ads are available under the AdWords Help topic "Using Remarketing to reach people who visited your site."

Monitoring Remarketing Ads

1. **Verify that your ads are running on the Display Network placements you specified, if you specified any.**

- Click the *Display Network* tab and then the p*lacements* tab on the submenu that appears. Click the plus sign (+) next to *managed placements* to open that section. Under the *status* column, hover over the *speech bubble icon* next to one of your placements to see diagnostic information.

- Pause or delete placements that are not performing.

2. **Verify that your ads are running on the webpages with content related to the topics you specified.**

- Click the *Display Network* tab and then the *topics* tab on the submenu that appears. Under the *status* column, hover over the *speech bubble icon* next to one of your topics to see diagnostic information.

- Consider deleting topics that are not performing.

The following provides suggestions for correcting various performance problems and for improving your ads:

4. **Your ad is not showing.**

- If your Remarketing list does not accumulate 100 visitors within the membership duration period, AdWords does not show your ad. (Click on *shared library* and then *audience* to see how many entries you have on your list.)

- Ads sometimes do not appear until 24 hours after creation.

5. **Your Remarketing list is empty.**

- Check the Remarketing tag on your website code. Confirm the tag's spelling, spacing and URL. (The code should appear immediately above the </body> tag.)

- Check your Remarketing list. Confirm that the URL in your Remarketing list exactly matches the webpage's URL.

- If you communicate with your programmer via email, be aware that some email programs change the format of tags during transmission. Search for "How to add the Remarketing tag to your site" in AdWords Help for more information.

6. **Your Remarketing list is not growing.**

- Ensure your webpage has traffic. If people are not visiting the webpage, your Remarketing list does not grow. Check that you have ads or keywords driving traffic to webpages you are trying to remarket.

- Consider whether the webpage is worth tagging. If it is, develop ads to drive more traffic to the page. If not, consider adding it to another *Remarketing list* if that is appropriate or ignore it for the time being.

- Ensure your Remarketing list is open (not closed or paused).

- Check the *membership duration* for your Remarketing list. AdWords drops visitors who do not return to your site within the duration period specified. Determine whether the duration period is too short.

- Check that you use *and* and *or* correctly in your combination Remarketing lists.

6. **Refer to Basic Display Network Ads for suggestions for monitoring and improving Display Network ads.**

To expand your Remarketing campaigns, consider the following:

7. **Grow your Remarketing lists.** The more people who come to your website, the more people you have to market to via Remarketing. Use email campaigns, online articles and traditional marketing channels such as direct mail, print ads, etc. to attract people to your webpages.

8. **Create text and image ads for your campaign.** Try multiple display ad sizes, and test the different formats to determine which works best for your campaign.

9. **Remove any Campaign Level language, location or geographic restraints.**

10. **Reduce or increase the** *frequency cap* **to see whether more or fewer impressions before the same visitor help.**

11. **Consider** *ad scheduling.* Try showing your ads during those times of the week or day when your shoppers are most likely to be online.

12. **Consider changing your** *ad rotation.*

13. **Review the suggestions for Monitoring Display Ads and Growing Display Network Ads.**

THE GOOGLE SHOPPING NETWORK

The Google Shopping Network shows thumbnail-size ads on the Google.com search results page when you enter a search term for a product. Ads also show when you enter a search term and click the Shopping menu option.

Google Shopping Listings

Google Shopping Ads appear in a panel of images on Google.com or on a page of image ads on Google Shopping (an option under the Google.com input box). These two venues make up the Google Shopping Network.

- For *Google Shopping* product listings, you submit a file of product information, and AdWords creates a *listing* automatically for your product when someone searches for your product or a unique word related to your product category (e.g., a brand name or a synonym).

- *Google Shopping* uses the *cost-per-click* (CPC) bidding model unless you are using the *Conversation Tracking* feature and the *enhanced cost-per-click* (ECPC) bidding model or the *conversion optimization* feature and the cost-per-acquisition (CPA) bidding model.

- *Google Shopping* shows many *product listing* (Google calls them *product listing*, not ads) at the same time.

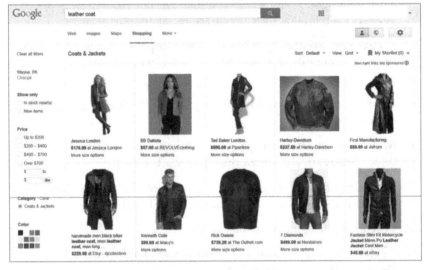

FIGURE 6.19 Google Shopping listings

Generally, listings include a brand name or product description, a price and the store name and, if room permits a notation that more options, sizes, etc. exist.

Google Shopping has several important features that you should consider before your start setting up your Google Shopping campaign, since these options impact the way you setup your Google Merchant account and feed.

You need to determine the following:

- **Whether you want to list products sold on your website and/or products sold in your store.** You can list both, but you must use a separate feed for each.

- **Whether you want to identify certain characteristics of ad searches by adding programming codes, called ValueTrack parameters, to your URL.** Results are shown in Google Analytics (not Google AdWords). Search in AdWords Help for "Track clicks with ValueTrack" for instructions.
  - ValueTrack can capture more than 20 different data elements. "Keyword" is one of the most helpful.
  - To capture the keyword that brought a searcher to your site, add a forward slash, question mark and keyword={keyword} to the URL in the ad: www.examplewebsite.com/?keyword={keyword}
  - You must use Google Analytics to see the results. AdWords does not show them.
- **Whether you want to use** *location ad extensions* **with your listings.** (You should!) This adds your company name, address, phone, etc. from your Google My Business account to the bottom of all your listings. You must have a Google My Business account to use location extensions.

Setting Up Google Shopping

You may need the help of a programmer to setup a Google Shopping campaign. The following are the basic steps:

1. Activate a Google Merchant Center account. Through the Merchant Center you:
   - **Link your AdWords and Merchant Center accounts and indicate your** *file transfer protocol* **(FTP) option for uploading files.** (If your Google Shopping feed is between 20MB and 1GB, you should upload it using FTP, an upload application that runs between servers, outside of your browser and, thus, runs faster. Files over 1 GB must be split into multiple files and uploaded.) Search in AdWords Help for "Submit data feeds via FTP" for instructions.
   - **Submit your inventory** *feed(s)*. You must submit separate feeds for website and store inventories.
   - **Submit a** *special offers feed* **if you want to use a promo code to give your buyers a free gift or a discount (either a flat amount or a percentage) at checkout.** You must contact Google to apply and be approved for this feature. Search on Google.com for "Merchant promotions interest form" for more information.
   - **Activate the option to use the** *Schema.org microdata* **tags to mark prices and availability data on your webpages.**

- **Also, you can download the *application program interface* (API).** The API lets you update your feed online, in real-time, at the Merchant Center. You can use the API between periodic uploads of your feed. It requires some technical competency.

2. **Build a feed (file) of the inventory items you want to sell.**

Refer to the topic "Beginner's guide, data feed overview" in AdWords Help for the latest requirements. These requirements change periodically. The following gives you only a basic overview of the feed.

- **Your feed contains a line item for each of your products.** For each line item you provide some 20–50 attributes such as product description, prices, along with links to wherever you store product images (your website, Flickr, Bucket, etc.).

- **Google accepts several programming formats, such as a spreadsheet or XML file.** Spreadsheets must be saved as in a text (.txt) format or converted to a zipped (.zip, .gz or .bz2) format before uploading.

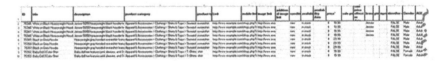

FIGURE 6.20 Google Shopping feed

- **Google has exacting and rigid standards for every field in the data feed.** You must comply with the latest version of the feed format and specifications.

Basically, the feed supports the following attributes:

a. *Identifying information*: a unique *ID* number for the item that does not change over time; an enticing *title* for the item; a *description* rich with keywords; a product category from Google's 6,200+ pre-defined *lists*; your own *product types* and *link*(s) to the product's landing page, your mobile landing page and the URL for your product *image,* among other items.

The title and description fields are especially important because AdWords uses them to determine if your product is more relevant than other advertisers' products to the searcher's query. Make sure these fields are rich in keywords.

b. *Pricing and availability*: the item's price and availability status (e.g., in stock, available, out of stock, preorder) and its sale price and effective dates, if appropriate.

c. *Unique identifiers*: UPC, EAN, JAN, ISBEN or other industry numbering schemes, along with two of these four: the *brand* (required for apparel), the *global trade ID number* (GTIN) and/or the *manufacturer's part number* (MPN) and/or the *identifier exists?* field.

Enter *false* in the *identifier exists?* field if your product(s) does not have an industry numbering scheme, as is the case with custom-made goods. AdWords constructs a numbering scheme for you.

Leave the field blank if your product has an industry numbering scheme.

d. For an item of *apparel*, the *size, size system, gender, age, size* and *color*: when you have the same product in different sizes and colors, you create one line item for each different color, size, etc. and give them all the same *master item identifier*.

Thus, a dress in five sizes and four colors becomes 20 line items, each bearing the same master item identifier. Google uses the master item name to check that you have the dress in other sizes and colors if a customer asks for one.

e. *Tax and shipping*: for taxes, you can enter a tax amount for each line item or, at the account level, you can submit a tax amount or tax chart or you can opt to use the state tax rates Google obtains from a third party.

For shipping, you can use a flat rate, the daily UPS, the standard non-retail FedEx rates, the United States Postal Service rates or a table of your own rates—but be sure to include the shipping weight of each item in your feed!

f. *AdWords attributes*: if you use a third-party software application to track your AdWords, you can include a more precise *destination URL* for each line item.

g. *Custom labels (0–4)*: you can use up to five free-form, user-defined fields to define, monitor, report or bid on products. Suggested uses include:
   — Profit margin (e.g., so you can know to bid higher or low profit margin so you know to bid lower).
   — Special handling costs (e.g., requires dry ice, so you know to keep bids low because costs are high).
   — Warranty type.
   — Not discountable.
   — Not returnable.

295

h. *Additional attributes*:

— Excluded destination: where you exclude an item from a destination URL.

— Expiration date: where you indicate the date when an item stops appearing.

For a full list of feed fields, search in AdWords Help for "Products feed specification."

- **Before you build your feed, consider how you want to advertise and promote your products.** Think about your product lines, their profit margins and the best sellers. This will help you determine how to group products for easily-running sales and promotions.

  Next, consider how to use the product type and custom label attributes to best advantage. You may want to use the custom labels for profit margins (use a percentage; high, medium, low; or 1–5 scale), best seller (1–5 scale) or seasonal (spring, summer, etc.). This can save you re-working your feed later. (Realize you cannot anticipate every advertising opportunity, so consider the opportunities for the next few months and then move forward.)

- **As a best practice for small businesses, use the simplest upload scenario.** That is, put all the products you want to advertise into your Merchant Center feed and opt to advertise "all products" in your campaign settings. When you want to add or delete products, upload a new feed. You cannot change your product feed through AdWords.

- **For larger businesses with a programming staff, Google offers an application program interface (API) called the** *content API for shopping.* The API lets you find, insert, update and delete items online in your Google Merchant Center account, in real-time. This means you can mark items as out-of-stock immediately and change prices on the fly (if you are also changing your website).

  Such practices require coordination with your website changes and careful attention to the process. Using the API also means you need to upload a new feed less often, which is helpful if you have hundreds of products and the feed takes hours to load and be approved.

  (For more information, search in Google.com or the Google Developer's website for "Content API for shopping.")

3. **Once you have your feed built in your selected format, you upload it to the Google Merchant Center.** Two separate feeds are required if you plan to advertise both products on your website (*online products*) and products available only in your store (*local products*).

Setting Up a Master Campaign

1. **Next, you setup a Google Shopping "master campaign" with a budget and a max CPC.**

   - Under the *campaign* tab, click the +*campaign* button. Select *Search Ads only* and *Google Shopping*. As part of the setup, you associate your Google Merchant Center account with the campaign.

   - Select your *shopping channel*, either *online* for products sold on your website or *local* for products sold in your store. You can check both, but you must have separate Google Merchant feeds for online and local products.

   - Set up any *delivery method (evenly, accelerated), ad schedule* or *negative keywords*. (You cannot setup *device bid adjustments* until you save your campaign and return to it using the *settings* tab.)

   - If you use third-party software or self-developed spreadsheets to track your sales by *destination URL*, ask your Google Merchant Center feed programmer for the *dynamic tracking URL* template.

2. **Once you save the campaign, AdWords creates an** *all products* **ad group.** The max CPC you set for the master campaign is carried to the ad group.

3. **Next, you can sub-divide the** *all products* **ad group into smaller product groups. A product grouping can be as broad or as narrow as you like.** Using the Google Categories attribute or your *product type* attribute is a best practice.

   You can subdivide a *product grouping* **into sub-groupings.** This is useful if you want to bid more competitively or run sales on certain products. Any item that does not fit one of your sub-groupings becomes part of an *everything else in* <*product grouping*>. This type of "nested list" ensures every product qualifies for a *product grouping*.

   - **To create your first-level product group, click the** *pencil icon* **to the right of the** *all product* **group to move to the** *subdivide all products* **panel.** Select the attribute you want to use to define your top-level product groups.

297

- **If you want to set a different bid for a product, you must create a product group for it.** To define the product group you use one of these attributes: (1) *item ID*: the identifier (id) for each product; (2) *brand*; (3) *Google categories*, a Google-defined list; (4) *Product type*, a list you define; (5) *custom labels* (one of five fields you define to label products) and (6) *condition* (i.e., new, used and refurbished).

- Repeat the process for each lower-level product groupings.

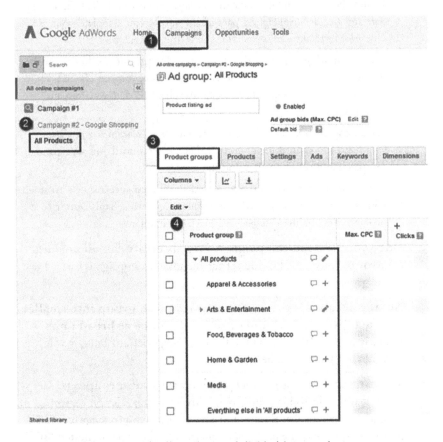

FIGURE 6.21 Ad group with all products subdivided into product groups

Note that the product groups are indented under All Product. Note also that the Arts & Entertainment group has an arrow next to it signifying that the group is further sub-divided.

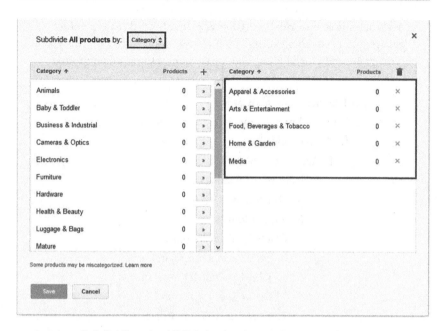

FIGURE 6.22 Subdividing the All Products ad group

This example shows the All Products ad group being sub-divided by *Google category*.

	Product group 🔲		Max. CPC 🔲	Clicks 🔲	Impr. 🔲	CTR 🔲	A·
☐	▾ All products	💬 ✏	-- ⬚	0	0	0.00%	
☐	Apparel & Accessories	💬 +	$0.01 ⬚	0	0	0.00%	
☐	▾ Arts & Entertainment	💬 ✏	-- ⬚	0	0	0.00%	
☐	▾ Hobbies & Creative Arts	💬 ✏	-- ⬚	0	0	0.00%	
☐	Artwork	💬 +	$0.01 ⬚	0	0	0.00%	
☐	Everything else in 'Hobbies & Creative Arts'	+ 💬	$0.01 ⬚	0	0	0.00%	
☐	Everything else in 'Arts & Entertainment'	💬 +	$0.01 ⬚	0	0	0.00%	
☐	Food, Beverages & Tobacco	💬 +	$0.01 ⬚	0	0	0.00%	
☐	Home & Garden	💬 +	$0.01 ⬚	0	0	0.00%	
☐	Media	💬 +	$0.01 ⬚	0	0	0.00%	

FIGURE 6.23 Subdivided product groupings

299

AdWords lets you nest up to seven levels to define *product groupings.* Establishing such deep levels of product groups gives you great granularity for bidding. Thus, you could setup product groupings such as:

1. All Products (Google Category)
    2. Arts and Entertainment (Google Category)
        3. Hobbies and Creative Arts (Google Category)
            4. Artwork (Google Category)
                5. Paintings (Product Type)
                    6. Old Masters
                    6. Impressionists
                    6. Celebrity Painters (custom label)
                        7. Tony Bennett (ID numbers)
                        7. John Lennon (ID numbers)
                        7. David Bowie (ID numbers)
                        7. *Every. Else / Celebrity Painters*
                    6. *Everything Else in Paintings*
                5. *Everything Else in Artwork*
            4. *Everything Else in Hobbies and Creative Arts*
        3. *Everything Else in Arts and Entertainment*
    2. *Everything Else in All Products*

The rules for setting up product groupings include the following:

1. A product cannot appear in more than one product grouping within an ad group. However, a product can appear in different ad groups.

2. If a product appears in multiple product groupings, AdWords first selects the campaign with the higher priority, then selects—and uses—the product listing with the highest max CPC bid.

3. If a product appears in two equally high-priority campaigns, the product listing with the highest bid is used.

4. If a product is not part of any *product grouping*, AdWords uses the max CPC from the *all products* ad group.

5. AdWords suggests bids for each product grouping based on your previous bid or, if you have no traffic yet, it shows the bids of other advertisers. AdWords shows this information in the *benchmark CTR* and *benchmark max. CPC* columns. Click *columns—customize columns* and add the *competitive metrics* (*benchmark CTR, benchmark max CPC* and *impression share*) to the *statistics table.*

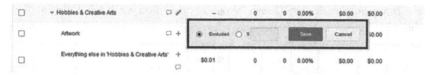

FIGURE 6.24 Excluding a Google Shopping product group

6. You can *exclude* a *product group* from being advertised by changing the *max CPC* to *exclude*.

- **You can add a promotional message (up to 45 characters) to** a *product group.* For example, "10% off through Saturday."

Setting Up a Sale Campaign

- **To run a sale on a product, create a new campaign.** Call this campaign your sales campaign and give it a *higher priority* than your master campaign. Next, create an ad group with your max CPC bid, start and stop dates and any promotional message you want to use. Finally, within the ad group, create a *product group* for the sale product(s), using one of the five attributes to define the group.

  By giving your sales campaign a *priority* **of** *medium* **or** *high,* **AdWords uses it instead of your master campaign.** AdWords always uses the highest-priority campaign that contains the product being sought by the searcher. By default, your master campaign has a priority of *low* and, thus, always provides your bid-of-last-resort.

  You can add a promotional message to your ad group. Promotional messages are shown with every item in the ad group. A promotional message should read like an alert, such as "limited quantities available." Google must approve promotional messages, which can delay your message. Google does not permit (1) capitalized words (except in a promotion code), (2) symbols (except $ and %), (3) shapes or double exclamation points in messages. You can include a promotional code if it does not have consecutive zeros. (Search in AdWords Help for "Editorial and professional requirements" for the latest rules.)

  When someone searches for your product between your start and stop dates, AdWords automatically uses your sales campaign and the bid set at either the Product Grouping Level, the Ad Group Level or the Campaign Level (in that order). After your stop date, AdWords reverts to using the master campaign for your max CPC bid, promotional message, etc. until you create another, higher priority campaign containing the product!

For more information on Google Shopping, search in AdWords Help for "Use shopping campaigns for a better way to promote your products." Also, search for and read, "Search products feed specification."

Before Google Shopping arrived, AdWords offered Product Listing Ads (PLAs), which they now call "regular product listings." If you have (or you inherit) a "regular product listing" campaign, search in AdWords Help for "Set up Shopping campaigns for Product Listing Ads" and read the section called, "Recommended steps for advertisers with regular Product Listing Ads campaigns."

Google is deprecating regular product listings in 2014; however, some documentation for them remains in Help. To complicate things further, some articles refer to Google Shopping listings as PLAs. Be cautious of information that does not seem to apply to Google Shopping; it may be a remnant from regular product listing.

Monitoring Google Shopping Listings

1. **To monitor your Google Shopping Listings, set the date range on the campaign management screen.**

   - To see data for a specific period, click the *date range* menu on the top right corner of the page and select the time period you'd like to analyze.

   - Also, be aware that complete data for yesterday is not available until 3 p.m. PT today.

2. **Review your *product groups* to:**

   - **Learn which products are selling. Track product listing information for each product and each attribute.** This lets you determine precisely which products are driving your sales within a product category.

   - **Use the *auto targets* tab to see how each product group is performing.**

   - Click the *dimensions* tab, then click *segment* and from the drop-down menu select *shopping categories* to determine the performance of different products by category, type, ID, brand, condition or custom labels. Use the *filter* button to narrow your selection.

     Learn whether your bids are higher than necessary or too low.

   - **Check your performance against the benchmark data of other advertisers with similar products.** AdWords provides you with an estimated average CTR and max CPC for all other advertisers (i.e., the sum of all CTRs divided by the total number of advertisers and the sum of all max CPCs divided by the total number of advertisers). Learn whether your ads are competing well against others.

- **Check your *impression share* and *percentage of impressions lost* because of insignificant bids or budget.**
- **Use the *bid simulator tool* to estimate the value of different bids.** (See Bid Simulator / Traffic Estimator Tool in Tools and Reports, p. 330.)

3. **If your ad is not appearing or is not appearing often enough, check the following:**
   - On the *ad* tab, check the *percentage served* column to see what percentage of the total impressions your ad received. Check the impression share column, too, if you have access to it.
   - Be aware that (1) more than one ad can appear for a single search and (2) your product listing can appear on Google SERPs as well as Google Shopping pages.

   If your *percentage served* is zero, your ad is not appearing. Check these possibilities:
   - A problem exists with your Google Merchant Center upload.
   - A billing problem exists or your budget is zero. Go to the *billing* tab and correct the situation.
   - AdWords has not approved a recently submitted product feed or readied it for use online.
   - Your product group (as you defined it by *brand, product_group, condition, adwords_grouping, adwords_labels and custom labels*) does not match the data in your feed. Check the descriptions in your feed.
     — Visit the Merchant Center to see the product data uploaded by your feed. Go to the *tools* tab and click *Merchant Center* to view your feed. (Only the account owner can edit the feed.)
     — The Merchant Center provides a dashboard showing your data's *health* (acceptability), *upload history* and *statistics, data quality* (errors, unacceptable items, inaccurate data, etc.) and product *statuses*.

To improve Google Shopping Listings:

1. **Bid competitively.** As always, the higher your bid, the higher your ad position and the more likely your prospect sees your ad.

2. **Optimize your product content.**
   - Be sure your feed includes fresh, accurate and comprehensive data about your products.

- Make your description rich in keywords.
- Provide all the information you can. Fill in every relevant data field in your data feed.
- Make sure your feed prices are in sync with your website prices. Google checks and will not advertise products with different prices on the website to those on the feed.

3. **Keep your feed format up to date.** Google makes changes often, so visit the Merchant Center Help Center often.

Search in AdWords Help for the topic, "Google Merchant Center, get started" for more information.

THE GOOGLE/ADMOB NETWORK

The Google AdMob Network is composed of app owners who agree to show ads on their apps in return for a percentage of the revenues from those ads. You can run several types of ads on the AdMob Network:

- *Ads on mobile apps*, which show ads for any product to people playing games, reading articles, watching movies, etc. on their smartphones.
- *Mobile App Install Ads* on the Display Network, which show ads for your app to people using the types of apps or specific apps your select.
- *Mobile App Engagement Ads* on the Display Network, which show ads to people who already own your app as they search for products or information offered by your ad (i.e., your ad reminds the searcher that your app fills their need).

The following provides key attributes of the ad types along with setup and monitoring instructions.

Ads on Mobile Apps

Ads on Mobile Apps **reach people using apps on their smartphones.** The app owner has opted into Google's AdMob Network, part of the Display Network.

You determine the apps where your ad appears. App viewers could be playing a game, reading news, watching a movie or YouTube video, when your ad appears.

- Only 1–3 ads appears on a mobile app, so real estate is very limited. This puts pressure on your ad to perform, so write it carefully.
- Sometimes bids for mobile apps are lower than for desktops (presumably, because of less competition). Often, they have better click-through rates.

304

You can specify categories of apps or individual apps where you want your ad to show.

- You can select your apps and app categories when you setup your ad, or you can use the *display planner tool* to find apps/placements in advance.

- If you specify a single, managed placement for your ad, try using the publisher's color scheme so your ad looks like it belongs with the app.

Your ad can be a text, images or app/digital (animated or video template). Experiment with different layouts to learn what works best with your audience.

You can use *ads on mobile apps*:

- To *remarket* to people who have visited your website previously.

- To advertise to people based on their *interests*.

- To show your ad on *YouTube's mobile* app (m.youtube.com).

- To advertise *your own* mobile app—an excellent way to reach people. who own your app and to advertise your new app.

Ads on mobile apps **must meet certain AdWords requirements.** To learn more, search in AdWords Help for "AdWords Help for Mobile Ads—what's the policy."

Setting up Ads on Mobile Apps

1. **Create a campaign.** Use the *Display Network only* campaign type and the *ads on mobile apps* sub-type.

   - If you are intending to advertise your own app, you should target the appropriate operating systems, device models and carriers. Click the *edit* link under *devices* to make those selections.

   - Be aware that Mobile App Ad campaigns cannot use *ad scheduling*, *ad delivery* and *ad extensions*.

   (Refer to Setting Up Basic Display Ad for discussion of campaign options.)

2. **Create an ad group.** Enter the following:

   - *Ad group name*: give your ad a descriptive name.

   - *Default bid amount*: enter the maximum you want to pay for your ad.

   - *Select the app store*: enter your app platform and name only if you want to advertise your app on mobile apps. Know, however, that the newer Mobile App Install Ads and *Mobile App Engagement Ads* provide more features.

- *Select your placements*: your choices include:
  — *All apps or all apps on* the Apple and/or Google platforms.
  — *Mobile app categories* panel. Select the categories you want on the Apple and Google platforms by clicking *add* next to the name.
  — *Search all apps* panel. Select the individual apps you want on the Apple and Google platforms by clicking *add* next to the name.
  — *Specific apps.* Enter the app using the required format.

In-Stream Video (Commercials) Ads	Cost-per-View bidding, with a skip button, with in-depth data by audience segment.	All three ads use the same routine. You check the version you want to use.
Overlay Banners (In-Display ad)	Cost-per-View bidding	1. *All Video Campaign* screen 2. Check the *In-Stream* format and/or
YouTube Promotions (In-Display ad)	Cost-per-View bidding	Check the *overlay banner* format and/or Check the *YouTube Promotion format*

- *Narrow your targeting further (optional)*: use this option to market to people based on their interests, age, gender, parental status or previous visits to certain of your webpages (Remarketing).

3. **Create your ad.**
    a. For an image ad, your entire advertising message must be on the image. AdWords does not show any copy.
        — To setup the ad, upload your image, give your ad a name, enter your *display URL* and *destination URL*.
        — If you want your ad to appear only on mobile phones (but not tablets) check the box next to *mobile*.
    b. For a text ad, you enter your headline, two description lines, *display URL* and *destination URL*.
        — If you want your ad to appear only on mobile phones (but not tablets) check the box next to *mobile*.

   c. For an app/digital content ad (which you use only if you are advertising your app on mobile apps), you select from the available templates.

     — You enter the unique element for your selected template:

       (1) For the app install ad template, you need an ad image.

       (2) For the Image app install ad template, you need an image bearing your message.

       (3) For the video app install ad template, you need a video on YouTube; because your ad plays automatically, you can set the number of seconds (1 to 5) the video plays before the viewer can close it.

     — Regardless of the template you chose, you enter:

       (1) *Your app platform* and *name/ID.*

       (2) Your headline and two description lines.

       (3) *Your landing page,* where your app can be obtained.

       (4) Whether you want to *exclude tablets.*

4. *Save* your ad.

5. Test your landing page with different types of mobile phones.

   Ensure that:

- The buy/sign-up button is big enough for the phone's small screen and is visible against the background.

- The site loads quickly.

- The site includes your phone number.

- The site meets AdWords design requirements; search in AdWords Help for "AdWords policies—AdMob ads" for requirements.

Monitoring Ads on Mobile Apps

1. **Review your costs-per-click volume.** Do not be surprised if your costs-per-click are lower for Mobile Ads. With somewhat less competition on mobile phones today than on desktops, your ad may be more successful. Thus, your click-through rate (and, in turn, your quality score and Ad Rank) may be better, which results in a lower cost.

2. **Determine which *placements* are showing your ad and bringing you customers.**

- To see where your ad is appearing, go to the *Display Network* tab and click *placements.* The app categories and apps you chose appear.

- To see the performance data for individual apps within a category, click the checkbox next to the category name and use the *See URL* drop-down menu to select specific apps. Review the data to see which apps perform better.

- Review the apps that bring you customers to determine as much as possible about the demographic, interests, etc. of people using those apps. Use that information to find more apps with users embodying those characteristics.

MOBILE APP INSTALL ADS

*Mobile App Install Ad*s let people download your app directly from you ad.

*Mobile App Install Ad*s run on mobile phones and tablets, using Google's AdMob Network (a segment of the Display Network). The AdMob Network is composed of mobile apps owners who have given Google the right to show ads on their mobile apps.

Show your *Mobile App Install Ad* on your own app to advertise your new apps to your current customers!

Sometimes bids for *Mobile App Install Ad*s are lower than for desktops (presumably, because of less competition) and, often, they have better click-through rates.

You can run *Mobile App Install Ad*s on the Search Network, Display Networks and on YouTube as banner ads. In addition, on YouTube you can run a video (commercial) with a banner ad before the featured video selected by the viewer from his or her mobile phone or tablet.

*Mobile App Install Ad*s must meet certain AdWords requirements. For example, if you are selling mobile apps such as ringtones, wallpapers, quizzes, etc., you must clearly state the price, billing interval and the fact it is a subscription. (To learn more, search in AdWords Help for "AdWords Help for Mobile Ads—what's the policy")

The AdMob Network supports apps available on Google Play (and soon on the iTunes Apps Store.)

To run *Mobile App Install Ad*s you need to know the following:

- Your app must reside in Google Play (or iTunes App store) and you need to have your Google package name (or iTunes app ID) on hand before you create your ad.
- You cannot run ads for Google Play apps and iTunes apps in the same campaign.
- Your ad automatically appears on devices that are compatible with your app's operating system and do not already have your app.

- If you plan to show your ad only on specific mobile apps, determine those placements before you start setting up your ad. Searching for them while in the ad group setup screen is tedious.

  Use the *display planner* tool to find apps/placements. The *display planner* tool provides a full list of Google Partner apps from which to select your preferences.

- **AdWords automatically treats Mobile App Install Ads for Android apps as if you use** *Conversion Tracking.* For iTunes apps, AdWords asks if you want to use Conversion Tracking for iOS apps, and you can activate it or not.

  (Your programmer will need to add a snippet of code to your app. Have him or her

FIGURE 6.25 Mobile App Install Ad on a mobile app

Note the *Mobile App Install Ad* at the bottom of the screen on this news app.

search in Google Developers website for "Mobile apps Conversion Tracking and Remarketing" for details.)

With *Conversion Tracking* in place,

— AdWords knows when someone uninstalls your app (whether it is on the Android or iTunes platform) and begins showing your ad to him or her again.
— The statistics table reports each download as a *conversion.*
— You can set a monetary value for a conversion and AdWords uses that value to calculate a value for your total conversions on the Statistics Table.
— For iTunes apps, you can enter the URL for your iOS app analytics so AdWords can post conversion information for you on your app platform.
— On the Search Network for an Android app, you also have the option to set a *target cost-per-acquisition (CPA),* the click cost that you want AdWords to meet, on average, as it bids on your behalf.

(Some bids go over the targeted amount but they are offset by other bids that are under the targeted amount.)

— On the Display Network for an Android app, you have an advanced option to set either a *max CPA*, an amount above which you do not want AdWords to bid, or a *target CPA*.

— You can opt out of *Conversion Tracking*. Go to *tools* and click *conversions* from the drop-down menu. Click the green dot beside your ad and select *remove*. Know that using *Conversion Tracking* is a best practice.

A legacy form of *Mobile App Install Ad*s continues to run under the *ads in mobile apps* campaign sub-type on the Display Network. (Another legacy version of *Mobile App Install Ad*s was called *promote in mobile apps*). You need to replace your ads with new *Mobile App Installs Ads* to take advantage of the additional features they offer (namely, the ability to run on the Search Network and YouTube).

MOBILE APP INSTALL ADS ON THE SEARCH NETWORK

Mobile App Install Ads on the Search Network show your ad to people who do not already have your app as they search for items on their smartphones related to your keywords.

The Search Network offers these special features for *Mobile App Install Ads*:

- On the Search Network your *Mobile App Install Ad* sends people to your website to learn more about your app, but you can include an *app extension* to let people download your app immediately.

- On the Search Network for an Android app, you also have the option to set a *target cost-per-acquisition (CPA)*, the click cost that you want AdWords to meet, on average, as it bids on your behalf. (Some bids go over the targeted amount but they are offset by other bids that are under the targeted amount.)

- If you do not use *Conversion Tracking* (i.e., you are advertising an iTunes app), your bidding method is *maximize for clicks* (CPC) and you can set a *maximum bid limit*. Alternatively, you can use a *flexible bidding strategy*, but your *Conversion Tracking* is automatic for Android apps.

- You can set start and stop dates for your ad.

- You can *exclude* tablets, which you want to do if your app is designed only for smaller screens.

- **When you enter your keywords, AdWords shows you search volumes, so you can fine-tune your keywords as you enter them.** Keep in mind that people often use different keywords when searching on a mobile device than they do on a desktop.

- **You can** *exclude* **your** *Mobile App Install Ad* **from running on apps altogether and have it run only on search results pages.** This is a campaign option so you need a separate campaign for ads you want to exclude from the ad mob network and ads you want to include on the ad mob network.

Setting Up Mobile App Install Ads on the Search Network

1. **Create a** *Search Network only* **campaign and select the** *Mobile App Install Ad* **subtype.** Setup the other campaign options to fit your needs.

2. **Setup your text ad.** AdWords picks up your app icon and download link from your app platform. You add your ad text and indicate whether you want to exclude tablets.

FIGURE 6.26 Search Network Mobile App Install Ad setup

3. **Enter your keywords.** AdWords automatically provides additional suggestions with volume counts.

4. **Test your landing page with different smartphones.** Ensure that:
   - The site loads quickly.
   - The sign-up form is very, very short and easy to maneuver on the phone.
   - The site includes your phone number.
   - The site meets AdWords design requirements; search in AdWords Help for "AdMob ads—what's the policy" for requirements.

311

5. **Add an *app extension* if you want people to download your app immediately without going to your app platform webpage.**

The *app extension* is added after your ad is saved. You can add it at either the Campaign Level or the Ad Level.

- If you are running multiple ads for the same app, setup your extension at the Campaign Level for easy attachment to each ad.

To add an *app extension* at the Campaign Level, Click *all online campaigns*, then click *ad extensions*. Click the *view* button in the next row of tabs and from the drop-down menu select *view: app extension*. Click + *extension* and the *new app* button on the select app panel. Add your app information.

The next time you want to add an app extension to any ad in the campaign, go to the *ad extension—view app extension* panel and your app will appear in a list of available app extensions. You need only click it to attach it to another ad.

- If you want to attach an *app extension* to a single ad, click the appropriate ad group in the left-hand menu and click *ad extensions*. Click the *view* button in the next row of tabs and from the drop-down

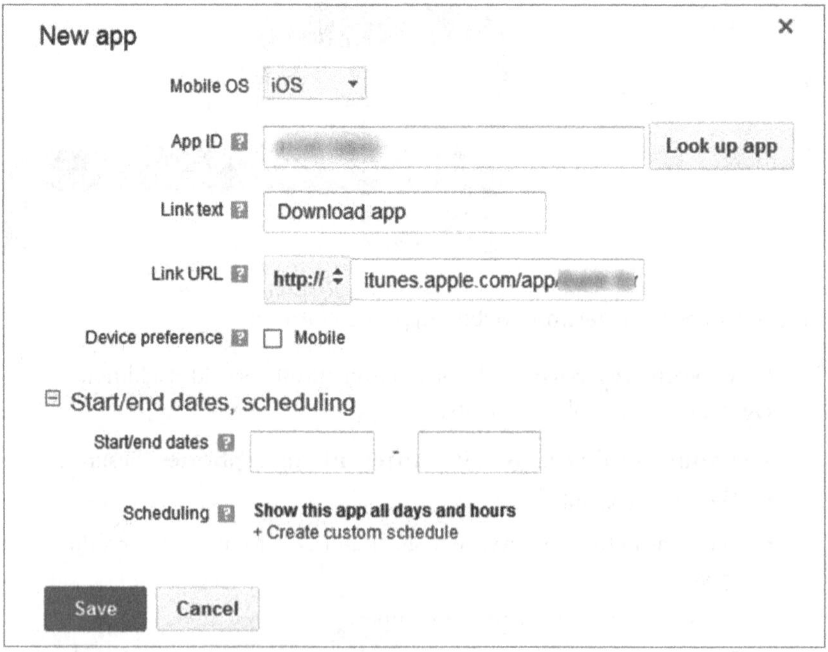

FIGURE 6.27 App extension setup for Mobile Install App Ad

menu select *view: app extension*. Click + *extension* and the *new app* button under the select app panel. Add your app information.

6. **If you want your ad to run** *only* **on** *search results pages* **(SERPs), exclude it from running on the Ad Mob network.** Click on your campaign in the left-hand menu, click the *Display Network* tab, select your ad group and click *campaign exclusions*. Select *placements*, then *lists*, then select *+list* and enter *adsenseformobileapps.com* to exclude mobile devices.

Mobile App Install Ads on the Display Network

The *Mobile App Install Ads on the Display Network* offers a few distinct advantages:

- **You have a choice of:**
  - An *App Install Ad*, which automatically picks up your app icon and customer reviews from your app platform. AdWords includes these with the headline, description lines and platform URL that you enter.

    Note that one version of the ad is animated, showing your headline and description as three separate lines appearing in sequence.
  - An *Image App Install Ad*, which uses an image you upload with your headline, description lines and your platform URL. The image must contain your entire ad message.
  - A *Video App Install Ad*, which places your overlay ad on your video, starts your video automatically and provides the ability to (1) go to your website, (2) install your app or (3) skip the video.

- **You can** *include* **or** *exclude* **tablets.** Exclude tablets if your app is not designed for that screen size.

- **You can exclude your** *Mobile App Install Ad* **from running on apps altogether and have it run only on Display Network webpages.** To do so, click your campaign in the left-hand menu, click the *Display Network* tab, select your ad group and click *campaign exclusions*. Select *placements*, select *lists*, then select *+list* and enter *adsenseformobileapps.com* to exclude mobile devices.

- **You can use** *Remarketing* **with** *Mobile App Install Ads.* If you use Remarketing, you can target people who have visited your website previously and, perhaps more importantly, people who have online search patterns similar to your previous visitors.

- **You can target your ad using any of the Display Network** *targeting methods* **along with these extra methods:**
  - *Installed app category*, which includes people who have installed apps from a category (or categories) of app you select

313

— *New mobile device*, which includes people who have the latest version of a mobile device (e.g., the iPhone 6 Plus(r))

— *Mobile app category*, which includes people interested in a certain category of app.

- **Your ad automatically appears on compatible devices, but you can target specific operating systems, devices and carriers.** This is especially helpful if you have an app that works only with the latest devices.

- *Mobile App Install Image Ads* **on the Display Network can show as banners and** *interstitial* **ads or as just interstitial ads.**

To show only as interstitial ads, you must exclude banner ads from the campaign. You cannot exclude banners until you save your campaign.

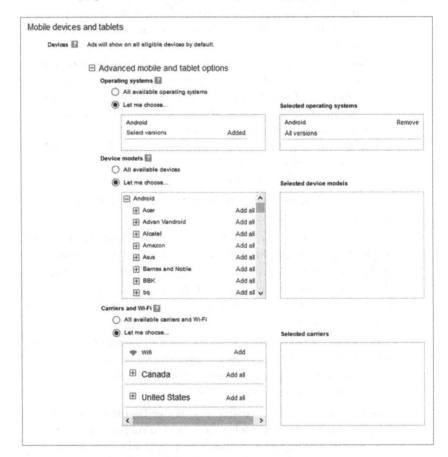

FIGURE 6.28 Display Network Mobile App device selections

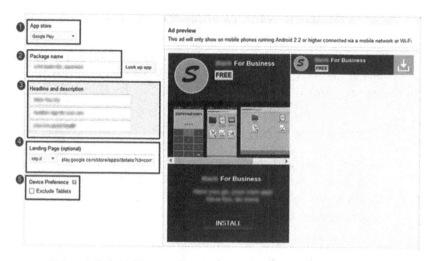

FIGURE 6.29 Mobile App Install Ad

The small ad in the upper right corner is animated. It uses three panels to show the headline and the two description lines.

Once your campaign is saved, click *Display Network* tab and then the red +*targets* button. Select your ad group and click *campaign placement exclusions*. Select *placements*, select *lists*, then select +*list* and add *GMob mobile app non-interstitial* as an exclusion.

Setting up Mobile App Install Ads on the Display Network

To deploy a *Mobile App Install Ad* on the Display Network:

1. **Setup a Display Network campaign(s) and select the** *Mobile App Install* **sub-type.** You will need your package name or app ID number if you have not advertised the app before.

    You may want to set a *frequency cap* to limit the number of times a person sees your ad in a day, week or month. This is especially important if you are running multiple ads or ad groups with overlapping targets.

    Be aware that *Mobile App Install* campaigns cannot use these campaign features:

    - Demographic, social media and experiments.
    - Advanced location settings.
    - Ad extensions.

315

2. **Create a Display Network ad group.** Give the ad group a descriptive name that reflects your theme and audience.

   a. **Select your *targeting methods*.** Remember that *targeting methods* are cumulative; thus, the more *targeting methods* you use the smaller your audience. Your choices are:

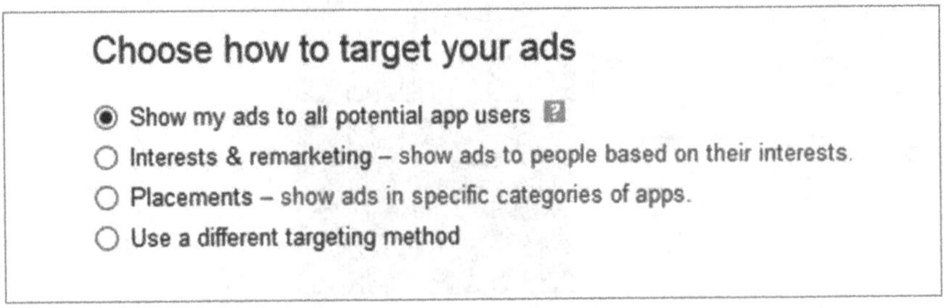

Choose how to target your ads

- ⦿ Show my ads to all potential app users ▣
- ◯ Interests & remarketing – show ads to people based on their interests.
- ◯ Placements – show ads in specific categories of apps.
- ◯ Use a different targeting method

FIGURE 6.30 Display Network target options for Mobile Install App Ads

— *Show my ads to all potential app users*: lets AdWords find apps for you.

— *Interests and Remarketing*: shows ads to people (1) based on their interests as indicated by the types of apps they downloaded previously, (2) whether they have new devices, (3) the *Remarketing* list on which they appear if you use Remarketing (4) and/or people with search profiles similar to those on your Remarketing list.

— *Placements*: shows ads on apps based on (1) app categories you select from the list AdWords displays, (2) individual apps you select from the AdWords categories or (3) apps you enter. As you select your *targeting methods*, AdWords shows the number of potential viewers. If no potential viewers show, contact your programmer and ask him or her to check whether your app is sending information to AdWords. (Ask your programmer to search "Mobile apps Conversion Tracking and Remarketing" for details.) If you created a list of placements using the *display planner tool*, enter those placements using the *add multiple placements at once* link under the *Placements* panel. Make sure your ad size is compatible with your placements. Different placements have different size requirements. If you specify a single, *managed placement* for your image ad, use an image that mimics the publisher's color scheme so your ad does not clash and look out of place.

— *Use a different targeting method*: shows ads based on age and gender.

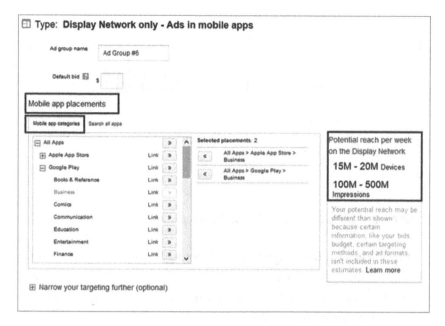

FIGURE 6.31 Display Network Mobile Install Ad placement options

    b. **Select your ad type.** Select either an *App Install Ad,* an *Image App Install Ad,* or a *Video App Install Ad.*

    For an *Image App Install Ad,* you must meet these requirements:
    — Have the legal rights to your image.
    — Have an image 320 × 50, 468 × 60, 728 × 90 or 300 × 250 pixels. Make sure your image meets the requirements of your placements.

As best practices:
    — Keep fonts big enough to read! As with all ads, use a catchy call to action.
    — Do not use a Flash image unless you know your placement(s) support it.
    — Use a transparent, 24-bit, .PNG image, so your background color shows through. Otherwise, you should set your background to match that of your image.
    — Consider adding your phone number. (You cannot use *call extensions* on *Mobile App Ads.*)
    — Experiment with different ad formats, ad copy, button text and colors to learn what entices your prospect.

    c. **Enter your ad details.**

317

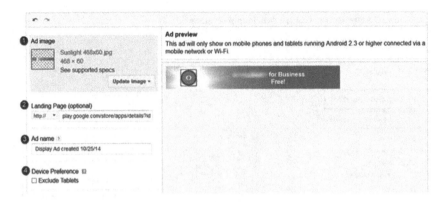

FIGURE 6.32 Mobile App Install Image Ad setup

3. **Test your landing page with different cell phones.** Ensure that:
   - The site loads quickly.
   - The *install* button is big enough for the phone's small screen and is visible against the background.
   - The sign-up form is very, very short and easy to maneuver on the phone.
   - The site includes your phone number.
   - The site meets AdWords design requirements; search in AdWords Help for "AdMob ads—what's the policy" for requirements.

4. **If you want your ad to appear only on Display Network websites and not apps, exclude your campaign from the Google/AdMob Network.**

Mobile App Install Ads on YouTube

You can advertise your app on YouTube as a banner ad or as a video-with-banner ad on YouTube's mobile app. YouTube's mobile app runs only on mobile phones and tablets—which means *Mobile App Install Ads* do not show on YouTube on desktops.

- **The YouTube app ad presents a *visit advertiser* link that takes the viewer to your website on Google or iTunes and an *install* button that takes your viewer to your webpage on Google Play or iTunes.**
- **The viewer can skip your Video Ad after five seconds.** You pay only if he or she watches for 30 seconds or to the end of the video, whichever is shorter.

318

- **Your ad can appear on:**
  - — The YouTube Search page.
  - — The YouTube Video pages.
  - — The Display Network Partner websites that permit videos.

- **Your video must reside on YouTube before you create your ad.**

- **You use video campaign** *targeting groups* **for YouTube banner or video-with-banner ads.** During setup you can define your *targeting group* based on age, gender, parental status and interests (affinity, in-market, other audience). After setup, you can add targeting criteria for video topics, keyword, placements, and Remarketing lists to your targeting group.

Setting Up Mobile App Install Ads on YouTube

To deploy a *Mobile App Install* Ad on YouTube:

1. **On the** *all video campaigns* **page, click** *+campaign* **and setup a new campaign.**

   (If *all video campaigns* does not appear as a choice in the left-hand menu, click *all online campaign* in the left-hand menu and then the red *+campaign* button. At the bottom of the options, click *online video*.)

   Aside from the normal data you enter for *location, language, delivery schedule and advance settings,* **you must:**

   - Select your network(s). The choices are all or any of these: YouTube Search page, YouTube Video pages or Display Network partner websites that permit videos.
   - Enter your YouTube video URL, if you have a video about your app.
   - Click the radio button next to *use Video Ad formats optimized for mobile app promotion*.
   - Enter your mobile app. Enter the URL of your app. AdWords automatically picks up the app name, icon, price, and ratings from your app platform to show next to the Video Ad and in the ad preview.
   - Select the devices to target. The default is all devices.
   - Optionally, set a *bid adjustment* (to increase or decrease your bid when your ad appears on a mobile device).

2. After you *save and continue* your campaign, you next setup your bid and targeting group (or select a *targeting group* you setup for a previous video campaign):

- Enter the name for your *targeting group*.

- Enter your cost-per-view (CPV) bid.

- Define your *targeting group*. If all of your desired criteria are not presented, you can refine the *target group* after you save your ad. (Go to the *targets tab* to make any needed changes.)

Monitoring Mobile App Install Ads

Installations of your mobile app show in different places depending on the ad type.

- For Search Network ads, installations show in the *conversions* column of the statistics table under the keyword tab.

- For Display Network ads, a breakdown of the app installations by *targeting method* is provided under the *Display Network* tab. Select the specific *targeting method* you want to view.

- For YouTube videos and banner ads, you can track installation on the *all video campaigns* page, under the *Segment* links by ad, network, targeting group, format within network, time, device, conversions and click type.

Performance data can be up to three days behind actual conversions. Information from people's phones and interactions between Google and your analytics tracking service can be delayed for many reasons.

1. **For Search Network** *Mobile App Ads*, **refer to Monitoring Basic Search Network Ads for monitoring suggestions.**

2. **For Display Network** *Mobile App Ads*, **refer to Basic Display Network Ads for monitoring suggestions.**

3. **For YouTube video and banner ads, refer to Monitoring All Video** *Campaign* **Video Ads for general suggestions.**

MOBILE APP ENGAGEMENT ADS

Mobile App Engagement Ads **send people from your ad directly to your app.** The more people download your app, the better your App Store ranking and, in return, the more people are likely to download your app.

If, for some reason, a person who does not have your app clicks your ad, your ad acts as a *Mobile App Install Ad* and takes the person to the App Store.

320

FIGURE 6.33 Mobile App Engagement Ad

To take full advantage of the advantages of *Mobile App Engagement Ads,* you need to use the Conversion Tracking and Remarketing features.

- *Conversion Tracking* records the number of actions driven by your ads, such as downloads or visits to different app pages.

- *Remarketing* uses cookies to show your ad to anyone who downloads your app, people who download a particular version, people who have not used your app recently, and people who viewed the sets of pages you specify.

- Both features require you to add *tags* (snippets of code) to your app. The *Remarketing tags* require uniform resource identifiers (URI) to mark the exact location in your app where your visitor is to land, and they must be constructed by your app programmer.

- You must re-release your app to users to deploy *Conversion Tracking* and *Remarketing*, once your app is tagged.

(See "Setting up Conversion Tracking" and "Add the Remarketing tag to your site or mobile app" in AdWords Help for detailed instructions.)

Mobile App Engagement Ads permit the use of *deep links*, links to specific screens or other locations within your app. Deep links use uniform resource identifiers (URIs) to specify a particular location within an app. If you want your ad to take your user to a specific screen or other location in your app, your programmer must establish a URI for that location. You must know the *scheme, host and path* of the URI for your ad. (See "Deep link" in AdWords Help for more information.)

Setting Up Mobile App Engagement Ads

To deploy a Mobile App Engagement Ad on the Search Network, do the following:

1. **Set up a Search Network campaign.**

    a. On the *all online campaign* screen, click the *campaigns* tab, click the red +*campaign* button, select *Search Network only*. Then, select the *Mobile App Engagement* sub-type.

    b. Click *add a new app* and enter your app platform and name.

    c. Your *bid strategy* is automatically set to *maximize clicks*.

    d. Enter your budget.

    e. Enter any other campaign options you want to use and click *save and continue*.

2. Create an ad group

    a. Name your ad group and enter your *default bid*.

    b. Enter your headline and description lines.

    c. Indicate whether you want to *exclude tablets* (and run only on mobile phones).

    d. Enter your app *deep link*. (Your programmer provides this information.)

    e. Enter your *keywords*. AdWords provides suggestions and search volumes.

3. **Setup *Conversion Tracking* if you are not already using it.** Once *Conversion Tracking* is setup, you can return to your campaign *settings* and enter a *target CPA*. The *target CPA* is the amount you want to spend, on average, for your clicks.

To deploy a *Mobile App Engagement Ad* on the Display Network:

1. **Install *Conversion Tracking* and *Remarketing* tags.**

    a. On the *tools* tab, select *conversions* from the drop-down menu. Select the type of conversion you want to track. (See "Setting up Conversion Tracking" in AdWords Help for detailed instructions.)

    b. If you want to change your bid strategy, click *advanced options*.

c. Make sure your tags are working before you proceed. Go to *shared library*, click *audiences* and click *view tag details* in the *Remarketing* box in the upper right-hand corner. If your tags do not appear in the validation tool, they are not working.

2. **Setup the audiences (*Remarketing lists*) for your ads.** If you want to advertise to everyone, you can skip this step. If you want to advertise to sub-groups of people who have your app, you must setup Remarketing lists.

AdWords pre-sets these *Remarketing lists* and asks you to associate either the app name, the specific tag:

* *People who did (or didn't) use an app recently*: a *Remarketing list* of people who used (or didn't use) your app within the time frame you specified.

* *People using specific versions*: a *Remarketing* list of people and the versions of your app they use.

* *People who took a specific action*: a *Remarketing list* of people and the action(s) they took.

* *Custom combinations*: combinations of any of the above lists. For example, people who haven't used the app recently but took a desired action in the past. (Note: this feature is being rolled out to AdWords users. The timeframe for making custom combinations available to all customers is not known.)

3. **Determine your *deep links*.** If you plan to have your user land in a specific place in your app, you need to know the uniform resource identifier (URI) of the location. Your programmer must establish the URI and let you know the *scheme*, *host* and *path*.

4. **Set up a Display Network campaign.**

a. On the *all online campaign* screen, click the *campaigns* tab, click the red *+campaign* button, select *Display Network only*. Then, select the *Mobile App Engagement* sub-type.

b. Click *add a new app* and enter your app platform and name.

c. Specify the appropriate operating systems, devices and carriers for your ad.

d. Your *bid strategy* is set to *Focus on Clicks* (CPC).

(Once you have met the minimum number of clicks required by Google to activate Conversion Track, you can change your bidding strategy to *Focus on Conversion* and use the *cost-per-acquisition* [CPA] bidding model or the *target CPA bidding model*.)

    e. Enter your budget.

    f. Enter any other campaign options you want to use.

    g. Click *save and continue.*

5. **Create an ad group.**

    a. Name you ad group.

    b. Enter your default bid.

    c. Your ad group automatically targets people who have your app. To refine your audience further, you can use your *Remarketing lists* from your Shared Library. Click the *Remarketing lists* tab and click the arrows beside the lists you want to use.

    d. Click *save and continue.*

6. **Create your ad.**

    a. Ads can include your app icon and an *Installed* badge to show users they already have your app.

    b. Enter your description lines.

    c. Specify your *link* or *deep link.*

    d. Customize the button to specify the desired action (e.g., "click to view," "learn more," "see choices," etc.).

Monitor Mobile App Engagement Ads

The performance data for your *Mobile App Engagement Ads* appears on the statistics table as impressions and clicks.

If you use *Conversion Tracking*, add the columns for converted clicks and conversions to the statistics table. Go to *columns—customize columns*, click *conversions* and add as many of the columns as you find useful.

1. To see a breakout by your desired actions, click the *segment* button and select *conversions by action name.*

2. Refer to Monitoring Basic Search Network Ads for general suggestions for improving ads if you are running search ads on mobile devices.

If your *Mobile App Engagement Ads* run on the Display Network,

1. To see a breakout by your targeted groups, click the *Display Network* tab and, then, the *interests and Remarketing* button.

2. Review the performance data for your *Remarketing lists* for your ads, ad group and campaign, *in turn.*

Check the *converted clicks* to see how many unique customers you received during the conversion period you set for *Conversion Tracking*.

Check the *cost/converted clicks* to see what a new customer costs you on average. Decide if this cost is acceptable.

Check the *click/conversion rate* to see what percentage of clicks result in a customer. This helps you estimate your future costs to meet your marketing goals. You can then determine if you have adequate budget to meet your goal.

Check the *view-through conversions* to see how many people who converted saw your ad but didn't click it. This tells you whether your ad is influencing conversions even though it may not trigger them.

3. Refer to Monitoring Basic Display Network Ads for suggestions for monitoring and improving ads if you have *Mobile App Engagement Ads* running on the Display Network.

Chapter 7

Tools and Reports

This chapter describes the major AdWords tools and reports that help you analyze AdWords results. Understanding the power of these tools and reports (which in actuality are online screens and spreadsheets much like those found in business intelligence applications) lets you identify the ads and options that drive performance.

More specifically, the chapter covers the major tools and reports, including those for keyword research, search-term frequency, competitive analysis, bid simulation and traffic projections. It covers the scope of their capabilities and recommends ways to resolve issues and find opportunities by slicing-and-dicing or drilling into data.

AdWords is an interactive application and, as such, gives new meaning to the words "tools" and "reports." Screens that show data usually let you change that data—making them tools and reports. Most screens are spreadsheets —making them reports and tools. Some screens let you view data projections— making them tools—but then let you download the data for further analysis —making them a report.

In AdWords, tools are programs that produce screens of data, and reports are screens of data that you can download, schedule or email. Do not bother to look for traditional reports—a formatted page with a place for your logo, a client name and columns of data that you print, for those of you old enough to remember such things. They do not exist.

The following describes the many programs and spreadsheets that help you create, manage and improve your AdWords ads.

AdWords editor: lets you download your account data as a spreadsheet, make changes, and upload the changes into AdWords. From the spreadsheet you can make mass changes, find duplicate keywords and solve other account-wide issues. Once you are satisfied with your changes, you can upload the changed items into AdWords to update the account data.

The AdWords editor is especially helpful to those managing accounts with many campaigns, ad groups and ads. Download the AdWords editor at www.google.com/AdWordsEditor.

Ad preview and diagnosis tool: lets you see your own ads as they look online. Rather than Googling your own ad and incurring a cost, run the ad preview and diagnosis tool so your view does not count in your click total. It also will tell you why your ad is not appearing. Enter www.google.com/AdPreview to go directly to the tool, or go to the *tools* tab and click *ad preview and diagnosis* on the drop-down menu.

Auction insights: lets you learn about the competition and the type of ads winning the auction for your keyword. Go to the *keyword* tab, check the box next to a successful keyword, click *details* and click *auction insights*. You can see the competitor's data broken out by device or time by clicking the *segment* button and *device* or *time* from the drop-down menu.

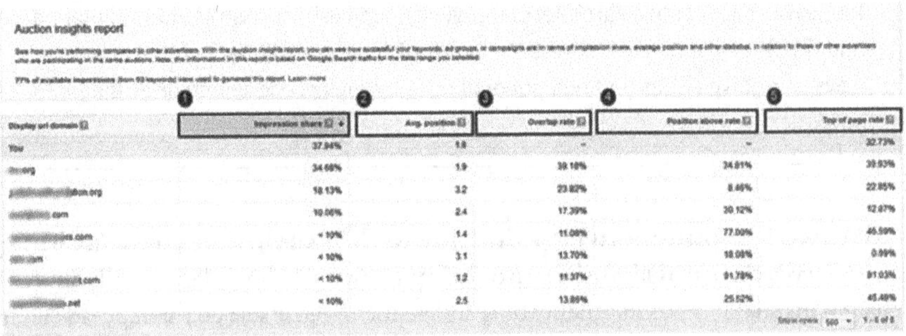

FIGURE 7.1 Auction Insights screen

The *auction insights* screen shows:

1. **Impression share**: your percentage of available impressions and how you compare to other advertisers. To improve your percentage, you must improve your bid or quality score and add as many *ad extensions* as possible.

2. **Average position**: your average position and how you rank against other advertisers.

3. **Overlap rate**: the percentage of time you and another advertiser show ads for the same query.

Auction insights report

See how you're performing compared to other advertisers. With the Auction insights report, you can see how successful your keywords, ad groups, or campaigns are in terms of impression sh who are participating in the same auctions. Note: the information in this report is based on Google Search traffic for the date range you selected.

77% of available impressions (from 93 keywords) were used to generate this report. Learn more

Display url domain	Impression share ↓	Avg. position	Overlap rate	Position above rate	Top of page rate
You	37.94%	1.8	–	–	32.73%
Computers	39.81%	1.8			32.14%
Mobile devices with full browsers	26.96%	1.7			37.26%
Tablets with full browsers	42.05%	1.7			32.50%
	34.68%	1.9	39.18%	34.81%	39.93%
Computers	40.89%	1.9	44.60%	34.41%	39.05%
Mobile devices with full browsers	13.59%	1.8	17.03%	42.90%	53.72%
Tablets with full browsers	< 10%	2.0	6.60%	33.82%	36.97%
	18.13%	3.2	23.82%	8.46%	22.85%
Computers	21.61%	3.2	27.59%	8.14%	21.73%
Mobile devices with full browsers	< 10%	2.5	6.80%	17.09%	42.97%
Tablets with full browsers	< 10%	2.8	4.00%	11.74%	28.76%
	10.06%	2.4	17.39%	30.12%	12.87%
Computers	< 10%	3.0	12.43%	22.65%	5.39%
Mobile devices with full browsers	26.10%	1.7	44.90%	45.78%	24.46%
Tablets with full browsers	21.29%	2.0	34.55%	29.78%	3.71%

FIGURE 7.2 Auction Insights report segmented by devices

4. **Position above rate**: the percentage of time another advertiser outbid you in an auction and took a higher ad position.

5. **Top of page rate**: the percentage of time your ad appeared at the top of the SERP, above the unpaid, organic results.

To improve your rankings:

1. Determine which advertisers are your most frequent competitors.

2. Execute a Google search aimed at viewing their competing ads and note the destination URLs.

3. Go to *tools—keyword planner—search for new keywords and ad group ideas* and enter a competitor's destination URL into *your landing page.*

4. Review the ad groups and keywords that Google suggests and see if your competitor is using keywords that you should add to your ad. Copy those keywords.

5. Go to *tools—keyword planner—get traffic estimates for a list of keywords* to use the *bid simulator* to determine the bid needed to outrank a competitor for either ad position or impressions. Change your bid accordingly.

Bid simulator: lets you see the bid curve for ads that ran on the Search Network during the previous seven days. To use the bid simulator, click the icon (⊯).

- On the *campaign* tab on the statistics table, under the *budget* column.
- On the *ad group* tab on the statistics table, under the *max. CPC* column.
- On the *keywords* tab on the statistics table, under the *max. CPC* column.
- Under *tools and analysis, keyword planner, get traffic estimates for a list of keywords.*

For an explanation of the bid simulator, see item C. in the *keyword planner* explanation that follows.

Campaign bid simulator: lets you see the bid curve for ads that ran on the Search Network during the previous seven days. To use the *campaign bid simulator*, click the icon in the *campaign* tab on the statistics table, next to your campaign. The *campaign bid simulator* works like the *bid simulator*. For an explanation of the *bid simulator*, see item C under the *keyword planner* explanation.

Change history: lets you view a list of changes you, or someone else, made to your budget, bid, keyword, status, distribution, targeting or ad during the period you specify. Go to *tools* tab and select *change history* from the drop-down menu.

Dimension reports: lets you review or schedule reports of the performance of your ad by campaign options, including: conversions (if you use *Conversion Tracking*), reach and frequency, time, destination URL, top movers, geographic area, user locations, search terms, paid vs. organic search, call details and free clicks (i.e., clicks that open a Video Ad). Click the *dimension* tab on the *all online campaigns* screen.

Keyword planner: lets you direct AdWords to use search data from the past seven days to show you:

- Potential ad groups ideas and associated keywords for the Search Network ads.
- Average monthly searches, competition level and suggested bid for the keywords.
- Drill down to the traffic estimator (bid stimulator) to see projected impressions, clicks, conversions and ad positions for various bids or daily budgets.

The *key word planner* lets you automatically add any of the ad groups or any individual keywords it displays to one of your existing ad groups or to a new ad group; this lets you create or expand campaigns quickly and easily.

Click on the *tools* tab and select *keyword planner tool* from the drop-down menu.

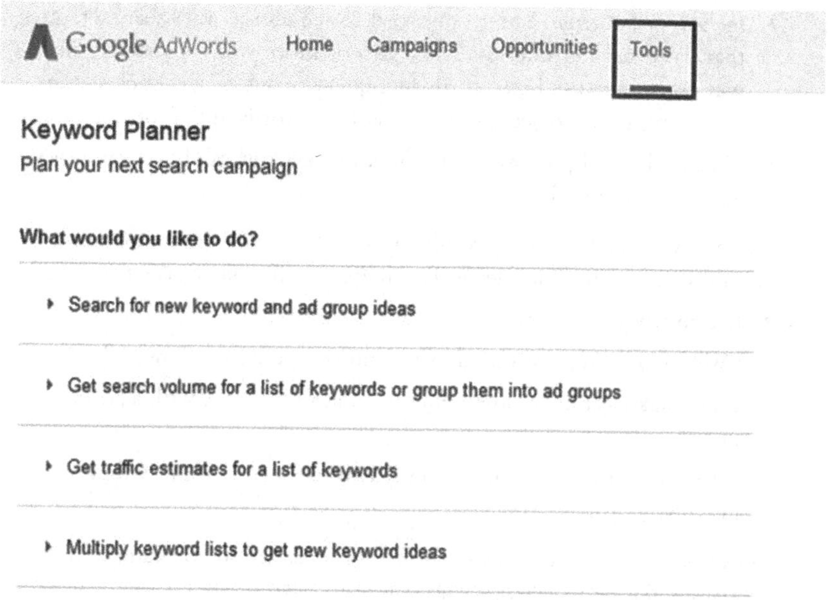

Keyword Planner

Plan your next search campaign

What would you like to do?

▸ Search for new keyword and ad group ideas

▸ Get search volume for a list of keywords or group them into ad groups

▸ Get traffic estimates for a list of keywords

▸ Multiply keyword lists to get new keyword ideas

FIGURE 7.3 Keyword planner

On the Keyword Planner shown in Figure 7.3, note the following different views:

1. *Search for new keywords and ad group ideas.* Use this option to start or expand campaigns or ad groups in one of three ways:
   - Enter a few of your most obvious keywords, and let AdWords provide dozens of related keywords, conveniently organized into ad group themes.
   - Enter your website page, and let AdWords determine the best ad group themes and associated keywords for your page. This is a super quick way to start a campaign.
   - Select a product category, a sub-product category and product types for your business and let AdWords find keywords for you.

   You can further refine your choices by:
   - Location, including all capabilities for defining locations seen at the Campaign Level. Use this for local or regional campaigns or for congressional districts.
   - *Language.* Use this for non-native language speaking groups within a county (e.g., Americans in France).
   - *Google and Google's Network partners.*

- *Include certain terms.* Enter one word to see all the ways searchers use that word in their queries. Enter two or more words to see all the ways searchers use both words in a query in any order. Enclose the words in quotes to see queries using both words in that order.

- *Negative keywords,* so keywords you know are not valid for your business are not considered.

Further, you can filter your results by search volume, bid, impressions, volumes and competition level. This helps you find keywords that are:

- Cheap (Bids below x).
- Overlooked (impressions above x and competition = low).
- Long-tails (search volume below x and bid below y, with a steady trend line).
- Emerging (search volume below x and bid below y, but with a trend line going up).

Download the filtered results and include *segments,* so you can see the trends for the keywords over the last year.

Finally, you can add ad groups and/or keywords to a plan. You can then review estimated impressions, clicks, conversions and ad positions for a plan by clicking the *review estimates* button and going immediately to the traffic estimator (described in item C).

2. *Get search volumes for a list of keywords or group them into ad groups.* This option functions similarly to *search for new keywords and ad group ideas* but includes the search volumes for the *exact match* of the keywords and the volume totals for the ad group ideas.

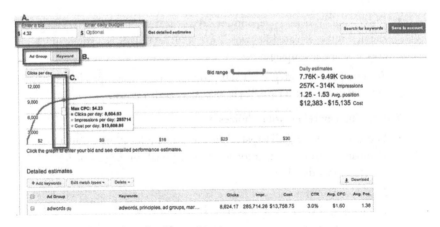

FIGURE 7.4 Bid simulator/traffic estimator

3. *Get traffic estimates for a list of keywords.* This option lets you see projected impressions, clicks, conversions and ad positions for various bids or daily budgets.

When you view option C, the above panel appears, showing the bid simulator/campaign simulator/ traffic estimator.

- Enter a bid and/or a daily budget (view A). The amounts do not matter; you are not making any commitment. Click *get detailed estimates* and the traffic estimator constructs a graph with a curve showing the relationship between bids and impressions.

- Click your mouse anywhere on the curve to have the selector (view B) appear. Slide the selector along the graph to see estimates for different bids. Note that the estimates are for the Search Network only, based on one week of historical data.

- Use the graph to determine where you can get the most impressions at the cheapest max CPC with a first, second or third ad position. This gives you a good starting point for formulating your bid and daily budget.

- Start with that bid to get the biggest bang for your buck; work up to that bid as you learn more about your customer or surpass that bid if you want to outshine the competition.

- Click the *keyword* button to see the estimates for your individual keywords.

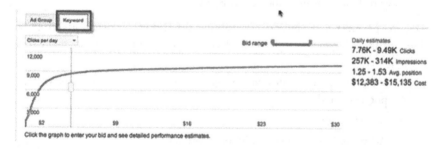

FIGURE 7.5 Bid simulator (view C)

The bid simulators do not run under the following conditions:

- Not enough data: your campaign is new or data from the last seven days is not available because your ads did not run.

- Campaign daily budget reached: your ad stopped running during the last seven days.

- Automatic bidding in use: the bid simulator does not run for campaigns using automatic bidding.
- Campaign not on Search Network: the bid simulator is used only for Search Network ads.
- Keywords not using the ad group default bid: the bid simulator uses ad group default bids, and they are not available if you are overriding them with keyword-level bids.
- Campaign experiment underway: the bid simulator does not work if an experiment is running.
- Product listing ads: the bid simulator does not handle product listing ads.

To learn more, search in AdWords Help for "Using traffic estimator to predict keyword performance."

4. *Multiply keyword lists to get new keyword ideas.* Use this option to make quick work of:

    - Adding one (or two) words at the front of a long list of keywords. For example, you can quickly add a brand name to your existing list of products.
    - Combining up to three lists such that every word appears next to every other word and in every word order.

    Once AdWords combines the words, it organizes them into ad groups and keyword ideas, as described in A, B, and C.

Display planner: lets you identify websites for Display Network ads based on different targeting methods. It finds advertising sites on the web that meet your criteria for:

- Website type (websites, videos, games, blog feeds, mobile apps, and podcasts) and/or
- Keyword, and/or
- Ad types (text, display, audio or In-Stream)
- Ad sizes supported, and/or
- Audience, including age, gender, household education, household income, location, language and/or device preferences.
- In addition, you can create a list of excluded placements.

The *display planner* lets you click the items you like and add them to your plan. With a single click you can turn *your plan* into one or more ad groups.

Click on the *tools* tab and select *display planner* from the drop-down menu.

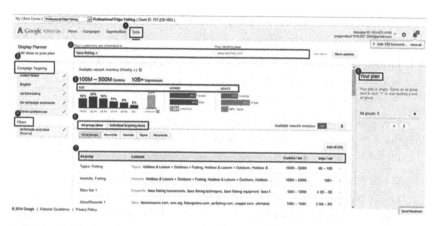

FIGURE 7.6 Display planner

The Display Planner shows potential ad group ideas and targeting methods.

On the *display planner* tool shown above, note the following numbers:

1. The *Tools* menu choice. The *display planner* resides on the Tools drop-down menu here.

2. Shows the keywords and topics you say your audience enjoys or alternatively, your landing page URL.

3. Shows your campaign options for country, language, ad scheduling and keyword inclusion/exclusion options.

4. Provides *filtering* options to include/exclude websites, ad size, mobile apps and/or videos.

5. Estimates the size of the available weekly (optionally, monthly) inventory of searches by age, gender and device.

6. Provides a tab for *ad group ideas*, as in Figure 7.6, which shows topics and placements grouped by a common theme, as you would do for an ad. Alternatively, you can view the *individual target ideas*, which simply provides lists of keyword, topics, placements, etc. from which you can pick appropriate items.

7. Shows AdWords recommendations, based on its historic data, for possible ad groups for your campaign. Recommendations cover the various targeting methods (i.e., topic, interest keyword, mobile app and placements).

   For each *idea*, AdWords also presents the *traffic volume* and *impressions*. *Traffic volume* represents the number of cookies AdWords placed on the computers of people who clicked an ad and visited a website.

335

Click on an *idea* (shown by AdWords in blue) to move to the *individual target idea*, to view the specifics.

8. Provides double arrows (>>) at the end of each *ad group ideas* and *individual target ideas* line to let you move an entire *ad group idea* or *individual target idea* into *your plan*.

   Your plan can include items from different targeting methods and, if you do, your estimated traffic reflects the narrowing that multiple targeting methods impose.

   If you enact *your plan*, AdWords adds your choices to an existing ad group unless one or more of your choices differ from your existing ad groups. Thus, if you select an ad format of 600 × 300 and none of your existing ad groups target that ad format, AdWords creates a new ad group, using the ad text from your existing ad.

9. Provides a button to download your choices to your PC to review with other people.

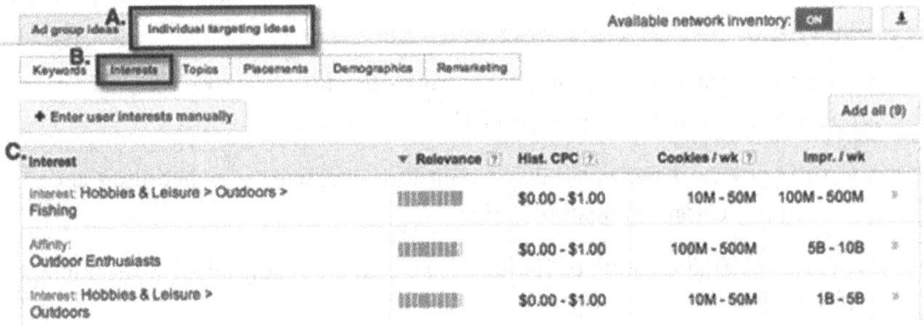

FIGURE 7.7 Display planner tool results
The Display Planner showing individual targeting ideas.

On the *individual targeting idea* panel shown in Figure 7.6, note the following:

1. The button to show the *individual targeting idea*.

2. The menu choices for *individual targeting ideas*. You can switch between ideas for *keywords, interests, topics, managed placements, demographics* or *Remarketing lists*.

3. The results for your *individual targeting idea* choice. The individual line items show the relevance of this idea to your audience and/or website, the historical *cost-per-click*, the number of cookies applied each week, and the number of impressions shown each week. Finally, double arrows let you add that ad group idea to your plan.

336

Be very careful selecting ideas. AdWords' recommendations may not match your ad needs. (For example, that Table Tennis Equipment is included for a website selling fishing equipment.)

Paid and organic report: lets you see new, potentially valuable, keywords for your ads and websites. The report shows search terms that evoke your website on Google's search engine results page (SERP) but do not appear as keywords in your ads and, conversely, keywords that trigger your ads but do not evoke your website for a top SERP placement. Aligning the keywords in your ads with those in your website can improve your quality score.

To activate the paid and organic report, you must associate your AdWords account with your Webmaster tools account. To view the report, go to the *ad group* tab, click the *dimensions* tab and select *paid and organic report* from the drop-down list.

To learn more, search in AdWords Help for "Measuring paid and organic search results."

Recommended budget tool: lets you obtain AdWords' recommendations for your budget. It is available only after your campaign is running. Go to *settings* tab—*bidding and budget* section—*budget*—*view rec. budget*.

Search terms report: lets you see the search terms that triggered your ad. Go to the *keyword* tab for the ad you want to review. Click on the *details* button above the statistics table.

Traffic estimator: lets you see projected impressions, clicks, conversions and ad positions for various bids or daily budgets. The traffic estimator is part of the keyword planner. See C under Keyword Planner.

Chapter 8

Glossary

This chapter provides definitions for terms used in AdWords, including many data elements and phrases with meaning specific to AdWords.

AdWords uses a number of terms specific to Google. Most are obvious, but not all. The following is a quick reference.

Adjusted max CPC A term used in this document to represent the actual amount you agree to pay for a click *after* AdWords applies any relevant *custom bid* and/or *bid adjustment* to the max CPC you originally set for a keyword.

AdSense Google's program for content providers (such as e-zines publishers) who make space available on their websites for Google ads in return for a portion of the money paid to Google by the advertiser.

Ad rank A score representing the relevancy and competitiveness of the ads. AdWords computes an ad rank for your ad each time your ad competes in an auction. Ads with the highest ad rank take the highest positions on a webpage. Google does not reveal the actual formula for computing an ad rank, but some researchers think it is "*quality score* × Mnx CPC."

AdWords Google's program for advertisers who pay to have their ads shown either when people run a search for the advertiser's product or when a Search Partner or an AdSense website owner runs content using keywords the advertiser specified.

Avg. CPC: average cost-per-click The average amount of money *you* spent for a click related to a particular keyword. An average is useful, since the exact amount varies for each impression. (Avg. CPC = total-amount-of-money-you-paid-Google-for-clicks divided by the-total-number-of-people-who-clicked-on-your-ad.)

Auction The process (or algorithm) Google uses for selecting ads to show on a search results page or an AdSense webpage. The exact algorithm is a trade secret; however, theoretically, the algorithm considers the search term, matches it with advertisers' keywords, determines the maximum bid it can obtain, given the remaining budgets of the advertisers, and selects the ad of the advertiser whose previous track record of success (i.e., quality score) is the highest.

Bid adjustment A means of raising or lowering your max CPC by a certain percentage for different devices (e.g., a mobile device or desktop), specific locations and/or specific days and hours. For example, you can lower your Max CPC by 10 percent for mobile devices if ads on mobile devices are less productive for you.

Bid price The amount you will pay/did pay for a click-through. It can be equal to or less than the default maximum bid you set for the ad group or the override amount you specified for the keyword involved.

Budget The amount of money you allocate to an ad group for the day. Google may be slightly over or slightly under your budget on any given day; however, over a month, the average will not exceed your daily budget. Lowering your budget in the middle of a day may result in that day being over your budget, since Google attempts to spread your budget in keeping with your campaign delivery choice (i.e., show ads evenly over time, show ads as quickly as possible).

Budget status The amount of money spent this month. Check the period for the data being shown for your campaign. It appears in the upper right-hand corner of the campaign page.

Campaign status An indicator that the campaign is active and ads are being shown is paused and ads are not being shown or is deleted and ads are not being shown and are not expected to be shown again (even though data for the ads remains available).

Clicks The number of times a viewer has clicked on your ad and gone to your landing page. Google does not count multiple clicks from the same computer on the same day.

Click-through The act of clicking on an ad and going to the ad owner's landing page. Google does not count multiple clicks from the same computer on the same day.

Click-through rate (CTR) The percentage of people who clicked on your ad out of all the times your ad appeared to someone. (CTR = people-who-clicked divided by the-total-number-of-impressions.)

Conversion rate (1-per-click) The percentage of unique visitors who pressed the "Buy" button on your landing page out of the total number of unique visitors. 1-per-click means AdWords counts a visitor only once, even if he or she visited the site more than once.

Conversions (1-per-click) The number of unique visitors who pressed the "Buy" button on your landing page. 1-per-click means AdWords counts only one click per visit, even if that person made several different purchases.

Conversion Tracking A campaign option that shows you what visitors do after they click on your ad. Conversion Tracking reports show which ads and keywords bring you buyers and the average cost-per-acquisition (CPA) and many other useful insights.

Cost/conversion (1-per-click) The total cost of clicks during the period, divided by the total number of purchases. In itself, this statistic means little, since the cost of a click varies for every visitor. However, over time, this number tells you whether your costs are trending up or down or remaining steady. 1-per-click means AdWords counts a person only once even if that person visited multiple times.

Cost-per-acquisition (CPA) The total cost of acquiring a customer (i.e., the total money spent on an AdWords ad divided by the total number of buyers). You must use AdWords Conversion Tracking to obtain a CPA.

Custom bid A means of raising or lowering your max CPC by a certain percentage for one of your targeting methods (i.e., topics, *managed placements*, gender or age). You can apply a *custom bid* for each item in one targeting method. For example, you could apply a percentage increase to your max CPC for each *managed placement* you selected.

Daily budget A campaign option specifying the maximum amount of money you agree to spend on the campaign each day.

Default maximum cost-per-click (CPC) The maximum amount you agree to pay for a click on your ad. You set this amount at the Campaign Level, but you can override it at an Ad Group Level and/or at the Keyword Level.

Display Network A group of websites participating in Google's AdSense program. Most participants are publishers (i.e., online magazines and news sites).

Experiment A test you can run on your AdWords campaign to let you compare the impact of changes to keywords, bids, ad groups and placements. Experiments help you understand the potential impact of changes to your campaigns. They enable you to make more informed advertising decisions and, thus, to lower the risk of new strategies.

Control/control split: The portion of your campaign where your original ad is used.

Experimental change: Any change to keywords, bids, ad groups or ad text you want to test.

Experiment size: The percentage of auctions randomly directed to your control ad versus the percentage of auctions randomly directed to your experimental ad.

Experiment split: The portion of your campaign where your new ad (your experimental change, as AdWords calls it) is applied.

Random-auction experiment: AdWords experiments are random-auction. AdWords randomly chooses to use either your control ad or your experimental ad. By randomly choosing which ad to use on an auction-by-auction basis, your ads each receive a fair sampling of auctions over time, which enables you to evaluate the impact of your changes.

Statistical significance: AdWords calculates a statistical significance based on the number of auctions your campaign participates in and the differences in impression share between the control item and the test item. AdWords provides one to three icons in your campaign to indicate 95 percent, 99 percent or 99.9 percent confidence that differences in the two ads are meaningful and not just due to chance.

First page bid estimate The estimated cost-per-click bid that could elevate your ad to the first SERP. AdWords calculates it using the ad rank and bids of your competitors after your ad has run a short time.

Global searches The number of searches worldwide for a particular keyword.

Image ads Ads permitting text and images (pictures or drawings).

Impression (Impr) The number of times your ad appears. An ad displayed 100 times online has 100 impressions (regardless of whether any viewers read or clicked on it).

Keyword matching An ad group option specifying how Google matches your keyword with the searcher's term: exactly (keyword must be in brackets), partially, as when your keyword(s) appear in order in the searcher's term(s) or broadly, as when your keyword(s), a synonym or a variation of your keyword appears somewhere in the searcher's term.

Landing page A webpage especially designed to fit with your AdWords ad. Usually it contains an offer to buy your product or, alternatively, to sign-up for more information. It must have a "back" button, and it cannot have pop-up ads.

Local searches The number of searches executed by people in your geographic area as defined by the area you specified in your campaign options or, else, your Google account.

Location A campaign option that limits display of your ad to your selection of country, region, state or city.

Page rank A ranking algorithm used in early Google days to determine where to list your website on the SERP. It now has little impact on your website placement on the SERP because Google has replaced it with an algorithm that uses some 500 attributes. Page rank is independent of your AdWords ad rank or *quality score*.

Pay-per-click An online advertising channel, like AdWords, where the advertiser pays a fee each time someone clicks on an ad and goes to the advertiser's website. Google AdWords and Bing Search Advertising are the two major channels.

Percent served The number of times this particular ad—as opposed to other ads in the ad group—appeared out of the total number of times your ad qualified to appear.

Product groups Subdivisions of the all products ad group created when you use Google Shopping and upload your inventory file to the Google Merchant Center.

Quality score A score computed by AdWords ranking the relevance of your ad and landing page along with your click-through record of accomplishment, historical keyword performance and whether visitors bought or, at least, spent time looking, rather than left immediately.

Search partners Website owners who permit Google to display Search Ads (text only) on their websites. AOL and EarthLink are two examples.

Search term The word or phrase a customer inputs into Google to initiate a search.

Split-testing See Experiment.

Status The current state of an ad is active, pending approval, paused or deleted. ("Deleted" means only that the ad is not running; AdWords retains the data for a "deleted ad.")

Pending: Inactive but scheduled to begin at a future date.

Ended: Inactive because it is past its scheduled end date.

Suspended: Inactive because your prepaid account balance has run out. (Google no longer supports prepaid accounts in the U.S., so this situation occurs only with older accounts and non-U.S accounts.) Suspended accounts do not show ads or accumulate new costs until you add additional funds. Go to the *Billing* tab.

Limited by budget: Active, but showing ads only occasionally due to budget constraints. You can place your mouse over the bubble next to this status to see your "Recommended budget."

Time period The period specified on the campaign page. The period defaults to the current year-to-date, but you can change it to any period from one day to or from initiation.

Index